Classroom Assessment in Multiple Languages

A Handbook for Teachers

Margo Gottlieb

Foreword by Kathy Escamilla

FOR INFORMATION:

Corwin

A SAGE Company

2455 Teller Road

Thousand Oaks, California 91320

(800) 233-9936

www.corwin.com

SAGE Publications Ltd.

1 Oliver's Yard

55 City Road

London EC1Y 1SP

United Kingdom

SAGE Publications India Pvt. Ltd.

B 1/I 1 Mohan Cooperative Industrial Area

Mathura Road, New Delhi 110 044

India

SAGE Publications Asia-Pacific Pte. Ltd.

18 Cross Street #10-10/11/12

China Square Central

Singapore 048423

Program Director and Publisher: Dan Alpert

Senior Content Development Editor:
Lucas Schleicher

Associate Content Development Editor:
Mia Rodriguez

Project Editor: Amy Schroller

Copy Editor: Colleen Brennan

Typesetter: Hurix Digital

Proofreader: Dennis Webb

Indexer: Integra

Cover Designer: Rose Storey

Marketing Manager: Maura Sullivan

Printed in the United States of America

ISBN 978-1-5443-8460-3

This book is printed on acid-free paper.

20 21 22 23 24 10 9 8 7 6 5 4 3 2 1

Contents

Visit the companion website at
https://resources.corwin.com/AssessingMLLs
to download printable versions of the resources.

Foreword

Across the entire U.S. from California to Connecticut from New Mexico to New York education discourse is dominated by a contradiction relating to Multilingual Learners no matter their native language(s) or culture(s). This is especially true for children whose native language is bilingualism/multilingualism. Schools and communities take great pride in their increasingly diverse communities while at the same time attributing poor academic outcomes in their community schools to this same linguistic and cultural diversity. This apparent contradiction can be directly attributed to the dominant use of English only high-stakes tests to rank and rate Multilingual Learners, their teachers, and their schools. This contradiction is so profound that while schools and teachers are mandated to give standardized tests and other assessments, many have little faith in the legitimacy of their outcomes, and fewer still use the outcomes to guide instruction. Educators, with good reason, doubt the validity of these top-down assessments, but policy makers continue to enact policies based on misguided and, at times, almost blind faith, in the value of these assessments creating yet another contradiction and a decades old narrative questioning whether the growing linguistic and cultural diversity in our country is a blessing or a curse. Moreover, even though there are a large and growing number of bilingual and dual language programs in the U.S., the vast majority of Multilingual Learners find themselves in programs where English is the dominant or only language of instruction, thereby legitimizing the exclusive use of English tests as measures of achievement. Even in dual language programs, teachers often feel pressure to get children ready for English only high stakes tests and outcomes in English are frequently the sole basis on which the efficacy of these programs is judged. Over the past few decades, the term assessment has come to be used synonymously with testing and because testing and assessment are used interchangeably, teachers and others see classroom assessment as preparation for the test and thus focus almost exclusively on English assessment.

Added to the above, the sad reality is that it is often thought that assessments in languages other than English serve no useful purpose in programs serving culturally and linguistically diverse students. Bilingualism and assessment of it is absent in language assessment testing in the U.S. Considering all of these contradictions, the author herself begins the book by questioning why the field might need another book on assessment given the fact that "Equity, or as the case may be inequity, is a prominent issue that comes to mind when addressing the large-scale testing involving multilingual learners" (p. 3).

In this book, Margo Gottlieb masterfully demonstrates why the field, in fact, does need another book on assessment especially for Multilingual Learners. She acknowledges the current contradictions and has skillfully steered the narrative away from its current oppressive emphasis on high stakes English only testing determined by policy makers and non-educators and turned the focus inward to schools, classrooms, teachers, families and children and more importantly to the importance of more valid and useful assessments for Multilingual Learners. As she rejects monolingual ideologies in assessment practices, she replaces this ideology with one that promotes multilingualism as a right. She states, "There is a moral imperative of promoting and infusing multilingualism and multiculturalism into classroom practices in lieu of maintaining a monolingual stance" (p. 21). She fortifies her argument by stating that, "referencing and leveraging multiple languages and cultures from the vantage point of Multilingual Learners is a healthy alternative to monolingual ideologies that view English as the norm" (p. 24).

While the book acknowledges the current problems with assessment and testing of Multilingual Learners, it does not get bogged down in what's wrong with the field, but focuses on possibilities for assessment practices that are asset oriented, feasible and have the potential to expand our discourse relating to measuring what Multilingual Learners know and can do. It is the feasibility of many of Gottlieb's suggested assessment strategies, along with an approach that is varied and does not presume that one assessment practice fits all, that readers of this book will no doubt find appealing and useful in teaching and better understanding Multilingual Learners.

The book begins by acknowledging the problem with the widespread use of the label English Language Learners (ELLs) for Multilingual Learners. The current ELL labeling system limits what we know about Multilingual Learners, thereby further exacerbating the perception that monolingual assessment practices are sufficient to understand this population. Gottlieb provides a rich description of the within and cross-language diversity of the group better labeled as Multilingual Learners and argues that assessment and testing should illuminate what these students know and can do in all of their languages and then, in each chapter, provides concrete examples of multilingual assessment practices that progress from theory and research support to practice. Important to her suggestions is the assumption that assessment and instruction must be aligned.

Throughout the book it is clear that the author has deep knowledge of assessment and testing practices and their chronic and historic issues with regard to Multilingual Learners. More importantly, the author is someone who has clearly been in and around teachers and schools and knows the on-the-ground burning issues about assessment that teachers and schools face on a daily basis and how collectively these issues mitigate against a greater variety of multilingual assessment practices. Each chapter begins with a vignette about an assessment issue that is often used as a rationale to maintain the status quo of English focused assessments and testing. These issues are ubiquitous in the field and include "Tests for state and local accountability are only in English;" "I only speak English—I need a translator;" "My colleagues don't understand the value of multilingual assessment;" "My students only use their home language to socialize" and "Learning in multiple languages confuses children and teachers." No doubt readers of this book have heard many of these same arguments for English only assessment at their schools and in their communities multiple times. This book takes on each of these perceptions and others and provides powerful counterarguments to each one including supporting literature and research to support the counterargument. In addition to identifying the pervasive problem, she proposes concrete and actionable solutions that can easily be implemented to create classroom based and schoolwide assessment practices to be more inclusive of Multilingual Learners.

Discounting the current assessment system that places accountability and academic achievement at the center of the assessment frameworks and as the core objectives and reasons to do assessment and testing, this book places Multilingual Learners at the center of the educational assessment system and proposes an assessment system guided by three important and related propositions stated with critical prepositions for differentiation. Specifically, she proposes that Multilingual Learners themselves, not accountability, be at the center of assessment systems and she labels this system *assessment as learning*. In this framework, students, not policy makers, become the leaders in their own learning and work with teachers to achieve academic and other educational goals. Gottlieb argues that, "Students are our most important source of information and yet current assessment practices have negated or minimized student participation... Until recently, there has been little attention to how the multiple languages of multilingual learners can contribute to their well-being in school and beyond" (p. 61). The second part of the framework titled *assessment for learning* is defined as the interaction between students and teachers to negotiate educational goals and paths for achieving them. The relationship between student and teachers is meant to be one in which goals for learning and growth can be mutually negotiated. The third aspect is *assessment of learning* and this includes the products, performances, or projects used to determine that the learning has indeed taken place. The entire framework provides opportunities for assessments in multiple languages using strategies that can be implemented across grade levels.

The assessment framework of *as, for,* and *of* presents significant new information to the field and is important because it puts Multilingual Learners at the center, but also because it broadens the term assessment beyond the very narrow way it is currently defined. The framework is comprehensive and inclusive and can be used with any of the languages that Multilingual Learners speak, it can be used in various types of language programs (e.g., English only, ELD, bilingual or dual language programs), and it can be used with any age level of Multilingual Learner.

The book acknowledges the importance of and need for the various types of content and academic testing currently mandated by states and districts including content assessment, assessments of language proficiency and various readiness assessments (e.g., the ACT/SAT). However, the book is not limited to assessment and testing as it relates to academic achievement. Rather, it suggests that classroom and school assessments in multiple languages (including translanguaging) can be opportunities for teachers and others to get to know students vis-a-vis their academic and personal interests, their attitudes about school and their languages, their opportunities to use their languages in and out of school, their motivation, and their ability to engage in self-assessment. Too often teachers, especially in English medium instructional programs, are unsure about how to include and value children's non-English languages in the classroom in concrete and visible ways. This book provides tangible guidance into how to create assessment systems that enable understanding of the whole student instead of only a fraction of the student who is only visible as an English learner.

The current practices in which assessments, tests, and school accountability policies are created by policy makers and publishing companies are notably challenged in this book, with the author's stance that schools, no matter what programs are offered to Multilingual Learners, should expand their assessment practices. Significantly, Gottlieb suggests that assessment systems for Multilingual

Learners should include local level dialogues with stakeholders to decide **who** should be involved in deciding **what** assessments should be used and with **whom**. Specifically, while the current high-stakes top down system is unlikely to change in the near future, Gottlieb advocates for assessment practices that include the multilingual learner families, their students, and their local contexts in deciding the totality of the assessment systems.

In this comprehensive view of assessment practices, accompanied by a plethora of assessment strategies for many languages and across many grade levels, Gottlieb has demonstrated why the field, particularly the field as it involves the teaching of Multilingual Learners, needs another assessment book, particularly a book like this. In this work assessment and testing are aligned closely with instruction and instruction is based not just on the state and local standards but also on what students and families know and want to learn. The value for multilingualism and multiliteracy and the many definitions of these concepts are foundational to this book even as they are still largely aspirational in the field. Gottlieb has illustrated how emerging knowledge and proficiency in multiple languages can be valued and documented in diverse programs for students at all ages and in many languages. Assessment, in this work, is a process and not an event.

For many in our field, one of the biggest impediments to social justice is our current high-stakes monolingual English assessment system. Even as we posture that we believe multilingualism and multiculturalism to be advantageous to individuals and communities, our school practices, particularly our assessment practices, contradict our purported values. There is much in this book to help ensure that multicultural assessment becomes more of a reality without overburdening already stressed teachers and school systems. The book contributes original and concrete strategies for teachers and administrators with regard to how to include multilingual strategies as a part of routine daily practices in schools and expands assessment to include socio-emotional assessments as well as academic, language, and content assessments. For administrators and coaches this book includes a plethora of checklists and performance-based assessment strategies that expand how we view what students know and can do beyond paper and pencil assessments. Done in multiple languages, these assessments could serve as the empirical evidence needed to change attitudes toward multilingualism at a school or district level in order to institutionalize more equitable assessment practices. The book mounts a powerful argument to counteract the current pervasive deficit notions about Multilingual Learners and can be used to advocate for reform and expansion of the limited views of assessments in so many of our country's schools. It could be a useful text in teacher education programs to guide future teachers in learning about equitable assessment practices. In this book the author calls for the results of assessment to result in a plan of action for how to take action on behalf of Multilingual Learners and their families with an admonition that taking action must include the voices of the students and their families. This book quite likely could serve as a catalyst toward the beginning of an enlightened discourse around assessment that will benefit Multilingual Learners.

—Kathy Escamilla, Professor
University of Colorado, Boulder

Preface

Why Is Assessment in Multiple Languages Necessary?

> *To have another language is to possess a second soul.*
> —Charlemagne

> *Apprendre une autre langue, c'est comme le commencement d'une autre vie.*
> —Michel Bouthot

The Dilemma

But the tests for state and local accountability are in English!

Anita Velásquez is a third-grade dual language teacher in a mid-size school district. She is well aware that this is the inaugural year for her students to take annual state achievement tests in English language arts/reading and mathematics. In anticipation of these high-stakes measures, the district has decided, with little teacher input, to change its language policy. Although the administration has supported learning in multiple languages, it continues to believe that accountability rests only in English.

As a result, Anita and her colleagues feel the pressure from school leaders to spend more time instructing students in English. All the while, the teachers are knowledgeable of the strong research base that favors multilingual learners' biliteracy development. Having witnessed positive results in their own classrooms, the teachers remain steadfast to maintaining two languages for instruction and classroom assessment. Multilingual learners' portfolios with weekly entries that showcase and personalize their learning have proven to be a strong source of evidence for the students' learning and growing in two languages.

Now Anita's principal has scheduled a meeting with the dual language team so he can better understand the teachers' stance on promoting bilingualism and biliteracy for their multilingual learners, their families, and the school community. He is of the conviction that there is a positive correlation between the amount of instructional time in English and student high-stakes test results. The dual language teachers are indeed mindful of the power of English, but they have been swayed by research

(Continued)

(Continued)

and practice that multilingual learners are enabled and empowered when all their languages are tapped as academic, cultural, linguistic, social, and emotional resources for learning.

In preparation for the upcoming meeting, the teachers decide to make a multimedia presentation based on the latest research and practice. They comb the literature on learning in multiple languages and generate a list of researchers whose findings confirm the benefits of multilingualism and the worth of multilingual education. In addition, during their joint planning time, the dual language team gathers evidence of their multilingual learners' language growth and achievement in two languages. What other evidence might the team gather to convince school leadership to continue to support their multilingual learners' dual language development past the primary grades?

FIRST IMPRESSIONS

- In what ways does this scenario resonate with you or your colleagues?

- What is your stance for educating, in particular assessing, multilingual learners in multiple languages?

- How do your multilingual learners feel about the use or non-use of all their languages at school?

- How might you, your colleagues, and multilingual learners begin to think about evidence for growth and achievement in multiple languages?

Each chapter's opening scenario presents a present-day conundrum faced by educators of multilingual learners in K–12 settings. Often the scenario is based on a prevailing myth or misconception. Its purpose is to spark lively discussion among multilingual learners, paraprofessionals, teachers, and other school leaders, even schools as a whole, on how to enhance classroom and schoolwide assessment practices for multilingual learners. It is followed by First Impressions, such as the one above, with probing questions related to the dilemma.

WHAT IS THE PURPOSE OF THE BOOK?

Classroom Assessment in Multiple Languages: A Handbook for Teachers challenges the monolingual bias (a **monoglossic language ideology** that ignores the presence and contexts of multiple language use by multilingual learners) that pervades U.S. society and its educational psyche, especially when it comes to assessment. It is a cry for social justice that sets out to change language hierarchies in classrooms and schools by assuming that, at a minimum, bilingualism is the norm for multilingual learners. Most important, through transformative assessment practices in multiple languages, multilingual learners and their teachers become aware of their students' true identities and gain a better understanding of the complex world in which they reside.

The primary purpose of the book is to instill a multilingual mindset in educators; one that embraces the linguistic and cultural resources of multilingual learners. In addition, it is intended to illustrate how instruction and classroom assessment can proceed in multiple languages irrespective of the extent of teachers' knowledge and use of the languages.

WHY DO WE NEED ANOTHER ASSESSMENT BOOK?

Most assessment books for K–12 educators deal with assessment *of* learning—that is, issues surrounding high-stakes tests, the scores that are generated, **reliability**, **validity**, and the consequences from the inferences that are drawn from the results. **Equity**, or as the case may be, inequity, is a prominent issue that comes to mind when addressing large-scale achievement testing involving multilingual learners.

This book attempts to turn those tables around. What if multilingual learners had the freedom to interact in more than one language with their peers during classroom assessment? What if multilingual learners and their teachers in dual language settings had opportunities to use assessment data in multiple languages to make decisions?

In this assessment book, three approaches encourage stakeholders to be change agents and decision-makers. We present a second dimension of assessment *of* learning—that of classroom-based projects, performances, or products that are co-planned by teachers, with input from students, generally at the culmination of a unit of learning. It is readily coupled with assessment *for* and *as* learning to create a full and equitable compendium of assessment approaches. At present, few books emphasize assessment *for* learning, especially for multilingual learners in collaboration with their teachers; fewer yet include assessment *as* learning, which is primarily student-driven.

Generally, assessment for multilingual learners, if touched upon at all in a book, is tucked into a remote chapter or combined with other marginalized groups, such as students with disabilities. The number of assessment books narrows even more when multiple languages are brought into play. With the exploding numbers of educational programs that have introduced instruction in multiple languages, there is very little guidance as to how to systematically incorporate the assessment process that honors those languages in the classroom routine. There has not been (until now) a book exclusively devoted to classroom assessment of K–12 multilingual learners in multiple languages. *Classroom Assessment in Multiple Languages* is a much-needed resource that is devoted to how educators and multilingual learners can mutually value languages and cultures in instruction and assessment throughout the school day and over time.

WHO IS THE AUDIENCE FOR THIS BOOK?

The audience for this book is broad and varied, composed of teachers who are convinced of the virtues of **multilingual education** and the role of classroom assessment, those who simply wish to accrue some knowledge on assessment in multiple languages, and those who are skeptical of multiple language use by multilingual learners at school, especially for assessment purposes. In addition to teachers, the book is intended for other instructional leaders (such as coaches), community liaisons, and school leaders (such as coordinators, directors, and principals), all of whom wish to improve teaching and learning for multilingual learners. Educators at the ground level need to have the resources and ammunition to support multilingual learners' engagement in classroom assessment in multiple languages.

Just as important is a call for multilingual learners, our primary stakeholders, to interact in meaningful discussion with peers and teachers in the language of their choice as part of becoming empowered. **Multilingual learners** encompass a wide range of students in K–12 settings who are or have been exposed to multiple languages and cultures on a consistent basis in or out of school. It is an assets-based term that accentuates the positive roles of language and culture in their lives. Lastly, we also reach out to teacher educators who are responsible for increasing the participation of preservice and inservice teachers in multilingual education. In Figure 1 we list the primary stakeholders and state the potential impact of this book on them.

FIGURE 1 The Appeal of a Book on Classroom Assessment in Multiple Languages to Educators and Multilingual Learners

AUDIENCE/STAKEHOLDERS	THEIR RESPONSIBILITY INCLUDES....
Multilingual learners	Becoming owners of learning and defenders of their languages and cultures as they embark on the pathway of becoming autonomous learners
Dual language/language education teachers	(Co)instructing and (co)assessing multilingual learners in one or more shared languages throughout the school day
Dual language/language education coaches	Facilitating and giving concrete feedback on planning, enacting, and evaluating assessment practices for multilingual learners in one or more languages
Dual language/language education co-ordinators and directors	Overseeing schoolwide language programs, helping craft and disseminate language policy and curriculum; formulating with other stakeholders a set of principles for assessment in multiple languages
General education teachers working with multilingual learners	Co-planning, co-teaching, and co-assessing multilingual learners with language teachers/coaches who may or may not share the languages of their multilingual learners; planning, teaching, and assessing multilingual learners in content-area classrooms
School leaders (e.g., principals, curriculum directors)	Overseeing schoolwide educational programs and ensuring that the mission, vision, and values of the school are upheld for multilingual education; creating a schoolwide language and assessment policy with teachers and the community
Consultants/teacher educators in institutions of higher education	Priming preservice and inservice teachers in teacher preparation programs in the theory, pedagogy, and practice for working with and assessing multilingual learners in multiple languages

WHAT CAN WE EXPECT FROM THIS BOOK?

Overall this book crosses the fields of general education, language education, and classroom assessment, as most multilingual learners are members of several classrooms during the school day. As a result, educators who delve into this book, whether singly or in collaboration with other teachers or school leaders, will be able to:

- Understand the rationale and cite evidence for the value and advantages of classroom assessment in multiple languages for their multilingual learners

- Add to their toolkit of classroom assessment practices in one or multiple languages

- Be more precise and effective in their assessment of multilingual learners by embedding assessment *as*, *for*, and *of* learning into their instructional repertoires

- Realize how social-emotional, content, and language learning are all tied to classroom assessment for multilingual learners

- Guide multilingual learners in having voice and choice in the assessment process.

HOW IS THIS BOOK ORGANIZED?

The Preface and each chapter begin with a scenario of an issue pertinent to multilingual assessment or one that attempts to dispel a myth surrounding the education of multilingual learners. It is followed by First Impressions, a set of questions that stimulate discussion of the reader's immediate reactions to the dilemma illuminated in the scenario. From this point, after the introductory chapters, each chapter is framed around the enactment of a phase of the assessment cycle.

Chapter 1 introduces the world of multilingual education and multilingual learners. It clarifies confusing terminology that seems to prevail and provides a rationale for the preference of the term multilingual learners when referring to students and multilingual education when speaking of educational programs. In it, we argue for a more assets-based orientation when speaking about students who interact in multiple languages and a description of language programs in which they participate.

Chapter 2 treats the complexity of assessment in multiple languages and teases out, step-by-step, how a multiphase assessment process interacts with assessment *as*, *for*, and *of* learning. Classroom examples illuminate each phase of the assessment cycle, and educators become aware of how to incorporate the three approaches into assessment in their setting. Furthermore, we begin to envision how the student perspective adds to the richness of the assessment process.

Chapters 3 through 7 incorporate linguistic and culturally relevant considerations for assessing multilingual learners in multiple languages for each phase of the assessment cycle: (1) planning, (2) collecting and organizing information, (3) interpreting information and providing feedback, (4) evaluating and reporting information, and (5) taking action. With a detailed description of how to prepare for and enact classroom assessment in multiple languages, students, teachers, and other school leaders can then apply these new tools, tips, and resources to their individual contexts.

The central focus of the book is on maintaining a balance among the assessment approaches *as, for,* and *of* learning and their application to multiple language use throughout the assessment process. There are also two subthemes that are woven throughout the pages, namely, how (1) multimodal communication can optimize multilingual learners' opportunities to access challenging content during instruction and assessment, and (2) translanguaging, the natural interplay between languages, can be an acceptable classroom instructional and assessment practice.

Toward the end of each chapter are actionable tips for younger and older multilingual learners, teachers and other school instructional leaders, as well as school leaders. Additionally, there is a suggestion for how to tackle the dilemma of each chapter. Lastly, a set of resources (e.g., surveys, checklists, **rating scales**, and self-assessments) invites readers to duplicate them for professional learning and classroom use or to access them on the book's website.

HOW DOES THE BOOK CONTRIBUTE TO SOCIAL JUSTICE AND EQUITY FOR MULTILINGUAL LEARNERS?

Multilingual learners deserve meaningful and fair assessment that generates useful information for improving teaching and learning in linguistically and culturally sustainable classrooms and schools. Anything less is neither equitable nor just. We assert that largely missing from this equation is the examination of the language, conceptual, and social-emotional development of multilingual learners and assessment of that growth in multiple languages. When multilingual learners are able to show what they know and can do using their full linguistic and academic repertoires, we enhance their prospects for success in school and beyond.

I should know—I have been one of those classroom teachers in search of fair and equitable ways to assess the growing numbers of multilingual learners in school. My career as a language teacher began in a large urban center where each year waves of immigrants would appear at the school's doorsteps. Unfortunately, these young, bright, enthusiastic students were soon stifled by not being able to demonstrate their full capabilities. In contrast, while most of today's multilingual learners have been born in the U.S., the issue remains: How can we elevate the status of classroom assessment in multiple languages in schools, districts, and states?

The opening scenario of the Preface previews one of the primary tenets of the book: multilingualism is desirable and advantageous, especially for **minoritized students**. To capitalize on this **heteroglossic language ideology**, we offer ideas for how educators can maximize opportunities for inclusion of multiple languages in their classroom assessment without adding time—no matter how many multilingual learners, the number of languages students speak, and the cultures they represent.

WHAT ARE SOME SPECIAL FEATURES OF THIS BOOK?

There are a couple of unique features of this book which hopefully will be helpful to you, other educators, and multilingual learners. First, educators' self- and co-assessment and multilingual learners' self- and peer assessment are built into the chapters to allow for ongoing personal reflection and to promote interaction and deep discussion of the issues. Second, in addition to Resources for Teachers and Other Instructional Leaders, in each chapter there are Resources for Multilingual Learners to be shared with the learners.

WHAT ARE SOME TIPS FOR ASSESSMENT IN MULTIPLE LANGUAGES?

Assessing multilingual learners is complicated; assessing multilingual learners in multiple languages even more so if you don't set the ground rules early with your students. Here is some general advice on what you can do at the beginning of the school year to start to form a mindset for instruction and assessment in multiple languages.

Guidelines for Assessing Multilingual Learners in Multiple Languages

1. Acquaint yourself with each and every one of your students and try to understand the impact of crisis, trauma, and stress on their individual and families' lives.

2. Become familiar with the patterns of language use of your multilingual learners, in English and their other languages, such as those obtained from My Personal Portrait (see Chapter 1, Resource 1.3).

3. Make sure that your multilingual learners are comfortable using multiple languages by creating and maintaining a warm, inviting, and safe classroom (and school) environment.

4. Develop a language and assessment policy for the classroom with your multilingual learners around the role and use of multiple languages (e.g., their use of glossaries, tech tools, interactive practices with peers) and have multilingual learners share it with family members, other teachers, and school leaders.

5. Allow multilingual learners to use multiple languages for specific purposes for instruction (e.g., clarifying information or ideas with others who share their partner language), even if instruction is in English; make sure to carry these instructional routines over to classroom assessment.

6. Remember that the language(s) of assessment should reflect the language(s) of instruction of each content area and that translanguaging (the natural exchange of multiple languages acknowledging multilingual learners' full linguistic repertoire) allows for enhanced expression of multilingual learners.

7. Negotiate multilingual learners' preferred use of multimodal communication (e.g., visual, digital, tactile, aural) in the design and assessment of classroom projects.

HOW MIGHT WE FACE THE ISSUE?

In this section, we revisit the central issue of the chapter and pose questions that bring the content to the forefront of discussion (and often courageous conversations) for students, teachers, and other school leaders. Based on the issue, we suggest that teachers carve out time from individual lessons to personalize learning for multilingual learners and to connect the issue to their lives. Time might also be devoted to professional learning, whether in person or online, through learning communities or extensive networks, to air some of the inherent controversy of the issue. Here is a sampling of questions around the issue of multilingualism and classroom assessment.

For Younger Multilingual Learners

- How many languages do you speak at home? Which ones? With whom?

- What do you like to do in school? What do you like to do when *not* in school? Which languages do you like to use?

- What is your favorite way to show teachers what you have learned—by talking to others, by writing, or by drawing?

- Do you use more than one language(s) at school? When or where?

For Older Multilingual Learners

- How do you define yourself as a language learner? What are some of the ways you use your multiple languages?

- What is your favorite type of assignment in school? Do you think in one or more languages when completing your assignments?

- What is your preferred way of showing your teachers what you know or your evidence for learning—by speaking, writing, illustrating, or a combination of ways?

- Do you use more than one language in school? When? With whom do you prefer to use your different languages, or at times, do you like to use both together?

For Teachers and Other Instructional Leaders

- Which terms has your school adopted to refer to multilingualism and multilingual learners? Do you agree with the terminology? If you don't, what might be your rationale for change and how might you pose it to the community, school board, or school leaders?

- Which considerations (linguistic, cultural, academic, experiential) do you take into account when assessing multilingual learners? How do you secure that information about your students?

- With whom might you collaborate, including your students, to accomplish short- and long-term goals of providing more equitable classroom assessment for multilingual learners?

- Why is assessment in multiple languages so critical for the equity of multilingual learners?

For School Leaders

- Do you dare to defy your colleagues who disagree with your school's values or position on multilingualism? If so, what evidence can you use to support your stance? How might you convince your colleagues of your position?

- How might you and others update your school's mission and vision to be more representative and inclusive of multilingualism, equity, and social justice; then, how might it be realized through an instruction and assessment policy?

- In your school, what is the current relationship between multilingual education and classroom assessment in multiple languages? Should it be revisited?

- What suggestions might you and others make to integrate principles of multilingualism and multiculturalism into instruction and classroom assessment?

HOW MIGHT WE RESOLVE THE DILEMMA? SUPPLEMENT HIGH-STAKES TESTS IN ENGLISH WITH COMPREHENSIVE MEASURES IN MULTIPLE LANGUAGES!

At the close of each chapter there is always a resolution to the dilemma introduced in the opening scenario. In this instance, we side with the third-grade dual language teachers who insist on more equitable measures to reflect the languages of instruction rather than solely relying on tests administered in English, a language in which multilingual learners are not fully versed, as the barometer of success. Anita and her dual language colleagues are committed to continue using multiple languages for instruction and assessment so that their multilingual learners can produce counterevidence to that of the forthcoming high-stakes tests in English. They plan to communicate to their principal that classroom assessment must be seen through the lens of multilingual learners!

WHAT HAS HAPPENED TO OUR MULTILINGUAL LEARNERS?

Upon completing the manuscript, our universe was turned upside down by the introduction of the novel COVID-19 virus. It would be remiss if one of the most galvanizing events of our lifetime was not acknowledged and its impact on K–12 education, in particular, multilingual learners and their families, was not addressed in some small way. As of this writing, we can only imagine what the new normal will ultimately be and how education will have to change to ensure the health and safety of students and educators.

Although the message of the book has not been altered, how we look at the world has. We are more dependent than ever on processing and producing information online and maintaining our distance in person. During these most difficult times, our roles as educators have expanded tremendously; not only are we instructional leaders, but counselors, psychologists, social workers, and advisors. Many of us are also home schooling our own children and taking care of households while assuming our teaching responsibilities.

We are constantly assessing multilingual learners' language and academic development, but what has become readily apparent is that assessment also entails social-emotional development. Knowing that multilingual learners will have spent the greater part of a year at home where languages other than English often prevail, it becomes crystal clear why assessment in multiple learners is justified and needed more than ever.

Let's examine some of the factors that have been influencing multilingual learners during late winter through spring of 2020 and the additional stressors on their lives—namely, economic, health, and safety—that have come to make our young learners so delicate. Although many students may be resilient, countless multilingual learners and their families are already marginalized and compromised. Schools are more than places of learning; they often serve as support systems for the most vulnerable students. Now is the time for instructional and school leaders to rise to the occasion and discuss sensitive issues about school closure, underscoring the intersections of race, culture, poverty, and accessibility.

Understandably, educators want to help. What can classroom teachers, support staff, or school leaders do to help multilingual learners emerge from this crisis? It is more important than ever to have information and resources available in multiple languages to multilingual learners, their families, and, to the extent feasible, throughout the community. Here is a series of tips for:

Fostering teachers' and other educators' communication with multilingual families:

1. Be empathetic and understanding of the unforeseen circumstances that COVID-19 has brought, such as changes in living arrangements, along with the accompanying emotional and economic upheaval.

2. Inform families and multilingual learners of their rights (e.g., in school, multilingual learners are a protected class) in language(s) they thoroughly understand.

3. Help families surmount economic hardship, to the extent feasible, such as listing food pantries and hours of operation in the community or where to pick up "grab and go" meals.

4. Set up or tap into a hotline of available social and medical services, preferably in multiple languages, and advice, such as when and where to seek assistance.

5. Understand that those families who are working may be doing so in unsafe environments, such as meat packing plants or agricultural areas, or must rely on public transportation.

6. Share symptoms and first steps in combatting COVID-19, safety measures, and when it is advisable to go to clinics or hospitals.

7. To the extent feasible, provide local community and school updates on a regular basis.

8. Download and share information from trustworthy websites.

9. Make the school website inviting and in the languages of family members.

10. Help family members share the joy and benefits from story telling and singing songs from other cultures in multiple languages.

Supporting teachers and other educators of multilingual learners:

1. Make the inequitable equitable.

2. Recognize that the digital divide is growing and greater than ever; it might be difficult for students to secure internet access (e.g., in some districts, school buses go to parking lots to set up hotspots for students to download materials), if, in fact they have devices.

3. Arrange for models, such as peers, to interact with other students in English and their partner language.

4. Offer tutorials on new material through software programs and online tools.

5. Find online resources (e.g., websites, apps) in multiple languages to advance learning.

6. Realize that there are multilingual learners who are homeless or living in very cramped noisy conditions with multiple generations with no room to work.

7. Use flipped-learning strategies where teachers post videos of interest as an entrée to students' new learning experiences.

8. Encourage and gently push multilingual learners; be empathetic, optimistic and calm, no matter what their circumstances.

9. Understand that many family members, including multilingual learners, may not be well-versed in technology.

10. Remember that parents/guardians are students' first teachers. Provide assignments that engage families, understanding that in some households there may be only one parent and that person may not be familiar with the concepts being taught or the teaching approaches being used.

11. Be cognizant that there are cultural innuendoes in materials and different cultural perspectives that should be leveraged to maximize learning opportunities for multilingual learners.

12. Brainstorm ways to co-plan and co-assess with colleagues in virtual meetings.

13. Don't be surprised at the mobility rate of your students; more than likely, families are seeking more secure living quarters with relatives.

14. Protect your multilingual learners and their families from discrimination and racism.

15. Activate students' prior knowledge and connect to their experiences before pursuing new learning.

You might ask, where does assessment fit into today's upside-down inside-out classroom? The last set of tips offer ideas for teachers of multilingual learners for collecting, analyzing, and sharing information with students and other educators to help move learning forward.

Ideas for seamlessly embedding classroom assessment in multiple languages remotely during times of unrest and re-entry into brick and mortar schools:

1. Get to know your students more deeply by having them maintain reflection logs, not only to reflect on content-based material but also to express their personal reactions (whether oral, written, visual, or digital) to the current situation.

2. Pair multilingual learners of shared languages virtually so that they may interact with each other and engage in activities together.

3. Have multilingual learners design products or create projects from everyday household materials or what may be in their immediate environment based on criteria for success.

4. Encourage students to self-assess and monitor their own learning.

5. If *all* multilingual learners have cell phones, use them as a resource to exchange photos, record videos, or engage in social media to respond to questions.

6. Have multilingual learners record their feelings in multiple languages (as an emotional outlet), whether or not their teachers are fluent in the language.

7. Tap educational websites serving multilingual learners for assessment ideas.

8. Pay attention to how your state is screening and identifying English learners.

9. Have a toolkit of different measures or instructional activities and tasks to use when brick and mortar schools resume so that you can easily and readily assess what multilingual learners can do in multiple languages.

10. Connect realistic, yet challenging, assignments to students' lives and interests; think of alternate ways of grading, if necessary at all.

Please use these ideas and those of your own as a backdrop to contextualize instruction and assessment for multilingual learners in multiple languages. After all, "our shared humanity is a call for education equity" (Burris, 2020, n.p.).

About the Author

Margo Gottlieb, PhD, is Co-founder and Lead Developer for WIDA at the Wisconsin Center for Education Research, University of Wisconsin–Madison, having also served as Director, Assessment and Evaluation, for the Illinois Resource Center. She has contributed to the crafting of language proficiency/development standards for American Samoa, Commonwealth of the Northern Mariana Islands, Guam, TESOL International Association, and WIDA and has designed assessments, curricular frameworks, and instructional assessment systems for multilingual learners. Her professional experiences span from being an inner-city language teacher to working with thousands of educators across states, school districts, publishing companies, governments, universities, and educational organizations.

Highlights of Margo's career include being a Fulbright Senior Specialist in Chile and being appointed to the U.S. Department of Education's Inaugural National Technical Advisory Council. TESOL International Association honored Margo in 2016 "as an individual who has made a significant contribution to the TESOL profession within the past 50 years." Having presented in 20 countries and across the United States, she relishes having opportunities for extensive travel and cherishes her global friendships.

Margo's widespread publications comprise more than 90 chapters, technical reports, monographs, articles, and encyclopedia entries. Additionally she has authored, co-authored, and co-edited 14 books, including *Language Power: Key Uses for Accessing Content* (with M. Castro, 2017), *Assessing Multilingual Learners: A Month-by-Month Guide (2017), Assessing English Language Learners: Bridges to Educational Equity* (2nd ed., 2016), *Academic Language in Diverse Classrooms: Definitions and Contexts* (with G. Ernst-Slavit, 2014), *Promoting Content and Language Learning* (a compendium of three mathematics and three English language arts volumes co-edited with G. Ernst-Slavit, 2013, 2014), *Common Language Assessment for English Learners* (2012), *Paper to Practice: Using the TESOL English Language Proficiency Standards in PreK–12 Classrooms* (with A. Katz & G. Ernst-Slavit, 2009); and *Assessment and Accountability in Language Education Programs: A Guide for Administrators and Teachers* (with D. Nguyen, 2007).

This book is dedicated to Helena, my Greek Macedonian 'adopted' grand-daughter, living in the UK, whose multiple languages and cultures help define her spirit and joyful being. Much credit goes to her multilingual multicultural parents whose linguistic identities have also been shaped from experiences they have accrued in many lands across the globe. My wish is for all multilingual learners to be able to share the sheer delight and pride in their languages and cultures as is portrayed in this young child.

CHAPTER 1

Who Are Multilingual Learners and Why Assess in Multiple Languages?

Als je me labelt, ontken je me.

Once you label me, you negate me.

—Søren Kierkegaard, 1849

The Dilemma

But the term English learners *doesn't accentuate what our students can do!*

After a happy early childhood experience in a small community center close to home, Juanito and other entering kindergartners enroll in the neighborhood elementary school. The young learners have become accustomed to a play-based environment where they interact with each other in multiple languages. Family members are warmly welcomed and children's bilingualism is celebrated as parents "help sustain their child's interest in using all the languages they hear by being enthusiastic and playful about multilingualism" (Cuéllar, 2019, n.p.).

As other new kindergartners to Einstein Elementary School, these same **dual language learners** (as they are referred to in early childhood education) are screened with an English language proficiency test to identify their current language development status. As a result of this policy of testing only in English, many of these dual language learners are now labeled **English learners**, the legal term applied to multilingual learners who qualify for English language support.

What began as a joyful relationship-building time for young learners is soon cast aside and replaced by a perception of what kindergartners are lacking: English. At Einstein, no attempt is made to ascertain the children's use of their other languages, their (pre)literacy development in their other languages, or types of activities that help spur conceptual development in their other languages. It appears that the only information that kindergarten teachers receive about their incoming class of multilingual learners is the students' English language proficiency levels.

Families and teachers have drafted a petition for dual language learners to have educational continuity as they transition from preschool to Einstein. A committee has also been formed to investigate initiating dual language education at the school. One of the first steps taken by the group is to develop a schoolwide and classroom language policy for instruction and assessment in multiple languages.

Mr. George, the principal, believes that the federal term English learner *is just fine and an accurate label for these students. He has also assigned it to describe the teachers and program as well as instruction and assessment practices. Given his "one student, one language" mentality, Mr. George sees no reason to have "readiness" measures for incoming kindergartners in languages other than English.

The teachers and community, however, think otherwise and are determined to change the principal's mind. They much prefer the umbrella term multilingual learners *to represent the entire range of students who interact in multiple languages and cultures. Having a more comprehensive portrait of incoming students will certainly be helpful for teachers' planning instruction and classroom assessment. What can the kindergarten team do to convince Mr. George?*

- In what ways does this scenario resonate with you?

- What is the terminology used in your setting to represent multilingual learners, their languages, cultures, and programs?

- How does the current terminology positively or negatively impact classroom instructional and assessment practices?

- How might you advocate for instruction and assessment in multiple languages when faced with resistance?

Short and Fitzsimmons (2007) assert that "English language learners must perform *double the work* of native English speakers in the country's middle and high schools" (p. 1). This powerful statement is an awakening to teachers of the reality that **multilingual learners** face every day at school. However, it doesn't quite capture the magnitude of the educational challenges that confront multilingual learners who are participating in dual language, bilingual education, or other educational programs where learning in two languages is the classroom norm.

The reality is that not only are *multilingual learners* (the term inclusive of English language learners in this book) in these contexts being immersed in grade-level content and language simultaneously, they are doing so in multiple languages! More and more multilingual learners are participating in language education programs that are striving to meet the goals of bilingualism, biliteracy, biculturalism, and their most recent pillar, critical consciousness (Palmer, Cervantes-Soon, Dorner, & Heiman, 2019). Yet, rather than having an **assets-based orientation** to education, reports from **large-scale assessment** still tend to demoralize multilingual learners by emphasizing what these students lack, that is, English language proficiency (Gándara, 2015). Then there is the cry of the eternal achievement "gap" between multilingual learners and their fourth- and eighth-grade peers as determined by the National Assessment of Educational Progress (NAEP) reading scale scores (NCES, 2013).

Let's make a pact and look at multilingualism in a positive light; as Wong (2016) suggests, let's use multilingualism as a tool for closing the achievement gap. The pages before you attempt to turn the negativity that has prevailed in U.S. schools and society, namely, the view that multilingual learners are a liability, a problem in need of fixing (Escamilla, 2016), into a more positive strength-based stance where language is viewed as a right and resource (Ruíz, 1988). In doing so, we present ways to overturn terminology and labels that cast a negative light in favor of concepts that accentuate a multilingual/multicultural presence in classrooms and schools. We suggest how school and classroom language and assessment policies pose ways in which teachers, other instructional leaders, and multilingual learners alike can agree on how to accentuate opportunities for infusing multilingualism into curriculum, instruction, and assessment to become an educational way of life.

WHAT IS THE TERMINOLOGY (AND LABELS) FOR MULTILINGUAL LEARNERS AND THEIR TIE TO ASSESSMENT?

There is a tremendous variability in what constitutes **multilingual education** and the students who participate in such programs. Multilingual education invites and embraces multiple perspectives that stimulate deep thinking in multiple languages. Educators involved in multilingual education must be mindful of the inequities in policies that surround multilingual learners, must advocate on their behalf, and must combat against discriminatory practices. And yet, when it comes time for assessment, there is still a lot of misconceptions to dispel. Let's define some basic concepts before we launch into the assessment process.

Multilingual Education

We consider the concepts of multilingual education and **multilingualism** to be an extension of Cenoz and Gorter's 2015 definition: "multilingual education refers to the use of two or more languages in education, provided that schools aim at multilingualism and multiliteracy" (p. 2). In essence, *multilingual education* is an umbrella term that refers to the design of teaching and learning opportunities with multilingual learners in mind, whether for just a few students or a majority of the student body, no matter what their linguistic and cultural mix.

Multilingual education is more than a superficial treatment of linguistic and cultural diversity and greater than an appendix or a patch to extant curriculum. Multilingual education operates within a sociocultural context that can be described as part of comprehensive school reform that reaches down to every classroom. At its heart, multilingual education is critical pedagogy that represents social justice, important for all students, teachers, and educational leaders (Nieto, 2018).

Multilingualism

Within a school context, multilingualism encompasses the use of multilingual learners' multiple languages and cultures as resources for curriculum, instruction, and assessment. Like many educational concepts, multilingualism is not monolithic with one set way of being (namely, you are either multilingual or not); in fact, the multilingual population is so diversified that it might be envisioned along a continuum (de Jong, 2019).

In today's world, we cannot avoid multilingualism as it is enmeshed in prominent 21st-century themes of globalization, technologization, and politicalization (Douglas Fir Group, 2016). Within the confines of this book, however, it is being treated as an educational phenomenon within the context of K–12 schooling. Simply stated, multilingualism, by referencing and leveraging multiple languages and cultures from the vantage point of multilingual learners, is a healthy alternative to monolingual ideologies that view English as the norm.

Multilingual Learners

Multilingual learners is an assets-based term that is descriptive of a wide range of students who are or have been exposed to multiple languages and cultures on a consistent basis in or out of school. Some have participated in language education programs, others have not. Some have multilingual and multicultural roots that are evident in their home life, others do not. There is as huge a variety of students as there are circumstances and situations for their multiple language use. Schools, often taking their cue from federal legislation, their state, and district, use different labels to categorize students; some are linked to funding sources, others are not.

Educators and scholars alike have grappled with how to attenuate or, better yet, eradicate **deficit ideologies**. As Kibler and Valdés (2016) remind us, language is not neutral, and the ways in which our institutions tend to manufacture terms to classify students can be detrimental to their well-being and carry life-long consequences. An interesting study by Umansky and Dumont (2019) points to significant differences in teacher perception in the labeling of English learners (ELs). Their findings suggest that the classification of primary grade students as ELs results in lower teacher perceptions of these students' achievement across content areas; however, if ELs participate in bilingual instructional settings, the impact is moderated.

Most labels for multilingual learners are based on monolingual constructs that tend to stigmatize rather than elevate the status of their language development (García, 2009b).

SOURCE: Brenda (2018), pp. 152–153.

Case in point, there are several designations for ELs (e.g., English language learners or **emergent bilinguals**), a subset of multilingual learners that fall under federal **accountability**. The range of multilingual learners and their most widely accepted labels by educators are shown in Figure 1.1. Multilingual learners who are currently ELs are listed in the right-hand column while others are on the left-hand side.

Title 1 of the **Every Student Succeeds Act**, the 2015 iteration of the Elementary and Secondary Education Act, requires annual assessment of ELs, long-term ELs, and ELs with disabilities in Grades K–12 for English language proficiency and in Grades 3–8 and once in high school for English language arts/reading and mathematics with science testing occurring three times during the students' school career. Although the vast majority of these students function in more than one language, there is generally no attention to their bilingualism in testing (Shohamy, 2011). Let's explore each of these subgroups with an eye toward assessment practices.

There has been increasing focus on the accurate identification, assessment, and referral of **ELs with disabilities.** Attention to this issue, in part, has been triggered by the disproportionate under- and over-identification of ELs, as compared to non-ELs, for all categories of special education services (National Academies of Sciences and Engineering Medicine, 2017). ELs with disabilities qualify for both language support and their named disability included in an **Individualized Education Program (IEP)**. This dual identification requires a multiphased assessment process that should involve multiple measures in the students' multiple languages.

FIGURE 1.1 The Compendium of Multilingual Learners

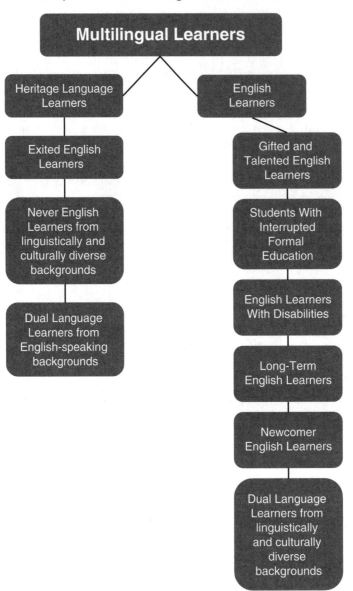

Long-term ELs (**LTELs**) are multilingual learners who are most likely in middle and high schools who have attended school for more than six years without having attained a prescribed threshold of academic language proficiency in English as determined by annual state testing. Some are **transnational** students who move back and forth between the U.S. and their family's country of origin or students born and raised in the U.S. who have received inconsistent schooling (Menken & Kleyn, 2009). Some LTELs are considered **students with interrupted formal education (SIFE).** Other SIFE students are refugees or migrants in Grades 4 through 12 who have sporadic attendance records, are transient, or are simply the product of discontinuity or inconsistency in educational programming. In fact, approximately 20% of the EL population is itinerant, students who tend to move so frequently they become lost in the system (Sahakyan & Ryan, 2018).

Newcomer ELs refer to multilingual learners born outside of the U.S. who have recently arrived at our shores and have enrolled in school within the past one to four years (depending on the state definition). Newcomer families have made their way here and to Canada from war-torn or politically unstable countries from around the world. Many have been traumatized and are under emotional duress for fear of persecution in their homelands. Individuals, such as unaccompanied minors, may also fall into this classification. Many **newcomers** attend specialized programs in middle or high schools with defined assessment procedures, including that of "native language literacy skills" (MAEC, 2019).

Just as important are those ELs who participate in *gifted and talented* programs. Local (district and school) policies often determine criteria for gifted and talented students with identification practices and assessment measures that, in large part, privilege **proficient English students**. Typically, identification involves the assessment of cognitive abilities in combination with **achievement testing** (Mun et al., 2016) in English. Absent is assessment in multiple languages, although an exploratory study recommended "creating alternative pathways to identification, allowing schools to use a variety of different assessment instruments (including **native language** ability and achievement assessments and reliable and valid nonverbal ability assessments) and to apply flexible criteria to ensure that students' talents and abilities are recognized" (Gubbins et al., 2018).

We cannot forget that there are other **minoritized students** in addition to the heterogeneous group of ELs exposed to multiple languages and cultures who are considered multilingual learners. First of all, there are **proficient English speakers** who have previously participated in language support programs, have met state exit criteria through assessment, and no longer qualify for language support services (*exited ELs*). In most states after four years post-participation, their educational status is officially changed; however, they continue to reside in multilingual/multicultural homes and communities. Others may be multilingual learners who perhaps are simultaneous bilinguals (who have been developing in two languages since birth) and, being English proficient, have never qualified as ELs (*never ELs*) as determined by initial screening measures.

Heritage language learners, students who come from home backgrounds with connections to multiple languages and cultures although they may not be proficient in a language other than English, are another group of multilingual learners. There are also multilingual learners who are members of indigenous communities (e.g., Navajo, Hawaiian, Arapaho, Chamorro) and are studying their heritage language for development, preservation, or maintenance (Kelleher, 2010).

In addition to these categories of multilingual learners, we need to recognize the growing numbers of students in dual language programs in the U.S. (namely, **dual language learners**) and in international contexts that are considered "elite" or "prestigious" with learners from "upwardly mobile, highly educated, higher socio-economic status" families (de Mejía, 2002). The most notable of these have been immersion programs, originating in Canada in the 1970s, designed for language "majority" students (Genesee, 2006; Lambert & Tucker, 1972). In the broadest sense, these students are also considered multilingual.

As you can see, the term *multilingual learners* is an inclusive one that describes a wide range of students who have been exposed to and interact in multiple languages and cultures. Consequently, in order to be sensitive to multilingual learner identities and their contexts for learning, assessment in multiple languages must be just as broad a classification scheme. Minimally, **classroom assessment** in multiple languages implies the reliance on two or more languages of equal status used in the collection, analysis, interpretation, and reporting of information to make instructional decisions.

Relax and Reflect: What terminology and associated assessment are part of your setting?

Let's revisit Figure 1.1 and select the subsets of multilingual learners that are identified as ELs (or ELLs, EBs, or DLLs) in your school. For each group of multilingual learners that you list from the left-hand side of the figure, such as the Newcomer example, jot down the assessment measures that determine their classification and the languages in which they are available. If there isn't enough information from the measures, think of next steps with your colleagues.

WHICH MULTILINGUAL LEARNERS	WHICH ASSESSMENT MEASURES	IN WHICH LANGUAGES
Newcomer ELs	• Language proficiency screener • Written description of an action picture • Welcome oral interview	• English • English and students' other language(s) • English and students' other language(s)
ELs with disabilities (IEPs)		
Gifted and talented ELs		
Long-term ELs (LTELs)		

WHAT ARE THE PREVAILING THEORIES OF LANGUAGE LEARNING?

Two theories of language learning reflect the dominant perspectives that have been taken by districts, schools, and the world of language assessment. A traditional cognitivist or structuralist view is one where second language acquisition is considered a linear process where students' language development is measured against a continuum from less to most proficient. This theoretical stance envisions language learning as a systematic prescribed sequence where the end point of the language proficiency scale means having reached the proficiency of an "idealized native speaker" (Douglas Fir Group, 2016). Figure 1.2 illustrates the

FIGURE 1.2   A Linear Progression of English Language Proficiency

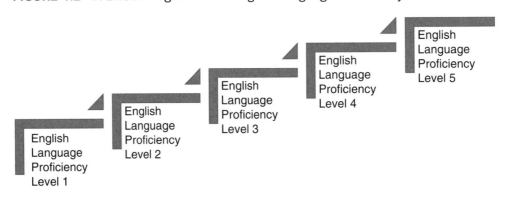

stair-step progression of this theory, from the lowest level of language proficiency (level 1) to the highest (level 5).

In recent years, structuralist theory with its claims that language development occurs in a prescribed sequence has been contested. Mahboob (2019) negates a native-speaking norm as an end goal for language learning, stating that it is imprecise and inappropriate. Likewise, Valdés (2005) and Phillipson (1994) call structuralist theory a "native speaker fallacy." These theorists replace emphasis on accuracy with a model of effectiveness where language development is sensitive to the context in which learning occurs.

Educational perspectives now see teaching and learning as cultural, social, and interactional (Hawkins, 2019). This more fluid sociocultural view of language development can be envisioned as a circle with interactive components against a backdrop of intersecting constructs of language, literacy, and culture (Nieto, 2018). Figure 1.3 shows a wheel of components, which helps define the different contexts for communication.

Put another way, according to sociocultural theory, language learning is contextually dependent. That is, language development is considered an interactive social process whereby multilingual learners learn to control increasing ranges of registers and **genres** that are influenced by a series of factors (Hammond & Gibbons, 2005). From this sociocultural perspective, students' variability in performance, in part, can be attributed to:

1. Their familiarity with particular situations or topics

2. Their interest and motivation

3. The purpose for messaging or communicating

4. The activities or actions in which students engage

5. The roles and stances that depict the identities of the students

FIGURE 1.3 Components That Affect the Context for Communication

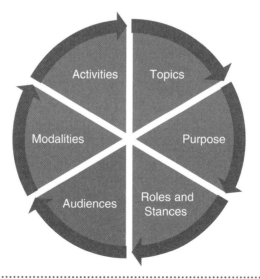

SOURCE: Gottlieb and Castro (2017), p. 25.

6. The modalities or ways of communicating (orally, visually, digitally, tactilely, or in writing)

7. The restrictiveness or flexibility of multiple language use

8. The understanding of cultural assumptions

9. The amount and appropriateness of **scaffolding**

10. The perceived audience or the participants in the interaction.

The field of language assessment has taken note of the theoretical movement toward more socially driven activity; as a result, it has broadened its scope. Bachman and Damböck (2017) have articulated how this dramatic shift has impacted the classroom. They state that "language assessment is no longer primarily viewed as a technical activity of obtaining **test** scores and analyzing these technically. Rather it is now viewed much more broadly as a socioculturally embedded process" (p. 1). In essence, assessment has moved beyond measurement instruments (i.e., **tests**) to activities that reflect the culture of the classroom and its primary purpose of improving teaching and learning.

One other aspect of sociocultural theory has direct implications for classroom instruction and assessment. With learning considered a more interactive process, a more dynamic and adaptive notion of assessment emerges with an expanded role of teachers and students. That is, for multilingual learners, classroom assessment has become increasingly learner-centered, more inclusive of student voice where students are co-contributors, in collaboration with teachers, to **learning goals** and accompanying evidence for reaching them (Gottlieb, 2016; Moss, 2008; Wajda, 2011).

Translanguaging

Have you ever observed your multilingual learners chatting on the playground, in the lunchroom, in the hallways, or study halls? What languages do you hear? Is it the students' **home language**, English, or an interweaving of both languages?

 Stop-Think-Act-React

Relax and Reflect: What is your school's theoretical basis for assessment?

In grade-level teams or professional learning communities, teachers and other school leaders should be encouraged to draw (literally) their representation of multilingual development (such as in Figures 1.2 and 1.3) to help better understand instruction and assessment for their multilingual learners. Each drawing should depict how a theory or combination of theories of language learning and assessment might be converted into practice in their classrooms and school. Each group of educators should have time to explain their theoretical orientation and together decide on the prevailing theory for supporting multilingual learners in their school.

"Bilingual kids mix languages and it's OK; it does not mean they are confused, they are just figuring it all out" (BilingualKidspot.com).

As an arm of sociocultural theory, **translanguaging** has been widely applied to language education and has helped shape the transformation and acceptance of multiple languages and languaging as part of schooling (García & Wei, 2018). **Translanguaging**, in essence, is the natural intermingling of languages for given purposes and audiences. For multilingual learners, it is indicative of a single linguistic repertoire rather than the maintenance of two or more independent language systems.

In school, translanguaging represents multilingual learners' access to and use of all their languages, irrespective of the language(s) of instruction (García, Ibarra Johnson, & Seltzer, 2017). In dual language and bilingual education classrooms that have a strong presence of two languages, assessment may be dynamic and fluid, inclusive of translanguaging, to show what multilingual learners can do with language(s) in different circumstances. Broadly speaking, we can say that translanguaging encompasses the linguistic practices of bilinguals (Otheguy, García, & Reid, 2015). In the upcoming chapters, we shall see how to apply this new respect for simultaneous use of multiple languages through translanguaging to classroom assessment.

 Stop-Think-Act-React

Relax and Reflect: What does translanguaging mean to you?

Ever since the notion of translanguaging came onto the educational scene in the U.S. (García, 2009a) it has stirred up controversy. Be an explorer and take note of the times you hear a mix of languages by multilingual learners and their teachers alike whether inside or outside the building. Ask students if they are aware of the languages that they use with different people and why they make the language choices they do. The information will be useful in formulating a classroom language and assessment policy.

WHAT IS A FRAMEWORK FOR CLASSROOM ASSESSMENT IN MULTIPLE LANGUAGES?

How might theory on multilingual development and language learning help inform the design of a framework for assessment in multiple languages? The research that supports sociocultural pedagogy in multilingual multicultural classrooms also points to having a coherent framework for sociocultural assessment (Smith, Teemant, & Pinnegar, 2004). We take this principle one step further by asserting that to be equitable, classroom assessment for multilingual learners must also be inclusive of the students' multiple languages and cultural perspectives.

Figure 1.4 offers such a classroom assessment framework where the multiple languages of multilingual learners are part of the fabric of assessment planning and practices. Ultimately, decisions are predicated on the purpose of assessment and multilingual learners' use of multiple languages that reveal their entire linguistic pool.

FIGURE 1.4 Framing Classroom Assessment in Multiple Languages

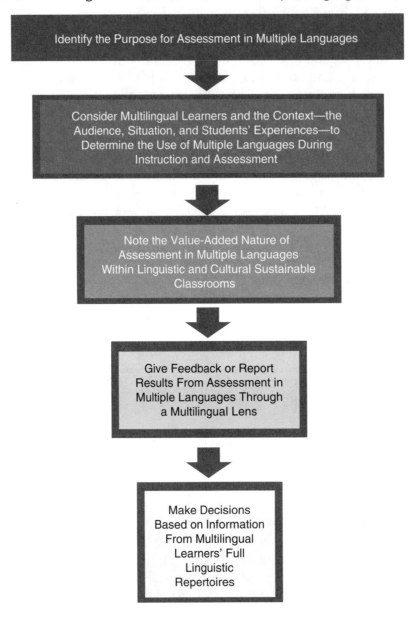

Identify the Purpose for Assessment in Multiple Languages

Consider Multilingual Learners and the Context—the Audience, Situation, and Students' Experiences—to Determine the Use of Multiple Languages During Instruction and Assessment

Note the Value-Added Nature of Assessment in Multiple Languages Within Linguistic and Cultural Sustainable Classrooms

Give Feedback or Report Results From Assessment in Multiple Languages Through a Multilingual Lens

Make Decisions Based on Information From Multilingual Learners' Full Linguistic Repertoires

HOW MIGHT WE CREATE A LANGUAGE AND ASSESSMENT POLICY?

Language policy is educational policy. Schoolwide language policies help establish coherent K–12 language programming for multilingual learners while also supporting the greater school community. School leaders, instructional leaders, school staff, community representatives, family members, and students should join in building consensus around how to portray their school as a haven for their multilingual learners, languages, and cultures.

A stunning example of how multilingualism has become engrained in the fabric of teaching and learning is the language policy of Lincoln International School (Asociación Escuelas Lincoln) in Buenos Aires, Argentina. Its teachers have crafted and adopted a set of belief statements and evidence-based practices as part of its language philosophy that exemplifies its values and highlights the strength of multilingualism. Some of these language-centered, research-based principles, such as affirmation and enrichment, have become enacted in the school's everyday practices. As multilingualism and multiculturalism are critical to family communication, cultural identity, making meaning, and thinking, the school promotes and reinforces their continuous development. Equally important, in learning through multiple languages as media of instruction, all students:

- Construct understandings about interculturalism and global interdependence

- Develop competencies in conflict resolution in socially responsible ways

- Formulate insights to facilitate movement across cultural and linguistic boundaries

- Respect multiple perspectives.

Policies, including those for language and assessment, designed and upheld by the school and local community, should reverberate in every classroom. Teachers, along with students, should make a pact at the beginning of year that spells out the parameters of multiple language use. Resource 1.1, Our Classroom Language and Assessment Policy, suggests routine language-centered activities where multilingual learners have opportunities to respond according to their typical language use. It can be used as a prototype to develop a language policy for classrooms with multilingual learners. Let students take the lead in describing situations for interacting in multiple languages, suggested in the resource, as the basis for crafting a language policy.

As an extension, multilingual learners should have opportunities to reflect on their personal preferences to formulate their own language policy; Resource 1.2 provides a range of options for students to draw from. For example, to what extent are multilingual learners using multiple languages to search through glossaries, use technology tools (e.g., apps), or discuss school issues with peers? Which language(s) are multilingual learners most comfortable with in exploring content topics and where might they search for information in multiple languages? Resources from multilingual learners' multiple language use could then be pooled to co-create a classroom language and assessment policy.

Students and teachers alike should share their classroom policy that spells out the roles and uses of multiple languages with peers, family members, other teachers, and school leaders. To the extent feasible, if not applicable to the entire school, a uniform language policy should be the norm across a grade level. In that way, multilingual learners' language preferences will be honored and they will have consistency and continuity in their languaging experiences. Equally important, **reliability** or consistency will be built into enacting classroom assessment practices that adhere to the language policy.

THE BIG QUESTION: WHY ASSESS IN MULTIPLE LANGUAGES?

We have finally reached the heart and soul of this book. Simply stated, but with huge implications for **equity** and social justice, assessment for multilingual learners that is only in English fails to represent the whole child and puts the students at a distinct disadvantage (Withycombe, 2019). By definition, multilinguals have the distinct advantage of having multiple languages and cultures at their disposal. We therefore offer ways in which assessment can inspire and capture multilingual learners' natural interaction in multiple languages to describe and document their full range of oral language and literacy practices. At the same time, we touch on multilingual learners' social emotional development. In doing so, we hope to instill change in classroom instruction and assessment wherever there is a multilingual learner.

Assessment in multilingual languages often requires creative applications of measures in English and other languages for determining multilingual learners' comprehensive language and conceptual development (García, Kleifgen, & Fachi, 2008). For example, in dual language contexts, multilingual learners may make an oral presentation in English while producing notes or a summary in their other language; they may read selections in one language and answer questions in another. If translanguaging, the natural intertwining of languages to promote making meaning, is an acceptable classroom policy, then by extension it should be expected and accepted for classroom assessment. Multilingual learners in general education classrooms can readily access multiple languages in researching topics electronically or when interacting with peers from the same partner language, whether the teacher is familiar with the languages or not, even if the end product is only in English.

Engaging Multilingual Learners in Assessment

From the first day to the close of the school year, students should be participants in classroom instruction and assessment. Purposeful interaction among students to explore and investigate issues of interest should be part of every classroom routine. The ultimate goal is for students to become leaders of their own learning through engaged assessment (Berger, Rugen, & Woodfin, 2014).

One of the initial investigations to introduce assessment to multilingual learners, from early grades through high school, is through surveys. Depending on their ages, students can be guided through the process of formulating and posing questions as well as compiling and displaying data. There are several purposes for collecting, analyzing, and graphing survey data on multilingual learners or all students in classrooms at the beginning of the year, such as in a "Who Are We?" project. Having multilingual learners become engaged in learning about each other has many advantages:

- You will become acquainted with your students on a personal level.

- You can set up social and language norms based on student preferences.

- Your students will have opportunities to interact in meaningful ways.

- Your students will get to know each other through their languages and cultures.

- Your students will be introduced to the essential components of assessment: planning, collecting, analyzing, interpreting, and reporting data.

- Your students will realize that they are integral to the functioning of the classroom and members of a community of learners.

Figure 1.5 (expanded in Resources 1.3 and 1.4 to be compiled by older students or read to for younger students) is an outline of topics that leads to a classroom

FIGURE 1.5   A Sketch of My Classroom Portrait by the Numbers

MULTILINGUAL LEARNERS	TOTAL NUMBER
1. Languages	
2. Countries of Origin	
3. Older Siblings; Younger Siblings	
4. Special Interests (e.g., broad categories such as music, sports, social media)	
5. Birthdays (by each month)	

portrait. Teachers may wish to guide the process and later collaborate with colleagues to do the following:

- Compare the perceptions of their students from former teachers against current data.

- Contextualize the data in the breakdown of English learners' language proficiency scores by English language proficiency levels.

- Contextualize the data in estimating multilingual learners' other languages by language proficiency levels.

- Determine the average growth of English learners' English language proficiency over the past 3 years.

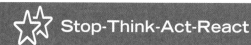

Stop-Think-Act-React

Relax and Reflect: How might you extend student engagement into deeper learning and assessment?

A survey that is planned and conducted by students is an entrée into promoting purposeful oral and written discourse in your classroom. It is also an introduction to **multimodal communication**, where students show their learning in different ways—orally, visually, tactilely, kinesthetically, digitally, or in writing. As a first entry in multilingual learners' assessment portfolio, teachers and students may wish to negotiate a preferred product in one or more languages that builds on the information from the survey. Options may include multilingual learners' creating:

- Montages
- Photo albums
- Videos
- Multimedia presentations
- Questioning or interviews of classmates
- Data plots
- Oral autobiographies
- Memoirs.

WHAT IS ASSESSMENT *AS*, *FOR*, AND *OF* LEARNING FOR MULTILINGUAL LEARNERS IN MULTIPLE LANGUAGES?

The trilogy—assessment *as*, *for*, and *of* learning—is a thread that is woven throughout the book. By centering on the assets of multilingual learners, we acknowledge and leverage their identities and power to become independent thinkers and beings through their multiple languages and cultures. Figure 1.6 shows the relationship among these three assessment approaches as a series of concentric circles.

As shown in the innermost circle, multilingual learners are the center of our educational universe and the force behind **assessment *as* learning**. **Assessment *as* learning** calls upon our students to become leaders of their own learning by assessing their own progress toward mutually agreed upon goals. The interaction between multilingual learners and their teachers or between teachers, the middle circle, in discussion and decision-making constitutes **assessment *for* learning**. **Assessment *of* learning** at a classroom level, represented in the outer circle, is shaped by teachers—individually, as a department, or grade-level team—with input from students and support of school leadership on projects, products, or performances at the close of a unit of learning. Inherent in all these approaches is the potential for assessment to occur in multiple languages (Gottlieb, 2016).

Assessment *as* and *for* learning is often represented as formative assessment purposes; it is differentiated here to recognize the active participation of students as independent thinkers and doers (in assessment *as* learning) and their interaction with teachers (in assessment *for* learning). During assessment *as* and *for* learning, multilingual learners should have opportunities for language choice; that is, all their languages should serve as resources to explore, expand, and delve into learning. Assessment *of* learning is often equated with assessment for summative purposes; it reflects what students have accomplished at the culmination of a period of instruction, typically, a unit of learning. Figure 1.7 offers an overview of features of assessment *as*, *for*, and *of* learning within the context of multiple language use.

FIGURE 1.6 The Relationship Among Assessment *as*, *for*, and *of* Learning

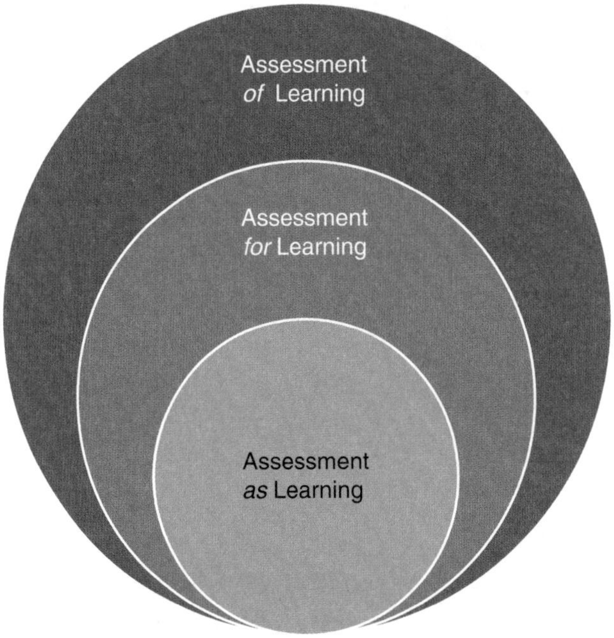

SOURCE: Gottlieb and Honigsfeld (2020), p. 143.

CLASSROOM ASSESSMENT IN MULTIPLE LANGUAGES

FIGURE 1.7 Comparing Features of Assessment *as*, *for*, and *of* Learning

ASSESSMENT AS LEARNING…	ASSESSMENT FOR LEARNING…	ASSESSMENT OF LEARNING…
Invites multiple language use to foster students' metacognitive, metacultural, and **metalinguistic** awareness.	Invites multiple language use to improve teaching and learning.	Invites multiple language use for determining growth in learning and attainment of learning goals.
Occurs on a continuous basis between and among students in multiple languages, facilitated by teachers until self-regulated by students.	Occurs on a continuous basis between teachers and students in multiple languages, as applicable.	Occurs at designated time intervals, such as at the end of units of learning, determined by teachers with input from students.
Is internal to student thinking and learning in one or more languages.	Is internal to instruction and teacher/student learning in one or more languages.	Represents the culmination of an instructional cycle in one or more languages.
Is individualized for students, with consideration for multiple language use.	Is individualized for students and classrooms, with consideration for multiple language use.	Is often standard where teachers follow the same procedures and criteria for success across classrooms.
Encourages students to co-construct activities in one or more languages.	Encourages teachers to create tasks and determine criteria for success with students, with consideration for multiple languages.	Encourages classrooms, grade levels, departments, or schools to design projects, with consideration for multiple languages.
Uses original student work in multiple languages as data sources.	Uses original student work in multiple languages, as applicable, as data sources.	Uses projects or end of unit testing as the primary data sources in multiple languages, as applicable.
Is intrinsically motivated by students, relying on their choice of language(s).	Is instructionally bound, with uses of multiple languages as agreed upon by teachers and students.	Is accountability centered, providing evidence for learning at the classroom, program, and school levels in multiple languages.
Relies on students as assessors and evaluators of their own and others' work.	Relies on immediate **descriptive feedback** to students based on criteria for success.	Relies on scores or feedback related to academic content and language development standards or learning targets.

ADAPTED FROM: Gottlieb (2016).

Relax and Reflect: How does your self-assessment of the three approaches of assessment fare?

Use the descriptors of assessment *as*, *for*, and *of* learning in Figure 1.7 (replicated in Resource 1.5) to evaluate the extent to which you or your teacher team might incorporate or have incorporated these three assessment approaches into your practice.

WHAT ARE SOME TIPS FOR CLASSROOM ASSESSMENT IN MULTIPLE LANGUAGES?

Multilingual learners are talented individuals who deserve every opportunity to learn in multiple languages. Their language proficiencies are going to vary, not necessarily based on test scores but on their personal and educational experiences, social-emotional factors, the situation, the audience, and the purpose of the message. Assessing multilingual learners is a complicated undertaking; balancing assessment in multiple languages even more so.

As an educator, you should set the ground rules early with your students for your classroom or with other teachers. Here are some suggestions to help form a classroom and school community that values instruction and assessment in multiple languages.

1. Become familiar with your multilingual learners' experiences and patterns of language use in multiple languages (such as those from this chapter's Resources). Have multilingual learners make an inventory of their language preferences for typical situations. Use the information for planning instruction and assessment as well as for giving **feedback** to your multilingual learners.

2. Make sure that your multilingual learners are comfortable using multiple languages by creating a warm, inviting, and safe classroom (and school) environment where students are encouraged to take risks. Create a classroom (and school) language and assessment policy with multilingual learners (and faculty) to agree on the parameters of multiple language use.

3. Given your classroom language and assessment policy, have your multilingual learners self-assess their multiple language use, perhaps by creating or using a **rating scale**, such as in Resource 1.2. Amend your policy based on student feedback on an interim basis as part of classroom meetings or student **self-assessment** and make adjustments, as warranted.

4. Per your classroom language and assessment policy, allow multilingual learners to use multiple languages for specific purposes (e.g., asking and clarifying information or ideas with others who share

their partner language), even if instruction is in English, and carry these routines over to classroom assessment.

5. Remember that the languages of classroom instruction and assessment should reflect the languages of your multilingual learners.

HOW MIGHT WE FACE THE ISSUE? INSTILL AN ASSETS-DRIVEN PHILOSOPHY IN YOUR CLASSROOM OR SCHOOL!

Multilingualism is a worldwide norm. Gaining acceptance of a multilingual stance in the U.S. when the power of English is ever present and xenophobia prevails in some environments is a challenge we face as an educational community. Federal terminology and policy simply do not account for multilingual learners' full linguistic repertoires and do not reflect the students' strengths. The future of education of today's children and youth rests in our hands; we must optimize the potential of multilingual learners by cultivating their most enduring assets—their languages and cultures.

To leverage students' languages and cultures at school, multilingual learners must have opportunities to have their voices heard. Encourage active participation and interaction among multilingual learners to share their perspectives. Take time to listen to student conversations about their feelings toward learning in multiple languages and their preferences for demonstrating what they know. Here are some questions to spark those conversations.

For Younger Multilingual Learners

- Do you use more than one language in school? Which ones? If yes, when do you use them and with whom?

- How do you feel when you use more than one language in school?

- What is best about having more than one language and culture?

For Older Multilingual Learners

- Do you feel positive or negative about the language program that you are participating in? Why? How might you change it?

- Do you feel that your languages and cultures are valued in school? Why?

- Would you like to be able to choose which language(s) to use to discuss ideas with your classmates, take tests, or to produce projects? Why?

In turn, instructional and other school leaders should take it upon themselves to advocate on behalf of multilingual learners by converting deficit-ladened terminology to language that is asset-driven. Use these questions as a starting point to engage in ongoing discussion about how to make multilingualism and multiculturalism the norm from which all of education flows.

For Teachers and Other Instructional Leaders

- Do you feel that the terminology used for English learners and their programs is fair and just? Why?

- Do you think that assessment is the culprit for perpetuating terms that have a negative connotation?

- How might you begin with your school, classroom, or grade/department to make changes to any negative terminology? How might you include multilingual learners and their families in deciding more appropriate terms?

For School Leaders

- Does your school have enrollment procedures that capture incoming kindergartners' use of multiple languages?

- How might you spearhead a schoolwide policy to collect information in multiple languages from multilingual learners at the beginning of a school year?

- How might you form professional learning communities to network with schools with growing numbers of multilingual learners in strengthening classroom assessment in multiple languages?

HOW MIGHT WE RESOLVE THE DILEMMA? ACCENTUATE WHAT MULTILINGUAL LEARNERS CAN DO!

How might classrooms and schools begin to recognize the moral imperative of promoting and infusing multilingualism and multiculturalism into classroom practice in lieu of maintaining a monolingual stance? After all, multilingualism is not the global exception, it's the rule. Isn't it about time that we join this international reality?

We suggest beginning a campaign of assessment in multiple languages with broadcasting the benefits of multilingualism and adopting positive terminology to describe multilingual learners and their educational programs. One clear-cut way to advance the assets of multilingual learners is to value their languages and cultures from the moment that students enter school. For multilingual learners and their teachers, assessment in multiple languages should be part of the initial enrollment process, proceed throughout the day, every day, and be engrained into the psyche of school. Hopefully the kindergarten teachers at Einstein school will be able to convince Mr. George, their principal, of the value of extending the development of multilingualism to their youngest learners.

Resources for Multilingual Learners, Their Teachers, and Other School Leaders

RESOURCE 1.1 FOR TEACHERS AND THEIR MULTILINGUAL LEARNERS
Our Classroom Language and Assessment Policy

Multilingual learners should have input in formulating a classroom language and assessment policy. Use this figure as a guide to help determine when you and your multilingual learners use English, their other language, or both languages (as in translanguaging).

WHAT WE CAN DO:	IN OUR OTHER LANGUAGE	IN ENGLISH	IN BOTH LANGUAGES
1. Ask and answer questions			
2. Do classroom routines, such as give or follow directions			
3. Read assigned materials or do research			
4. Explore the internet to investigate topics or issues			
5. Join in conversations with classmates			
6. Exchange ideas with classmates			
7. Engage in discussions			
8. Take notes or label diagrams			
9. Uses references, such as dictionaries			
10. Prepare and give presentations			
11. Produce projects with classmates			
12. Create criteria for success			
13. Engage in self-assessment			
14. Engage in peer assessment			
15. Give feedback to classmates			

RESOURCE 1.2 FOR MULTILINGUAL LEARNERS

My Language Policy (for Older Multilingual Learners)

Read "What I do" from the table, below. How often do you use multiple languages in your classroom: Not at all, Sometimes, Most of the time, or All the time? Put an X in one of the boxes.

Name:_____ Languages:_____

WHAT I DO:	NOT AT ALL	SOMETIMES	MOST OF THE TIME	ALL THE TIME
1. Ask and answer questions in class				
2. Follow classroom routines				
3. Read materials				
4. Explore the internet to investigate a topic or issue				
5. Join in conversations with my classmates				
6. Exchange ideas with my classmates				
7. Write notes				
8. Use bilingual dictionaries				
9. Prepare and give a presentation				
10. Produce a project with classmates				
11. Assess my classmates with criteria for success				
12. Give feedback to my classmates				

RESOURCE 1.3 FOR MULTILINGUAL LEARNERS

My Personal Portrait

Read the questions on the left. Circle the numbers and write in the answers on the right. You may wish to add a selfie or a picture of your family.

Name: _____

My Languages: How many languages do you speak? 1　　　2　　　3　　　4	Which ones?
My Languages: How many languages do you read and write? 1　　　2　　　3　　　4	Which ones?
My Family's Countries of Origin/ Cultures:	Outside the U.S., where is your family from?
My Siblings: How many brothers and sisters do you have? 1　2　3　4　5　6	How old are they?
My Special Interests: What do you like?	Music, sports, art, social media? Anything else?
My Birthday Month: In which month were you born?	January, February, March, April, May, June, July, August, September, October, November, December

RESOURCE 1.4 FOR MULTILINGUAL LEARNERS AND THEIR TEACHERS
My Classroom Portrait

Figure out the answers from Resource 1.3 for the whole class. Older students can determine the average number or just tally and give the total number. Then in small groups, students can make a bar graph of the numbers for each of the questions. Put all the information together to make a classroom portrait and produce a mini report.

1. **Our Languages:** How many languages do we speak?	Which ones?
2. **Our Languages:** How many languages do we read and write?	Which ones?
3. **Our Countries of Origin/Cultures:** Outside the U.S: how many countries do our families come from?	Which ones?
4. **Our Siblings:** How many brothers and sisters do we have? How many are older than us and how many are younger?	What are their ages?
5. **Our Special Interests:** What do we like?	Music, sports, art, social media? Anything else?
6. **Our Birthday Months:** In which month were we born?	How many in each month? January, February, March, April, May, June, July, August, September, October, November, December
7. **Our Question for the Class:**	

RESOURCE 1.5 FOR TEACHERS AND OTHER SCHOOL LEADERS

My Personal Use of Assessment *as, for,* and *of* Learning

Reproduce this figure and put an X in the cell(s) whose features are present in your classroom, a P in those which you plan to adopt, and an O for those which you do not plan to tackle. Compare your assessment practices with those of your colleagues, and think about how you might move toward more balanced representation of students and teachers.

ASSESSMENT *AS* LEARNING...	ASSESSMENT *FOR* LEARNING...	ASSESSMENT *OF* LEARNING...
Invites multiple language use to foster students' metacognitive, metacultural, and metalinguistic awareness.	Invites multiple language use for formative purposes.	Invites multiple language use for determining growth in learning and attainment of learning goals.
Occurs on a continuous basis between and among students in multiple languages, facilitated by teachers until self-regulated by students.	Occurs on a continuous basis between teachers and students in multiple languages, as applicable.	Occurs at designated time intervals, such as at the end of a unit of learning, determined by teachers with input from students generally in one language.
Is internal to student thinking and learning in one or more languages.	Is internal to instruction and teacher/student learning in one or more languages.	Represents the culmination of an instructional cycle in one or more languages.
Is individualized for students, with consideration for multiple language use.	Is individualized for classrooms with consideration for multiple language use.	Is often standard where teachers follow the same set of directions and procedures for or across classrooms.
Encourages students to co-construct in English and their partner language.	Encourages teachers to create tasks and determine criteria for success with students with consideration for multiple languages.	Encourages classrooms, grade levels, departments, or schools to design projects with consideration for multiple languages.
Uses original student work in multiple languages as data sources.	Uses original student work in multiple languages, as applicable, as data sources.	Uses projects or end of unit testing as the primary data sources in multiple languages, as applicable.
Is intrinsically motivated by students, relying on their choice of language(s).	Is instructionally bound, with uses of multiple languages as agreed upon by teachers and students.	Is accountability driven, providing evidence for learning at the classroom, program, and school levels in multiple languages.
Relies on students as assessors and evaluators, based on jointly constructed criteria for success.	Relies on immediate descriptive feedback to students based on criteria for success.	Relies on scores or feedback related to academic content and language development standards in relation to program goals.

CHAPTER 2

How Do We Get Started With Assessment in Multiple Languages?

Aprender a dudar es aprender a pensar.

Learning to doubt is learning to think.

—Octavio Paz

The Dilemma

But I only speak English… someone needs to translate!

It's the second semester and the junior high teacher team at Central School, a K–8 building, is preparing its students for high school. For many, especially multilingual learners, it's going to be a huge transition to unchartered terrain where multilingual education, rather than seen as a philosophy and way of being, is just another class that is confined to a maximum of two periods a day. Consideration of language and culture has not been infused into the general curriculum of the high school. In fact, World Languages is a department unto itself with current offerings consisting of English as an Additional Language, Mandarin for heritage speakers, as well as French, Mandarin, and Spanish as "foreign" languages.

The middle school grades at Central and the neighboring high school have recently had an influx of newcomers, some of whom have lived under traumatic stressful circumstances with uneven educational experiences. Their conditions have been exacerbated by sickness and discrimination upon their arrival in the U.S. The counselor, social worker, and middle school teachers are challenged by such a growing diversity of multilingual learners—their languages, cultures, continuity of education, experiential backgrounds, and upbringings. They are desperate to find translators and reach out to the high school to create a joint welcoming packet for the newcomers and their families, but are at a loss. However, right now they are faced with a more pressing issue.

The middle school team recognizes that before leaving Central School, all students are required to pass the U.S. Constitution test, a district directive taken seriously by the school. For multilingual learners born and raised in the U.S., it's not a concern. The team, however, is especially worried about the newcomers and English learners who are about to face alien concepts in a rather incomprehensible language—English. There simply isn't enough time to revamp the Social Studies curriculum to make it accessible to the students who require intensive support.

Quickly the teachers survey colleagues and their local social networks for answers. As they only speak English themselves, their first thought is that they need translators, desperately! But then they soon realize that translating the material, whether by a person, through the internet, or with an old-fashioned dictionary will not facilitate the understanding of such complex, abstract, and culturally sensitive concepts as democracy, freedom, or justice, which the newcomers have never experienced.

What can the teachers do to prepare their newcomers for such a high-stakes test when translation is not an option? Here are some suggestions they received:

- *Use multimodal communication on a consistent basis. Find audiobooks or videos on American history, look for artifacts, infographics, or posters that represent key concepts; rely on gestures during instruction or graphic organizers to present and reinforce ideas.*

- *Create a glossary for students and give multilingual learners more time to take the high-stakes test.*

- *Tap the community for speakers of the students' languages. Extend invitations to community members to interact with the students and help explain the concepts in sessions before or after school.*

- *Contact the local library to lend resources or community organizations for assistance.*

- *Create a buddy system with multilingual learners of the same partner language to help clarify or paraphrase concepts.*

- *Have eighth-grade students, including multilingual learners, craft practice tests in one or more languages and provide feedback along with test-taking strategies to the newcomers.*

If you or your colleagues are faced with a similar dilemma at your school, what might you do if you can't speak your multilingual learners' languages?

- In what ways does this scenario resonate with you?

- What are some considerations for assessment in multiple languages when you don't speak the students' language?

- Why is it important to know your multilingual learners' preferred language for assessment?

- How might you engage multilingual learners in the assessment process?

Multilingual learners are increasingly populating schools across the U.S. and around the world. Teachers cannot possibly be knowledgeable of all the languages the students speak or their cultural traditions. Yet it is critical that in school multilingual learners are able to express themselves in the languages of their choice and grow in developing those languages. Language plays a critical role in learning, no doubt about it. The question becomes "How can teachers leverage the assets of multilingual learners in instruction and assessment?"

Wherever there are multilingual learners, especially students who are (or labeled) English learners, newcomers, English learners with intensive needs, or long-term English learners, language takes on many roles. For example, in this chapter's introductory vignette we see how language, even when geared to the purpose of assessment, can serve as a:

- tool to meet specific needs and contexts

- vehicle to ensure that different populations are treated equitably

- resource to enrich learning environments

- means for students to see their own self-worth and value in what they are learning. (Reynolds, 2019)

In content classrooms, especially in middle and high schools, language is often invisible as teaching is geared to conceptual learning of the discipline and disciplinary practices. When thinking about these classrooms, especially where multiple languages are present, the many languages of multilingual learners can become integrated into instruction and assessment. Here is where a focus on one or more languages can be:

- connected to the community

- embedded in social activity

- reflected in varying cultural perspectives

- highlighted in disciplinary content

- one of many modes for communicating information, ideas, and concepts

- a means for clarifying misunderstandings and deepening meaning

- the lens for learning.

Stop-Think-Act-React

Relax and Reflect: What does language have to do with classroom assessment?

Take time to examine and contemplate the roles that language plays in your classroom. How are the multiple languages of your multilingual learners taken into account in instruction and assessment? How do you ensure that instruction and assessment are equitable, especially for your multilingual learners?

This book highlights the primacy of language, in particular, multiple languages in classroom assessment. The five-step assessment cycle, outlined in Figure 2.1, serves as the organizing frame for teachers and other educators of multilingual learners as they enact each phase of the process. This chapter encourages educators to think about assessment for multilingual learners in multiple languages, whether in dual language, developmental bilingual, or general education classrooms. Starting with the purpose for assessment, we share assessment activities across each phase of the cycle throughout the school year. Finally, we revisit assessment *as, for,* and *of* learning and unveil a multilingual multicultural curricular framework that captures these approaches.

FIGURE 2.1 A Multiphase Assessment Cycle for Inclusion of Multiple Languages

HOW DO WE BEGIN TO THINK ABOUT ASSESSMENT FOR MULTILINGUAL LEARNERS IN MULTIPLE LANGUAGES?

Assessment is a complex undertaking; when classroom assessment occurs in multiple languages, however, it becomes even more complicated. Multiple stakeholders, including teachers and other school leaders, instructional leaders, multilingual learners, and to some extent, multilingual families are all contributors to the classroom assessment cycle. To give an overview of what is in store, Figure 2.2 summarizes each phase of the assessment cycle, its primary stakeholders, and some related activities.

FIGURE 2.2 Suggestions for Stakeholders and Activities for Each Phase of Classroom Assessment in Multiple Languages

PHASE OF ASSESSMENT	PRIMARY STAKEHOLDERS	SELECT ACTIVITIES
Planning assessment in multiple languages	School and instructional leaders, including coaches and teachers, with input from multilingual learners and family members	• Develop school and classroom language and assessment policies. • Ensure a balance among assessment approaches and languages across the year. • Identify and match available resources to instructional goals. • Co-plan and co-design classroom assessment along with criteria for success.
Collecting and organizing assessment information in multiple languages	Teachers and other instructional leaders along with multilingual learners	• Gather baseline data. • Identify representation of multiple languages. • Select types and amount of evidence (e.g., number of portfolio entries). • Practice and conduct student-led conferences.
Interpreting assessment information and providing feedback in multiple languages	Teachers, other instructional leaders, individual multilingual learners and their peers	• Analyze data and reflect on results. • Have students engage in self- and peer assessment. • Match student language samples and projects against criteria for success. • Use feedback to improve teaching and learning.
Evaluating and reporting assessment information in multiple languages	Teachers, other instructional leaders, and individual multilingual learners	• Provide evidence for learning in multimodal ways. • Assess value or effectiveness of learning in multiple languages. • Convert evidence for learning into grades or narratives, as necessary. • Share results with families and the community.
Taking action based on assessment results in multiple languages	School leaders, teachers and other instructional leaders, individual multilingual learners, and family members	• Revise goals for teaching and learning. • Modify curriculum and instruction based on feedback. • Seek additional resources and connections to students and community. • Use evidence of learning to make a personal difference or impact on the community.

There is not a timetable associated with the phases for assessment. If, for example, a school is contemplating converting its current instructional models for multilingual learners into ones with more explicit instruction and assessment in multiple languages, the planning phase may take an entire school year or more. Planning would consist of a comprehensive series of activities and would include extensive teacher and community engagement. If, on the other hand, a school has a more mature dual language or dual immersion program, it might be ripe for taking accountability for multiple languages to a new level to ensure that assessment has equal status across languages. This shift might occur more quickly, but just as deliberately, across the phases of assessment.

WHAT COMES NEXT IN ASSESSING IN MULTIPLE LANGUAGES?

In thinking about instruction and classroom assessment in multiple languages, teachers, teacher teams, or professional learning communities may ask themselves (with questions duplicated in Resource 2.1):

1. What is my philosophy (or theoretical basis) for teaching multilingual learners?

2. What are some of the major themes or issues to explore with my students?

3. How can my students contribute their insights and perspectives to these themes or issues?

4. What are the connections of these themes to content and language standards?

5. How are we to incorporate our students' experiences and interests in the assessment process?

6. What will be the language(s) of assessment? What choices might our multilingual learners make?

Setting up assessment centers on identifying its overall purpose and how the information is to be collected and used. Figure 2.3 gives examples of different purposes for assessment for students, classrooms, and schools with consideration for multiple language use.

 Stop-Think-Act-React

Relax and Reflect: How might you conduct an assessment audit?

This activity is for grade-level/department teams, schoolwide, or even as a professional learning community. First, select the purposes for assessment from Figure 2.3 or add some of your own to examine. Then determine the evidence to be accrued for each purpose and whether it is be matched in one language (English) or in multiple languages (English + multilingual learners' other languages). The results of this investigation should provide insight into planning assessment in multiple languages for students, classrooms, and/or schools.

FIGURE 2.3 Purposes for Assessment for Multilingual Learners, Classrooms, and Schools

LEVEL OF ENACTMENT	PURPOSES FOR ASSESSMENT
Multilingual Learners	• Pinpoint student strengths in multiple languages according to the task and learning context. • Identify student learning needs in multiple languages in clear constructive ways. • Inform personalized instruction based on individual student progress. • Set and refine goals for learning; plan and manage next steps with teachers. • Self-reflect on learning in multiple languages.
Classrooms	• Match student-generated goals for learning in one or more languages to instruction and evidence of learning. • Determine growth in multilingual learners' language development and academic achievement in one or more languages over time. • Provide ongoing feedback to students to improve teaching and learning. • Inform one's teaching practice.
Schools	• Determine effectiveness of programs involving multilingual learners. • Monitor growth of multilingual learners' language development in multiple languages. • Determine growth over time in achievement of multilingual learners from information that is linguistically and culturally relevant. • Support the direction of schoolwide planning for ongoing systemic improvement.

Thinking about assessment means trying to figure out the richest and fairest data for decision-making. Figure 2.4 gives examples of how data for classrooms and schools can provide evidence for learning in multiple languages. It is replicated as Resource 2.2 with empty cells so that teachers and other instructional leaders can show the distribution of measures and languages across the school year—at the beginning, mid-year, and toward the end. Likewise, language and content teachers can collaborate on determining the needed information in multiple languages over the span of a year.

For Schools

With the rise of dual language programs across the nation, more and more schools are devoting resources to enrichment education for multilingual learners whereby students' multiple languages are being further developed while content instruction occurs in two languages (Wilson, 2011). Planning for the collection of information on multilingual learners should begin before the students walk in the front door of the school. Understanding the backgrounds of the students (such as those reported in Resource 2.3 for creating a student portrait) provides a context for interpreting assessment data.

FIGURE 2.4 Assessment for Multilingual Learners in Multiple Languages Throughout the School Year

	SCHOOL	CLASSROOM
Beginning of Year	Collection of baseline data of multilingual learners in (1) core content areas and (2) language development	Collection of (1) student oral language and content-based (disciplinary) literacy data and (2) multilingual learners' individual reporting of language use
Mid-Year	Co-ordination of data collection within and across classrooms; adjustment of schoolwide goals based on data analysis	Collection and analysis of (1) ongoing performance data of language and content, (2) student self- and peer reflection, and (3) data for adjusting grade-level and classroom goals
End of Year	Analysis of achievement and language proficiency data related to student subgroups; reviewing social-emotional and outcome data	Analysis of oral language and content-based (disciplinary) literacy; revisiting goals for teaching and learning

An assessment audit serves as a starting point for planning assessment activities throughout the school year. In addition, there are Resources at the close of this chapter which may be helpful for assessment in multiple languages. These resources can be tacked onto student enrollment forms (time permitting or if feasible), discussed at schoolwide meetings, addressed in professional learning events, incorporated into the opening days of classroom instruction, or used by teachers throughout the school year. They include the following:

- *A Sample Oral Language Use Survey for Multilingual Learners* (Resource 2.4) asks students to identify their use of one or more languages.

- *A Sample Literacy Survey for Multilingual Learners* (Resource 2.5) asks students to describe their literacy practices in one or more languages.

- *Guidelines for Collecting Oral and Written Language Samples* (Resource 2.6) provides directions for generating oral responses to compelling questions or providing first draft written responses to oral or written prompts.

- *Considerations for Assessment in Multiple Languages: A Checklist and Rating Scale* (Resource 2.7) is a comprehensive list of student characteristics that is intended to help prepare teachers and other school leaders for assessment and to better understand the factors that potentially impact the results.

For Classrooms

Teachers should research their multilingual learners' individual stories and identities to understand the circumstances for each student's language use. This information is a potentially rich data source for assessment in multiple languages. Ultimately, greater knowledge of the histories of each student will yield more equitable assessment, as results can be readily interpreted through multilingual learners' linguistic and cultural lens.

There are a variety of ways for teachers to collect student-level data, even though they themselves may not understand or speak the languages of their multilingual learners. As an extension of the classroom assessment column in Figure 2.4, Figure 2.5 shows assessment information from multilingual learners that is useful throughout the school year. As part of getting ready for the school year, teachers of multilingual learners should think about how to assess in multiple languages month by month (Gottlieb, 2017).

FIGURE 2.5 Assessment in Multiple Languages: Information From Multilingual Learners Throughout the School Year

ASSESSMENT ACTIVITIES OR ACTIONS WHERE MULTILINGUAL LEARNERS....	TIME OF SCHOOL YEAR
Participate as translators during home visits	Beginning
Complete individual student surveys, such as for oral language use and literacy in multiple languages (as in Resources 2.4 and 2.5), if not a school-level activity	Beginning
Provide individual student oral language and writing samples in multiple languages (as in Resources 2.6 and 2.7), if not a school-level activity	Beginning of the year and on an interim basis
Design sociograms (visual representations that map the relationships between students with others who speak and don't speak their partner language)	Beginning and mid-year
Maintain journal entries, diaries, or a collection of oral and written language samples (again, refer to Resource 2.6) relating personal stories (e.g., autobiographies or recounts of experiences or reactions to events)	Throughout the year
Participate in student-led conferences with teachers and family members	Mid and end of year
Interact with others in classroom team activities and discussions with peers in one or more languages	Throughout the year
Engage with classmates in multimodal projects, such as creating videos, podcasts, or iMovies in multiple languages	Throughout the year, perhaps on a monthly basis

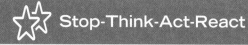 Stop-Think-Act-React

Relax and Reflect: How might multilingual learners contribute their expertise to assessment in your classroom?

Think about how you might design assessment throughout the year with your multilingual learners, whether you speak the languages of your students or not. First, you will better understand your multilingual learners and how their backgrounds are impacting their learning. Second, your multilingual learners, by participating in authentic and meaningful activities, will become assessment leaders in your classroom. Consider using this chart as a starting point for gathering information on your multilingual learners and their use of multiple languages. If you wish to be more specific, you might create a month-by-month timeline to map out applicable assessments for your multilingual learners.

MY MULTILINGUAL LEARNERS ENGAGE IN....	IN WHICH LANGUAGES?	DURING WHAT TIME(S) OF YEAR?

For Multilingual Learners

Students offer a critical perspective and insight into learning that are integral to the process of classroom assessment. In some circumstances, multilingual learners may feel comfortable communicating exclusively in one language or another. At other times, they may prefer to translanguage with peers to make meaning from content. As part of formulating a classroom language policy, multilingual learners along with their teachers should create a pact based on the preferences of students of how and to what extent the languages of instruction transfer over to the languages of assessment.

Classroom assessment is a deliberate multiphased process, not a test, in which teachers use evidence to adjust their instruction and students use feedback to amend their ways of learning. Within it, teachers need to decide at what points during instruction to collect assessment evidence to ensure that the process is not too complicated or time-consuming in order to yield just the right amount of information (Popham, 2009). To balance the distribution of the kinds of information that are important for decision-making throughout the school year and the languages for that evidence, we suggest planning around three approaches to assessment that are synonymous with learning.

HOW IS CLASSROOM ASSESSMENT *AS*, *FOR*, AND *OF* LEARNING USEFUL?

Let's revisit three approaches to assessment with an eye toward setting out a long-term plan based on the roles of educational stakeholders as sources of information for instructional decision-making. Assessments *as*, *for*, and *of* learning provide a vision for engaging in teaching and learning. Together the approaches offer a strong model of inclusion and equity for multilingual learners, their teachers, and other educational leaders.

Assessment *as* Learning

Students are our most important source of information, yet for years, the dominance of teacher-directed instruction and assessment has negated or minimized student participation. Until recently, there has been little attention to how the multiple languages of multilingual learners can contribute to their well-being in school and beyond. Yet the research substantiates the value of student engagement in learning with its social-emotional and academic benefits (Christenson, Reschly, & Wylie, 2012).

For multilingual learners at different levels of English language proficiency and achievement, it has been relatively easy to justify their passivity when English is the sole language of instruction and requisite for full participation in classroom life. Assessment *as* learning as a classroom practice places students in the center and broadcasts their voice, empowerment, and agency.

The time has come to change the practice of having multilingual learners peripheral to the mainstream learning experience. Assessment *as* learning should begin the first day of school when multilingual learners can interact with their peers in the language(s) of their choice to:

- explore topics or issues of mutual interest

- suggest criteria for success

- contribute to crafting classroom tasks or projects

- engage in self- and **peer assessment**

- explore multilingual resources.

Assessment *for* Learning

The connection between learning and assessment is becoming more tightly interwoven as teachers pay more attention to multilingual learners' language development within content learning (Gottlieb & Katz, 2020). As an approach, assessment *for* learning encompasses a range of practices that encourage teachers along with their learners to seek ways of documenting what they know and can do. In assessment *for* learning, multilingual learners negotiate with their teachers on a variety of issues, including what decisions are to be made based on what counts as evidence, in which languages, how the information will be interpreted, and what will be the form of reporting.

Assessment *for* learning might begin with teacher and student conversations that lead to collaboration in making mutually agreed upon goals. Both teachers and students are keenly aware of where the students are in their learning that is firmly anchored to grade-level **academic content standards** and, additionally for multilingual learners, their language proficiency/development standards in English and their additional language. What is of critical concern, however, is where students are to go next and how they plan to get there. Within a sociocultural context for learning, multilingual learners' experiences are to be built upon so that they have access to rigorous content through language and that assessment is fair and equitable (Swain, Kinnear, & Steinman 2011).

In assessment *for* learning, multilingual learners can interact with their teachers in English or their shared language(s) to:

- craft integrated **learning targets**

- co-construct criteria for success and types of acceptable evidence

- offer and incorporate feedback throughout the process

- negotiate a language policy for instruction and assessment.

Assessment *of* Learning

Assessment *of* learning at a classroom level is shaped by teachers, individually or as a department or grade-level team, with input from students. It represents democratized assessment that reflects what students have accomplished at the culmination of a period of instruction, such as a unit of learning. In essence, assessment *of* learning has a **summative assessment** purpose geared for internal accountability and documents student growth over time. As the other approaches, assessment *of* learning should be authentic and performance-based rather than test-driven (Sleeter & Carmona, 2017).

For classrooms, assessment *of* learning requires more planning than assessment *as* and *for* learning as it generally revolves around long-term projects. Depending on the presence of multilingual learners, there should always be options for multiple language use. Overall, assessment *of* learning should center on collaboration among teachers in:

- co-creating learning targets based on standards

- determining uniform criteria for success

- modeling and sharing evidence for products, performances, or projects

- incorporating linguistic and cultural relevance into products, performances, or projects.

HOW DO STANDARDS IMPACT ASSESSMENT IN MULTIPLE LANGUAGES?

In Chapter 1 we see two language theories that have implications for how we envision assessment in one or more languages. But where do standards fit in? Content and language standards, mandated in federal legislation along with aligned **high-stakes testing**, generally represent a single trajectory for learning. They have been conceptualized where one level of proficiency moves to the next one in lock-step order.

This view, however, is counter educational perspectives that see teaching and learning as cultural, social, and interactional (Hawkins, 2019). While standards remain part of the educational landscape as progressions for learning, classroom assessment has become more socially motivated and contextually embedded (Bachman & Damböck, 2017; Kaul, 2019; Moss, 2008). These two views of language, learning, and assessment come closer together, however, when we can express standards in sociocultural contexts rather than as isolated expectations.

Standards can serve both as a metric and as a tool for teachers and students in formulating and working toward common goals for learning (Gottlieb, 2009). Older students can set their own learning goals in multiple languages and self-assess their progress. Younger students can work with teachers to formulate mutually agreed upon goals in multiple languages and how they are to be met.

Student learning targets designated for a unit or for an entire semester that have been derived from standards can be expressed as "I can" statements. The added student participation and interaction in this process is indicative of another shift in classroom assessment, toward increased student-centeredness. By helping to formulate and understand expectations for learning (i.e., learning goals), multilingual learners are co-contributors in determining what counts as evidence for learning and the multimodal means for achieving it (Gottlieb, 2016; Wajda, 2011). Figure 2.6 shows how standards yield integrated targets for content and language for a unit of learning which, in turn, can be converted to student "I can" statements.

FIGURE 2.6 Setting Up Assessment With Students: From Standards to Integrated Learning Targets to "I Can" Statements

EXAMPLE CONTENT AND LANGUAGE STANDARDS FOR MATHEMATICS AND LANGUAGE ARTS	SAMPLE INTEGRATED LEARNING TARGETS	POSSIBLE "I CAN" STATEMENTS
Content: Apply and extend understanding of multiplication of fractions by whole numbers. **Language:** Explain how fractions work to solve everyday problems.	Solve mathematical problems involving fractional parts and explain how to use fractions in everyday situations.	"I can multiply fractions in following a brownie recipe for my class." (en español e inglés)
Content: Define the roles and influences of individuals in political systems. **Language:** Describe the overall structure of events, ideas, concepts, or information.	Identify the attributes of democracy in retelling biographies of famous people of the Civil Rights era.	"I can tell my friends about Rosa Parks's life and what she did for our democracy."
Your turn!		

ADAPTED FROM Gottlieb and Ernst-Slavit (2014).

HOW IS ASSESSMENT IN MULTIPLE LANGUAGES RELATED TO CURRICULUM DESIGN?

Curriculum is a dynamic and ever-changing way of organizing learning experiences. Why is there constant movement in curriculum? Because every year there are unique groups of students with different languages, cultures, histories, and understandings of the world; there are different configurations of classrooms with new and veteran teachers; and there are always new school, district, and state policies and practices to enact. School and instructional leaders have to be sensitive to the here and now of **curriculum design** in order to maximize opportunities for all students to learn.

Traditionally, curriculum has been envisioned as three phases: planning, enacting, and evaluating. More recently, it has been seen through a sociocultural lens. The idea of 'enacting' has replaced 'implementing' to reflect the potential agency of teachers and learners in the process. The heart of curriculum enactment is the classroom, the learning community, where the teacher is the catalyst for change (Graves, 2008).

In classrooms with multilingual learners in which instruction and assessment occur in two languages, curriculum design and enactment must include students' "funds of knowledge" (Moll, Amanti, Neff, & Gonzalez, 1992). Hence, culturally sustainable teaching leverages students' cultural resources. Incorporating linguistically and culturally relevance into curriculum includes:

1. positive references to families and communities

2. communication of high expectations to students and family members

3. learning within the context of languages and cultures

4. student-centered instruction that is built from their experiential bases

5. teachers as facilitators of learning (Ladson-Billings, 1994)

For multilingual learners, as all students, curriculum should not rely on prepackaged sets of materials but rather consist of a series of negotiated tasks between students and teachers. Figure 2.7 represents how lessons are folded into units of learning and how curriculum encompasses multilingual and multicultural contexts and perspectives.

 Stop-Think-Act-React

Relax and Reflect: How has curriculum evolved in your school?

Ask some veteran teachers about their perceptions of curricular change over time. What has been their view of language in relation to content? Have there been different materials and resources for instruction? Has technology been enhanced? How has assessment evolved to reflect these new realities?

Has there been an influx of multilingual learners from different places and circumstances, and if so, how has curriculum embraced the shift in student population? To what extent is today's curriculum better suited for multilingual learners—is there recognition of multiple languages and cultures, have student characteristics been embedded into units of learning, do multilingual learners engage with others to learn in meaningful and exciting ways? What can you do to ensure representation of the assets of multilingual learners in curriculum design?

FIGURE 2.7 Embedding Multicultural Contexts and Perspectives in Unit and Lesson Planning

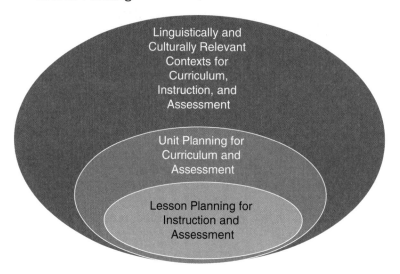

Today classroom assessment is viewed as a process, not an event, as it is an integral component of curriculum design and the instructional cycle (Cumming, 2009; Gottlieb & Katz, 2020). When assessment is integrated into curriculum, the planning process becomes more coherent (Graves, 2016). One principle for curriculum design for multilingual learners is to "adopt a positive, welcoming mindset and culture of learning . . . by advanc(ing) bilingualism and bi-literacy as assets to learning and capitalizing on ELs' home language(s), cultural assets, and prior knowledge" (Pimentel, 2018, p. 3).

With assessment in multiple languages having increased attention of schools comes the need for more coordinated curriculum and instruction. When first thinking about assessment in multiple languages, there are questions to ponder and discuss with colleagues, such as the following.

- To what extent should I plan for assessment in multiple languages— on an ongoing basis, intermittently, or only at prescribed times?

- If I teach in one language, how can I allow my multilingual learners to use other languages?

- If I allow my multilingual learners choice in their language use during instruction, should it or how might it carry over to assessment?

- Should it be permissible for my multilingual learners to use a language during assessment other than English if I don't know it? Why?

- Why should I allow my multilingual learners to rely on digital tools to access content in their preferred language?

- How do we set learning goals in multiple languages with our multilingual learners?

- How do I grade students who use multiple languages if I can't understand them?

The lessons within a unit of learning are influenced by considerations for assessment. According to Shepard, Penuel, and Davidson (2017), there are two guiding principles that shape classroom assessment: "First, make assessments coherent [by] integrating them with rich curriculum and effective instruction and second, ground this integration of curriculum, instruction, and embedded assessments in equity-focused research on learning" (p. 1). In formalizing curriculum inclusive of multilingual learners, we should also be aware of the role that translanguaging plays.

WHERE DOES TRANSLANGUAGING FIT INTO CURRICULUM, INSTRUCTION, AND ASSESSMENT?

In essence, translanguaging refers to language practices of bilinguals where bilingualism is treated as a resource and languaging is fluid, depending on the situation (Celic & Seltzer, 2011). Since the 2010s, translanguaging has had an increased acceptance in the education of multilingual learners in dual language, bilingual, or world language, and general education classrooms. When multilingual learners translanguage, it can either be spontaneous or planned; however, there should be some purpose behind it. Before formulating an assessment plan, teachers and other school leaders should be aware that translanguaging is multifaceted; it can be a(n):

… classroom or school language policy

… philosophy

… theory

… idiolect (a personal language choice)

… way of being (the practices of bilinguals)

… pedagogical approach

… political stance

… instructional strategy

… construct

… ideology.

▶ Signage on a Mexican restaurant window in Auckland, NZ

Relax and Reflect: How do you envision translanguaging and its implications for assessment?

In small groups, decide what translanguaging means to you and your colleagues. To what extent is translanguaging part of instruction and assessment in your setting? Given your position, how do you envision the usefulness of translanguaging for your multilingual learners?

If you believe that translanguaging should be viewed as a bonafide pedagogical practice, then it should be addressed within instructional and assessment spaces. Think about specific purposes for translanguaging within a classroom context and their application to assessment. Such purposes may include:

- building **metalinguistic awareness** by examining features between languages to facilitate and extend multilingual learners' meaning-making

- understanding the relationship between languages and cultures

- emphasizing an important point or concept in oral or written text

- constructing first drafts of reports, essays to promote deeper fuller understanding and communication of content

- expressing cultural norms, such as terms of affection or endearment when referring to family members.

HOW MIGHT WE FACE THE ISSUE? CREATE A MULTILINGUAL RESOURCE BANK

Assessment for multilingual learners in multiple languages is a classroom and schoolwide commitment. An array of stakeholders and resources are needed to facilitate student learning during assessment. The coordination of effort on the part of school and instructional leaders can maximize acceptance of assessment in multiple languages. An up-to-date multilingual resource bank can help educators quickly identify family and community members who can help translate or explain a cultural tradition. Here are some questions for stakeholders.

For Younger Multilingual Learners

- Who helps you learn in more than one language? at home? in school?

- Which classmates help you learn in English and your other language?

- How do you do your schoolwork thinking and using both your languages?

For Older Multilingual Learners

- How do your experiences in multiple languages and cultures help you be a better learner?

- Which resources do you typically use (e.g., dictionaries, technology) for learning in multiple languages?

- How might you use your multiple languages for career planning, after-school jobs, or internships?

For Teachers and Other Instructional Leaders

- Who might you turn to in planning assessment in multiple languages? Why?

- To what extent do you apply your school and classroom language policies to assessment? If you haven't had an opportunity to formulate a language and assessment policy with your multilingual learners, where might you start?

- How might you depend on other educators for assessment or co-assessment in multiple languages?

For School Leaders

- How might you engage other adults in your school to help assess multilingual learners in multiple languages?

- How might you enlist multilingual adults in your community to help in the assessment process?

- How might you devise and maintain a language bank of resources for your school (e.g., of bilingual psychologists, bilingual social workers, health services)?

- How might you create a network of school and community leaders to assist in solving issues revolving around assessment in multiple languages?

HOW MIGHT WE RESOLVE THE DILEMMA? ENLIST MULTILINGUALS IN THE ASSESSMENT PROCESS!

Thinking ahead about assessment in multiple languages can offset the last-minute stress of trying to secure help from bilingual individuals. If you are in a school setting with two or twenty-two languages, you can take steps to provide ample opportunities for multilingual learners to express themselves in the languages of their choice as they move toward creating a final product, producing a first draft, or engaging in conversation. Here are some ideas for tapping the multilingual resources in your classroom, school, and community that Central School is thinking of initiating.

- If you are a teacher or co-teacher in a dual language, immersion, or bilingual setting, you have bilingual resources at your fingertips, starting with the multilingual learners. Their linguistic and cultural richness should be a source and inspiration for enhancing curriculum and drawing from it to create student-led assessment. The students can take the lead in facilitating group discussions, reporting the consensus of a group, or stating preferences of their peers.

- If you are a teacher or co-teacher in school with a myriad of different languages, set up a schoolwide buddy system for multilingual learners. First, try to partner multilingual learners of the same language and grade level. If that is not feasible, create a multilingual resource bank of multilingual learners within the school and multilingual volunteers in the community.

- If you are the sole language teacher in a school with just a few multilingual learners, establish a rapport with classroom teachers and bring additional multilingual resources and materials directly to the students. You might also wish to connect with the multilingual learners' homes to gain an understanding of the students' life circumstances and experiences outside of school. Check out resources in the community, such as a community center, library, or after-school club for your multilingual learners.

- If you are a school leader, think how the school's visual arts center, resource center, or technology center may serve as a meeting point for multilingual learners and families for tutoring, mentoring, meeting, or networking. Depending on the geography of your district or school, you might enlist a safe place, such as a neighboring school (elementary with a middle or high school), to form an after-school club for sharing oral traditions in multiple languages, promoting multilingual literacy, or learning coding to promote digital literacy.

In this chapter we have endorsed multiple stakeholders—from multilingual learners to teachers and other school leaders—in using multiple languages for curriculum, instruction, and assessment. We have underscored the merit of having multilingual learners access content through multiple languages as they engage in assessment *as, for*, and *of* learning. Armed with resources, we have illustrated how to support multilingual learners and strategize assessment in multiple languages whether teachers and other educators are dependent on translators or are polyglots in their own right.

Resources for Multilingual Learners, Their Teachers, and Other Instructional Leaders

RESOURCE 2.1 FOR TEACHERS AND OTHER INSTRUCTIONAL LEADERS
A Planning Sheet for Assessment in Multiple Languages

With your grade-level team or department contemplate the following questions.

1. What is our philosophy (or theoretical basis) for teaching multilingual learners?

2. What are some of the major themes or issues to explore with our students?

3. How can our students contribute their insights and perspectives to these themes or issues?

(Continued)

(Continued)

4. **What are the connections of these themes to content and language standards?**

5. **How are we to incorporate our students' experiences and interests in the assessment process?**

6. **What will be the language(s) of assessment? What choices might our multilingual learners make?**

CLASSROOM ASSESSMENT IN MULTIPLE LANGUAGES

RESOURCE 2.2 FOR TEACHERS AND OTHER INSTRUCTIONAL LEADERS

Planning the Flow of Assessment Data for Multilingual Learners Throughout the School Year

How might you distribute assessment data across the school year? You are welcome to use this broad timeline or create one that better matches your school or district (such as quarters or month-by-month). Based on your distribution, how might you better ensure representation of your multilingual learners in multiple languages?

	CLASSROOM DATA	SCHOOL-LEVEL DATA
Beginning of Year		
Mid-Year		
End of Year		

RESOURCE 2.3 FOR MULTILINGUAL LEARNERS

My Multilingual Language Portrait

Instructions for the Teacher: My Multilingual Language Portrait may be part of the initial enrollment process or created within the first days of a new student's placement in a classroom. It may be inputted into a computer or iPad and then read to younger students; responses can then be individually recorded, either digitally or in writing. Multilingual learners who are literate in English could complete it independently or it could be read to older students in their other language (if feasible) by peers or paraprofessionals.

Name: _____ Grade: _____ Date: _____

The languages I speak: _____

The languages I read: _____

The languages I write: _____

1. **Who?** The languages you speak with different **people** almost every day, such as family members and friends. Do not put their full names, but rather their relation to you (e.g., mi abuela María):

I SPEAK A LANGUAGE OTHER THAN ENGLISH WITH …	I SPEAK ENGLISH WITH …	I SPEAK BOTH LANGUAGES WITH …

2. **Where?** The languages you speak at different **places**, such as at stores or the clinic:

I SPEAK A LANGUAGE OTHER THAN ENGLISH IN OR AT ...	I SPEAK ENGLISH IN OR AT ...	I SPEAK BOTH LANGUAGES IN OR AT ...

3. **When?** The languages you speak at different **times**, such as before school, at school, after school, or during the weekends:

I SPEAK A LANGUAGE OTHER THAN ENGLISH WHEN ...	I SPEAK ENGLISH WHEN ...	I SPEAK BOTH LANGUAGES WHEN ...

4. **What?** The languages you use to **read** at school or at home:

WHAT I READ IN A LANGUAGE OTHER THAN ENGLISH ...	WHAT I READ IN ENGLISH ...	WHAT I READ IN BOTH LANGUAGES ...

(Continued)

(Continued)

5. **What?** The languages you use to **write** at school or at home, such as a journal or notes:

WHAT I WRITE IN A LANGUAGE OTHER THAN ENGLISH ...	WHAT I WRITE IN ENGLISH ...	WHAT I WRITE IN BOTH LANGUAGES ...

6. **Which ones?** The language(s) you feel your best in and why:

MY LANGUAGE OTHER THAN ENGLISH ...	ENGLISH ...	BOTH LANGUAGES ...

7. **Which ones?** The language(s) you feel you *learn* best in and why:

MY LANGUAGE OTHER THAN ENGLISH ...	ENGLISH ...	BOTH LANGUAGES ...

RESOURCE 2.4 FOR MULTILINGUAL LEARNERS

A Sample Oral Language Use Survey for Multilingual Learners

Directions: Which language or languages do you use around your home, neighborhood, and school? You can follow as I read the questions. Put an X in the box with the language or languages that you use—your language other than English, English, or both languages. *Not Applicable* means that it doesn't apply to me.

My Name:_____ Date:_____

My Languages: _____

WHICH LANGUAGES DO YOU SPEAK…	MY LANGUAGE(S) OTHER THAN ENGLISH	ENGLISH	BOTH OR MORE LANGUAGES	NOT APPLICABLE
1. With your parents or guardians				
2. With your grandparents				
3. With your brothers and sisters				
4. With others who live with you				
5. With your caregivers (if any)				
6. With your neighbors				
7. With your friends				
AROUND YOUR NEIGHBORHOOD				
8. At the store				
9. At the clinic				
10. At a religious gathering				

(Continued)

(Continued)

WHICH LANGUAGES DO YOU SPEAK…	MY LANGUAGE(S) OTHER THAN ENGLISH	ENGLISH	BOTH OR MORE LANGUAGES	NOT APPLICABLE
11. At a market or restaurant				
12. When talking on the phone				
13. When expressing emotion				
AROUND SCHOOL				
14. Outside or on the playground				
15. In the lunchroom				
16. In the halls				
17. During free time				

SOURCE: Adapted from Gottlieb (2016), p. 34.

RESOURCE 2.5 FOR MULTILINGUAL LEARNERS

A Sample Literacy Survey for Multilingual Learners

What do you read and write when you are not at school? Put an X in the box to show whether you use your language other than English, English, or both languages. *Not Applicable* means that you do not use those materials for reading or writing.

BEFORE OR AFTER SCHOOL	IN MY LANGUAGE OTHER THAN ENGLISH	IN ENGLISH	IN BOTH LANGUAGES	NOT APPLICABLE
I READ …				
Maps (on my phone)				
Schedules (for school, bus, or train)				
Notes from friends (texts or emails)				
Information from the internet				
E-articles for homework				
Brochures/ pamphlets				
Magazines/news stories				
Short stories				
Poetry				

(Continued)

(Continued)

BEFORE OR AFTER SCHOOL	IN MY LANGUAGE OTHER THAN ENGLISH	IN ENGLISH	IN BOTH LANGUAGES	NOT APPLICABLE
Books				

I WRITE…				
Information on forms				
Lists (of things to do)				
Notes for my classes				
Texts or emails				
Answers to questions (for homework)				
Short stories				
Poetry or songs				

SOURCE: Adapted from Gottlieb (2016), p. 35.

RESOURCE 2.6 FOR TEACHERS AND OTHER INSTRUCTIONAL LEADERS

Guidelines for Collecting Oral and Written Language Samples in Multiple Languages

Gathering oral and written language samples, if possible, should be part of overall data collection upon entry in a school as part of the initial enrollment process. If not feasible, then teachers should collect these baseline data at the beginning of the school year. Here are some suggestions that can readily be converted into a checklist to set up for initial oral and written student samples.

Teachers should ease multilingual learners into the experience by having them:

- ☐ Choose their preferred language to start; then ease into the other language

- ☐ Choose whether to begin with oral language or written language sample

- ☐ Be comfortable with the situation, to the extent feasible

- ☐ Select from a set of action-packed, cross-disciplinary developmentally appropriate pictures, photos, graphics

- ☐ Become acquainted with any equipment or technology

- ☐ Choose to use technology for keyboarding (for students in fourth grade and beyond) or paper and pencil for their written sample

- ☐ Listen to instructions in two languages to maximize comprehension

- ☐ Practice by providing identifying and background information

- ☐ Ask clarifying questions in their preferred language

- ☐ Be introduced to student-friendly criteria on which they will be evaluated.

RESOURCE 2.7 FOR TEACHERS AND OTHER SCHOOL LEADERS

Considerations for Assessment in Multiple Languages: A Checklist and Rating Scale

As a school, you may treat the following considerations for assessment in several ways.

☐ *First,* you may wish to create a checklist. Check (√) signifies that you take this factor into account; zero (0) denotes that you haven't.

☐ *Second*, you may wish to convert the checklist into a rating scale. Check (√) means that you take this factor into account, zero (0) that you haven't, or plus (+) that you are considering this factor in your assessment practices.

☐ *Third*, you may take your +s on the complete list or for each set of considerations and prioritize them, starting with 1 as the top consideration. Then, individually, jointly with a co-worker, or as a group, develop a plan to launch your reform efforts on assessing multilingual learners!

1. Linguistic considerations; multilingual learners'
   - ☐ 1a. language(s) other than English
   - ☐ 1b. oral language proficiency in their language(s) other than English
   - ☐ 1c. literacy in their language(s) other than English
   - ☐ 1d. preferences and contexts of language use in English and other languages
   - ☐ 1e. English language proficiency
   - ☐ 1f. amount of exposure to English at school and at home

2. Cultural considerations; multilingual learners'
   - ☐ 2a. cultural (and religious) backgrounds
   - ☐ 2b. cultural traditions and perspectives
   - ☐ 2c. number of years and places educated outside the U.S.
   - ☐ 2d. number of years in U.S. schools
   - ☐ 2e. familiarity with mainstream (anglocentric) ways of being

3. Academic considerations; multilingual learners'
   - ☐ 3a. performance in content area classrooms
   - ☐ 3b. language(s) of instruction by content area or time allocation
   - ☐ 3c. language(s) of classroom assessment (by content area)
   - ☐ 3d. opportunities to learn grade-level content
   - ☐ 3e. opportunities to gain 21st-century skills (e.g., technology)

4. Experiential considerations; multilingual learners'
   - ☐ 4a. continuity of education within a year (mobility)
   - ☐ 4b. continuity of education from year to year
   - ☐ 4c. participation in and types of language education programs
   - ☐ 4d. allocation of language(s) by educational program
   - ☐ 4e. exposure to literacy experiences outside of school

5. Social-emotional considerations; multilingual learners'
   - ☐ 5a. exposure to trauma from cultural or religious conflict
   - ☐ 5b. exposure to trauma from separation (i.e., from parents, close relatives)
   - ☐ 5c. exposure to racial/ethnic discrimination
   - ☐ 5d. exposure to bullying
   - ☐ 5e. transiency/mobility/homelessness

CHAPTER 3

Planning Classroom Assessment in Multiple Languages

▶ A banner on a building in Berlin

Entre dicho y hecho hay gran trecho.

Things are easier said than done.

—Spanish proverb

The Dilemma

But my students just socialize in their home language!

Ana is entering her fourth year as a language specialist and this fall she also is becoming a part-time instructional coach for her school. She is genuinely pleased with how school leadership, along with the faculty and community, has moved from having a school climate that featured a transmission model, where teaching was imparted to students, to one in which collaboration is the norm where establishing relationships is paramount. Relationship building is visible in the partnerships that are continually being built between coaches and teachers, teachers and students, and teachers, students, and families.

Collaborative expectations and values have filtered down to classrooms. As in teaching, learning is now viewed as a social activity where interaction with others has become the source for co-constructing and sharing new knowledge and ideas. Classrooms are seen as communities of learners where learning occurs when its members actively participate in meaningful shared experiences (Rogoff, 1994). The collective expertise in classrooms is distributed through careful planning of experiences that are accessed and shared by everyone in one or more languages.

Changes in the classroom have brought about a new norm throughout the school. Multilingual learners are now linguistic and cultural envoys who interact with each other as they contribute to and engage in hands-on tasks. The expected silence of yesterday has been replaced with a buzz of activity where students are encouraged to discuss issues of personal importance and reach consensus on decisions. For multilingual learners the classroom has become a welcome safe space where students feel confident to experiment with language and to apply their cultural expertise. However, there is still some stigma for multilingual learners who engage in discussions in languages other than English.

As Ana has dual responsibilities, she is pleased that there is schoolwide joint planning time. Throughout the week, she partners with language and content co-teachers as well as grade-level and department teams. While the teachers who instruct in English are generally supportive of this social-oriented learning environment, they are afraid that if they allow their multilingual learners to interact in languages other than English, they will lose control. They fear that the students are busy socializing and deviating from their assigned activities. Among bilingual and dual language teachers there is apprehension about conforming to the strict language allocation assigned to each language that is required of some program models.

Yet the multilingual learners appear to be on task and gaining confidence in themselves as learners. It's time to start co-planning assessment for a curricular project of several weeks. The teachers are conflicted as to what extent multilingual learners should be allowed to use their language(s) of choice. What should they do?

FIRST IMPRESSIONS

- In what ways does this scenario resonate with you?

- In planning assessment, how do you capitalize on the linguistic strengths of your multilingual learners?

- How do you capture assessment within a linguistically and culturally sustainable curriculum design?

- How do you build assessment *as, for,* and *of* learning in multiple languages into co-planning with other teachers?

FIGURE 3.1 The FIRST PHASE of the Assessment Cycle: Planning Assessment in Multiple Languages

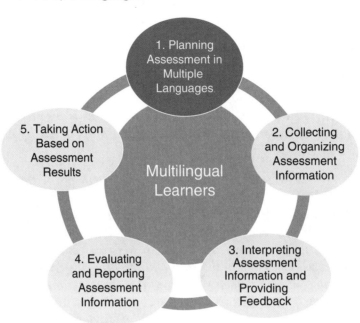

Multilingual learners think in and use multiple languages. It is most evident when they interact with peers of the same language group or when they participate in instructional programs that honor multiple language use. We organize the book around the assessment cycle in multiple languages as an ongoing process whereby multilingual learners have opportunities to access and become empowered by engaging in learning while educators become vested in multilingual learners and their linguistic and cultural assets. In other words, we promote assessment as a vehicle for linguistic and cultural equity and support for educators with multilingual learners.

This chapter focuses on the preliminary phase of the cycle, planning, as shown in Figure 3.1. It views the purposes for assessment (the why) as central to planning for assessment in multiple languages (the what) that are carefully crafted through curriculum design (the how). We illustrate the unfolding of instruction and assessment through a multilingual multicultural curricular model. In it, we see how integrated learning targets assist educators of multilingual learners to seamlessly blend content and language in assessment *as, for,* and *of* learning.

WHAT DOES CLASSROOM ASSESSMENT IN MULTIPLE LANGUAGES ENTAIL?

Classroom assessment involving multilingual learners is an iterative process that is part of curriculum and instruction where there is an ongoing dynamic interplay between language and content among stakeholders (Cumming, 2009; Gottlieb, Katz, & Ernst-Slavit, 2009). In recognizing that learning is inclusive of the broader communities in which multilingual learners live, classroom assessment must come to reflect that sociocultural reality. And, as instruction and assessment are shifting toward more student-centeredness and interaction, classroom assessment must allow for multilingual learners' enhanced participation in one or more languages as students take on increased responsibility for learning.

Classroom assessment in multiple languages may be:

- spontaneous (contingent), where teachers give immediate pointed feedback to students, redirect a lesson on the spot, or launch into a mini-lesson

- planned with students, where multilingual learners are expected to thoughtfully reflect on their learning and that of their peers

- interactive, where students and teachers discuss options for activities, tasks, and projects and accompanying evidence of learning

- performance-based, where multilingual learners engage in hands-on authentic learning that is inclusive of their languages and cultures.

Additional Purposes for Classroom Assessment in Multiple Languages

Returning to Figure 1.4 in Chapter 1, Framing Classroom Assessment in Multiple Languages, the first consideration in planning or co-planning assessment in multiple languages is to identify its purpose, audience, and use of information. Classroom assessment for multilingual learners has both formative and summative purposes. Formative purposes pertain to assessment *as* and *for* learning that are internal to everyday classroom practices among students or between students and teachers. Summative purposes for classrooms, associated with assessment *of* learning, also involve the interaction between students and teachers but are reserved for accumulated learning as demonstrated, for example, by projects or performances. Assessment *of* learning also refers to commercial tests and other measures that are part of district and state accountability, but that application, while recognized, is treated in the companion book for educational leaders.

The terms formative and summative can mistakenly refer to assessment outcomes or kinds of tests or strategies rather than purposes or processes. To avoid this misconception, we choose to use the trilogy *as*, *for*, and *of* learning to describe different approaches to classroom assessment and to underscore the importance of stakeholders (namely, students, students with teachers, and teachers) and their engagement in the process. In some contexts, **formative assessment** is indeed assessment *for* learning (see Black & Wiliam, 1999; Council of Chief State School Officers, 2018; Heritage, 2010; Stiggins, 2006; as examples), but we choose to separate and accentuate the critical role of students as decision-makers and leaders in their own right, thus assessment *as* learning. Figure 3.2 illustrates the relationship between these terms.

FIGURE 3.2 Assessment *as, for,* and *of* Learning as an Outgrowth of Assessment for Formative and Summative Purposes

Formative Assessment Purposes   Summative Assessment Purposes

Assessment *as* Learning   Assessment *for* Learning   Assessment *of* Learning   Assessment *of* Learning
by Students   by Students   for Teachers   for Districts and States
                           With Teachers   With Students

At times the purpose for classroom assessment for multilingual learners calls for multiple language use. At other times, expectations for assessment are met with a single language. Still other times, translanguaging, the simultaneous interaction between multiple languages, is acceptable and encouraged.

Sometimes the target for assessment is more content-related knowledge and skills expressed through language and other modalities. At other times, language is the vehicle of instruction within content. When instruction and assessment are indistinguishable, translanguaging can serve as a means for building multilingual learners' metalinguistic, metacognitive, and metacultural awareness.

Additional purposes for classroom assessment in multiple languages include:

- determining growth in multilingual learners' social-emotional development, biliteracy development, cross-cultural communication, and achievement within and across content areas

- enhancing linguistically and culturally relevant teaching and learning.

In Figure 3.3 we see more specific purposes for classroom assessment that have been tentatively classified according to units of learning and lessons. It is duplicated as Resource 3.1 for teachers and other school leaders to discuss the purposes within their own context.

FIGURE 3.3 The Purposes for Classroom Assessment for Units of Learning and Accompanying Lessons

PURPOSES FOR CLASSROOM ASSESSMENT IN ONE OR MORE LANGUAGES	UNITS OF LEARNING	INDIVIDUAL LESSONS
Provide standards-related evidence of language and content learning.	X	X
Show growth in multilingual learners' linguistic repertoire across content areas.	X	
Offer evidence for translanguaging as a pedagogical and assessment practice.	X	X
Improve teaching and learning.	X	X
Offer immediate concrete actionable feedback to move teaching and learning forward.		X
Target learning of individual content skills.		X
Build multilingual learners' metacognitive, metalinguistic, and metacultural awareness.	X	X
Help guide instruction in multiple languages.	X	X
Reflect on learning goals and integrated learning targets.	X	X
Support decisions based on multilingual evidence.	X	X
Plan subsequent instruction in multiple languages.	X	X
Foster student agency, identity, confidence, pride, and autonomy.	X	X

Relax and Reflect: For whom are the purposes for classroom assessment intended?

Revisiting the purposes for classroom assessment in Figure 3.3, you might notice a mix of stakeholders. There are those that pertain to students, others to teachers, and still others to school leaders. Think about how you might categorize and prioritize the purposes for your setting.

All purposes for assessment apply to multilingual languages. The classroom's or school's language policy, the context for learning, and multilingual learners' preferences should ultimately determine which language(s) to use. As a grade-level team or department, review Resource 3.1 (a duplicate of Figure 3.3) with the added column for the language(s) of assessment.

FIGURE 3.4 Curriculum Building: The Relationship Between the Purpose(s) for Assessment, a Unit of Learning, and Their Associated Lessons

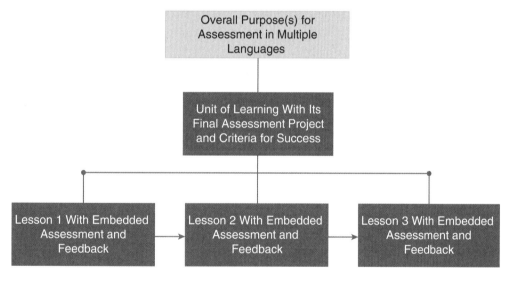

There needs to be a close relationship between the overall purpose for assessment and a unit of learning with its related lessons. Figure 3.4 illustrates that connection, and Resource 3.2 gives an example based on the essential question *How is the same fairytale portrayed in different cultures?* Resource 3.3 is a blank template for you to sketch out or modify an assessment plan for a unit of learning that integrates assessment.

HOW IS CLASSROOM ASSESSMENT AN EXPRESSION OF CURRICULUM DESIGN?

Designing curriculum which seamlessly wraps assessment helps students realize what's important to learning, what's needed to succeed, and how to accomplish it. As Sleeter and Carmona (2017) say, we must think of "students as curriculum" first, tapping the knowledge and experiences that they bring to school rather than subject matter or standards. If we are able to craft curriculum to fit multilingual students, we can instill multicultural perspectives and values rather than perpetuate normative cultural patterns that tend to marginalize multilingual learners.

For multilingual learners, planning curriculum must go beyond relevant or responsive to be linguistically and culturally sustainable. **Linguistic and cultural sustainability** (Paris, 2012) entails the preservation of languages, literacies, and other cultural practices of students and communities throughout schooling.

Another critical aspect of curriculum design unique for multilingual learners is the integration of language and content. First appearing in the ground-breaking book *Language and Content* (Mohan, 1986), the relationship between language and content was subsequently envisioned in a conceptual framework (Snow, Met, & Genesee, 1989). Today, researchers, policy-makers, and educators encourage the simultaneous building of disciplinary knowledge, conceptual understanding, and language competencies (Cheuk, 2016; Davison & Williams, 2013; Pimentel, 2018).

Features of Effective Curricula for Multilingual Learners

Curriculum should be designed to optimize students' potential for achieving the learning goals that have been carefully crafted by educators and students together. The following features illustrate the important role of assessment in multiple languages within linguistically and culturally sustainable curriculum (Suskie, 2018). Resource 3.4 converts these features into a rating scale to evaluate the extent that multiple languages have been considered in assessment and curriculum planning in your setting.

- Every learning goal sets up the context for assessment in multiple languages.

- Multilingual learners are afforded ample and diverse opportunities to access their full linguistic and cultural repertoires during assessment.

- Cross-linguistic and **cross-cultural considerations** are threaded throughout the unit of learning.

- Research-informed strategies on bilingualism and biliteracy push multilingual learners to achieve their goals through assessment.

- There are consistent challenging learning expectations for all multilingual learners regardless of their backgrounds and education status.

- Each lesson's activities build on the previous ones and contribute to forming a rich and meaningful culminating experience (i.e., performance, project, or product).

- The assessment experience at the close of a unit represents how learning goals are realized along with accompanying evidence.

- Assessment invites student voice in multiple languages.

Stop-Think-Act-React

Relax and Reflect: What does your curriculum look like for multilingual learners in your setting?

Curriculum, whether for individual content areas or cross-disciplinary as in STEAM (science, technology, engineering, arts, and mathematics), can take on many forms. To what extent is your curriculum inclusive of multilingual learners, their languages, cultures, and perspectives? To what extent is your curriculum equitable for all students? How might you augment your current curriculum to ensure its linguistic and cultural sustainability?

A Model of Curriculum Design for Multilingual Learners

In planning for learning, whether in one or multiple languages, there should be a direct connection among curriculum, instruction, and assessment. Figure 3.5 is an example of a model that is specifically designed for teaching and learning in multiple languages. Mirrored components reflect the parallelisms between curriculum that is enacted at the unit level and instruction that occurs at the lesson level. Assessment *as*, *for*, and *of* learning serves as the cement that brings cohesion, alignment, and continuity to curriculum and instruction.

Embedded Language Expectations for Systemic Planning, Enacting, and Justifying Outcomes (EL ESPEJO) is a linguistically and culturally sustainable curricular model that exemplifies the interplay among content, language, and culture. As shown in Figure 3.5, the curricular components for units of learning are replicated in parallel lessons. Together they highlight the linguistic and cultural contexts for learning that are drawn from multilingual learners' resources—their "funds of knowledge" or household, community, and classroom practices (González, Moll, & Amanti, 2005), which converge with their "funds of identity," a set of resources shaped by lived experiences essential for self-definition, self-expression, and self-understanding (Esteban-Guitart & Moll, 2014).

Let's unpack the curricular components of EL ESPEJO to illustrate how the planning phase for assessment in multiple languages might be organized. Presented below, the curricular side of the model unfolds as a unit plan with a series of steps from 1a to 1e.

Planning Assessment for a Unit of Learning in Multiple Languages: An Exemplar

This unit of learning designed for young multilingual learners (examples are adapted from a Grade 3 dual language team from Chicago Public Schools) explores language and culture in multilingual multicultural fairytales, a theme of interest to 8-year-olds. The steps and guiding questions follow the curricular

FIGURE 3.5 Mirrored Components for Planning and Assessing Learning for Multilingual Learners

Embedded Language Expectations for **S**ystemic Planning, **E**nacting, and **J**ustifying **O**utcomes: EL ESPEJO

UNIT PLANNING INCLUSIVE OF MULTIPLE LANGUAGES AND PERSPECTIVES: PLANNING FOR LEARNING AROUND A COMPELLING QUESTION, THEME, OR ISSUE AND THE OVERALL PURPOSE(S) FOR ASSESSMENT			
1a. Classroom/ Grade-Level Products, Projects, or Performances	1b. Community and Environmental Resources for Learning (Funds of Knowledge)	1c. Coordinated Language and Content Standards and Disciplinary Practices	1d. Integrated Learning Goals for Content and Language With Cross-Linguistic, and Cross-Cultural Considerations	1e. Language Expectations Associated With the Compelling Question, Theme, or Issue

CLASSROOM ASSESSMENT *AS, FOR,* AND *OF* LEARNING

| 2a. Classroom Learning Tasks and Activities | 2b. Student and Family Resources for Learning (Funds of Identity) | 2c. Coordinated Language and Content Standards and Disciplinary Practices | 2d. Integrated Objectives (Targets) for Content and Language With Cross-Linguistic/ Cross-Cultural Application | 2e. Oral, Written, Visual, Tactile, and Digital (Multimodal) Responses to the Compelling Question, Theme, or Issue |

2. Lesson Planning Inclusive of Multiple Languages and Perspectives: Moving Learning Forward Based on Feedback From Assessment

ADOPTED FROM Gottlieb and Hilliard (2019).

components of EL ESPEJO while the italicized text provides thematic examples. Resource 3.5 provides a blank plan of the steps for curricular design.

1. Identify the overall purpose(s) for assessment in multiple languages.

Why assess? or What should the information yield? The purpose for assessment should guide the crafting of the other components.

For this third-grade language arts unit, multilingual learners will:

- *Narrate a fairytale in Spanish and English*

- *Identify linguistic and cultural differences in oral and written text.*

1a. Negotiate a final product, project, or performance with students.

To what extent does your purpose(s) match the end project, product, or performance? The interests of the students should be paramount in determining how to express their learning.

Multilingual learners will produce and narrate a multimedia presentation (e.g., animated cartoons, slide shows) or a performance (e.g., videos, enactments) of a multicultural fairytale in multiple languages, including a self-assessment checklist of comparative story elements.

1b. Name community resources that contribute to the unit.

How might we tap families' funds of knowledge? How do we directly connect the experiences of the students with their families and communities for the capstone project or final event?

Family oral stories passed down from generation to generation and multilingual books from the neighborhood library will be the bases for selecting multilingual multicultural fairytales.

1c. Identify relevant content and related language standards.

Which academic content standards and language development/proficiency standards best match the purposes for assessment and the final project, performance, or product?

Language Arts Standards for Grade 3 in Spanish and English:

> *Recount stories, including fables, folktales, and myths from diverse cultures; determine the central message, lesson, or moral and explain how it is conveyed through key details in the text.*

> *Recuentan cuentos, incluyendo fábulas, cuentos populares, y mitos de diversas culturas; identifican el mensaje principal, lección o moraleja y explican cómo se transmite en los detalles clave del texto.*

> *Compare and contrast the themes, settings, and plots of stories written about the same or similar characters.*

Comparan y contrastan los temas, ambientes y tramas de los cuentos escritos sobre los mismos personajes o personajes similares.

Determine the meaning of words and phrases as they are used in a text, distinguishing literal from nonliteral language.

Determinan el significado de palabras y frases que se utilizan en un texto, determinan el lenguaje literal del no-literal.

Language Development Standards for Grade 3 (from https://commoncore-espanol. sdcoe.net/Portals/commoncore-espanol/Documents/2018_09_18_K-12_SLD_ Standards_Translated.pdf? ver=2018-09-18-101554-827) in Spanish and English:

Interpretativo: Escuchar activamente el español hablado en una gama de contextos sociales y académicos.

Interpretive: Listen actively to spoken English in a range of social and academic contexts.

Leer atentamente textos literarios e informativos, y analizar los medios multimedia para determinar cómo se transmite el significado explícito e implícitamente a través del lenguaje.

Read closely literary and informational texts and analyze multimedia to determine how meaning is conveyed explicitly and implicitly through language.

Productivo: Expresar información e ideas oralmente en presentaciones formales sobre temas académicos.

Productive: Express information and ideas in formal oral presentations on academic topics.

1d. Design integrated goals for learning that include cross-linguistic and cross-cultural considerations.

How might you negotiate student learning goals with your multilingual learners?

Goals or targets for learning should be drawn from:

- Multilingual learners' linguistic and cultural knowledge, experiences, and interests

- Language development/proficiency standards and content (state academic) standards

- Multimodal resources for communication (textual, visual, aural, and digital)

Integrated learning goals/targets for the proposed unit on fairytales:

To demonstrate metalinguistic awareness, multilingual learners will identify differences in language use in a familiar bilingual fairytale in Spanish and English (e.g., once upon a time/había una vez) and discuss the similarities and differences between languages.

To demonstrate metacultural awareness, multilingual learners will identify and discuss the cultural similarities and differences in Spanish and English of a familiar bilingual fairytale (e.g., actions of the characters, description of traditions).

To demonstrate understanding of a multicultural narrative, multilingual learners will recount a bilingual fairytale with vivid descriptions that highlight the elements of the story (i.e., the central theme, characters, setting, and events) using multimodal communication of their choice—orally, writing, illustrating).

Learning goals provide tangible and mutually agreed upon criteria by teachers and students that take the mystery out of assessment. Integrated learning goals for multilingual learners encompass students' language development in conjunction with disciplinary knowledge of the content areas (Cheuk, 2016). For a unit, learning goals should be SMART (Doran, 1981), representing Specific, Measurable, Attainable, Relevant, and Timely expectations. In essence, for multilingual learners, integrated learning goals exemplify the language, knowledge, and concepts embodied in teaching and learning.

Cross-Linguistic and Cross-Cultural Considerations

Linguistic and cultural sustainable classrooms and schools beg equitable assessment in multiple languages. Incorporating cross-linguistic and cross-cultural considerations into the learning experience for multilingual learners increase relevance, add meaning, and help build relationships between home and school. In addition, the unit itself becomes a more authentic and valid representation of a multilingual multicultural context for learning.

Here are some ideas for including cross-linguistic and cross-cultural considerations into curricular planning *(with examples from the fairytale unit)* that can carry over to assessment.

- Honor and leverage different perspectives that represent multiple cultures *(e.g., have students note cultural differences in the same fairytale across languages).*

- Have multilingual learners summarize the major events *(of the fairytale)* in one language and then compare the presentation of events in the other language.

- Have multilingual learners hunt for idiomatic expressions and **cognates** in oral and written text in different versions *(of the fairytale)* to accentuate the roles of language and culture in conveying meaning.

- Acknowledge the value and advantage of having various cultural meanings for different story elements *(e.g., different endings for the same fairytale depending on the culture, different expressions that carry the same meaning).*

1e. State language expectations

Learning goals should always be shared with students to help them formulate language expectations; they should also serve as the basis for **success criteria** for the unit. Here are language expectations as outlined in step 5 of EL ESPEJO that have been converted to student-friendly "I can" (Puedo) statements in Spanish for third-grade multilingual Spanish/English learners.

Puedo comparar el sentido de frases en español con las que encuentro en inglés en mi cuento de hadas. Puedo explicar cómo las frases son semejantes y diferentes.

I can compare the meaning of sentences in Spanish with those in English in my fairytale. I can explain how the sentences are similar and different.

Puedo relatar unas diferencias entre la cultura latina y la cultura estadounidence en mi cuento de hadas a mis compañeros.

I can tell some differences between the Spanish culture and the American culture in my fairytale to my classmates.

Puedo recontar un cuento de hadas en español e inglés. En el recuento incluyo el tema, los personajes, el lugar, los eventos de la historia, y detalles lleno de color.

I can recount a fairytale in Spanish and English. In the recount, I include the theme, characters, place, historical events, and colorful details.

To be effective in planning assessment, especially when multiple languages are involved, there must a match between the purpose(s) for assessment (selected from Figure 3.4), integrated learning goals, and the final product, project, or performance. Figure 3.6 illustrates this relationship.

Integrated learning goals as a planning and reflective tool can help students build their capacity to learn, discern what is important to their own learning, and become more self-sufficient independent learners. In that way, multilingual learners gain confidence in pursuing more challenging tasks to express their growing conceptual understanding and linguistic prowess. Integrated learning goals for multilingual learners who are engaging in learning in multiple languages should center on:

- ideas or concepts rather than isolated vocabulary or grammatical forms

- comparative expressions of language use

FIGURE 3.6 The Relationship Among Purpose(s) for Assessment, Integrated Learning Goals, and Final Projects for Units of Learning

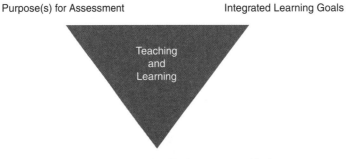

Purpose(s) for Assessment   Integrated Learning Goals

Teaching and Learning

Assessment Products, Performances, or Projects

- coupling of content-related actions with associated language

- effectiveness of communication rather than correctness

- student–student interaction for specific purposes

- multiple cultural perspectives

- negotiation of meaning with others.

Planning classroom assessment involves a thoughtful deliberation among teachers, with input from multilingual learners. Depending on the context for learning, learning goals should reflect the languages of instruction. For example, if striving for biliteracy in a dual language setting, multilingual learners, along with their teachers, should co-construct learning goals that apply to both English and the partner language. If the goal is achievement in particular content areas, such as mathematics, science, or social studies, then two languages might serve as the media of instruction, but the learning goal itself is not language specific. In this instance, classroom assessment should be in the language(s) of instruction with the option of having multilingual learners use one or more languages per their agreed upon classroom language policy.

 Stop-Think-Act-React

Relevant Resources: What are some templates to use for creating integrated learning goals?

A series of resources at the close of this chapter offers ways to think about how to craft integrated learning goals and targets in multiple languages. Resources 3.5 and 3.6 list the steps for planning units of learning in multiple languages and for a set of lessons. You are welcome to adopt or adapt these resources.

PLANNING CLASSROOM ASSESSMENT *AS, FOR,* AND *OF* LEARNING FOR CURRICULUM AND INSTRUCTION

In the model EL ESPEJO, classroom assessment *as, for,* and *of* learning straddles curricular units and their mirrored lessons. Assessment *of* learning generally plays out for the unit as a whole while assessment *as* and *for* learning are more descriptive of everyday classroom occurrences.

Assessment *of* Learning

Multilingual learners' final projects, performances, or products are evidence of learning. In the case of the fairytale unit, multimedia presentations, such as producing animated cartoons, videos, or slide shows, and performances, as in re-enactments, dramatizations, or plays, represent the culminating experience that the students can craft.

The final project is planned and built lesson by lesson across the course of the unit. Teachers may choose to get together to form criteria for success or perhaps project descriptors with different weights. They may plan with or share them with their multilingual learners so that the students are aware of the expectations from the beginning.

There is no reason why assessment *as* and *for* learning cannot be embedded into assessment *of* learning. Multilingual learners can express decisions they have made regarding their progress toward finalizing their end-of-unit project As in assessment itself, multilingual learners can communicate through multiple modalities, such as a personal journal, dialoguing with their teacher, or online. Here are some ideas generated by students:

"I am going to read my fairytale con mucho cuidado. Then I will retell it to a friend."'

"I want to use both my languages to show what is important to me."

"My partner and I have a plan for our project. We want to act out Caperucita Roja (Little Red Riding Hood)."

Assessment *for* Learning

Within the classroom context, planning for assessment might include strategies that represent lesson targets; other times, assessment is more spontaneous in response to peers or teachers to the situation at hand. Assessment *for* learning generally occurs within a lesson but also might occur on a daily basis as a classroom routine, such as submitting an exit slip. Here are some strategies facilitated by teachers that might yield useful information as part of assessment *for* learning:

- *Open-ended questioning* has few constraints in answering with no anticipated outcomes. This strategy is ideal for multilingual learners across language proficiency levels and languages as the students have control over what they say or write (e.g., "Tell me about your fairytale").

- *Undirected think-pair-share* and other collaborative moves allow students to be creative thinkers in questioning and responding to their peers in one or more languages (e.g., "Share with your partner who is your favorite character in the fairytale and why").

- *Think-alouds* between students and teachers could be approached in several ways. One strategy would be to connect multilingual learners' previous work or past experiences to the work at hand and to elaborate on how the learning target might be met (e.g., "I know all about Cenicienta. I have seen the video and my abuela has read me the book"). When the work is underway, students should be given opportunities to articulate in their preferred language and approach to learning (e.g., through visuals or personal conversations with teachers) to make sure their target is in reach.

Assessment *as* Learning

Classroom time each day should be devoted to building student ownership by encouraging productive student talk in pairs or in small groups, whether in person or virtually. Through critical questioning, multilingual learners gain a sense of trust and community. The following ideas can help spark student–student interaction, the cornerstone for assessment *as* learning.

- *Student–student conversation* captures student curiosity and emotions as they communicate with each other (through text, orally, or digitally).

- *Student self-reflection* promotes **metacognitive awareness** (thinking about and regulating one's thoughts) in multilingual learners' preferred language(s).

- *Peer assessment* allows classmates to give feedback to each other based on mutually agreed upon criteria, such as using a checklist or a rating scale, in the language of their choice.

- *Socratic seminars*, student-led discussions generally for older students, invite the group-appointed leader to ask open-ended questions based on a rich text with real-world connections. Students engage in active listening of their peers, think critically for themselves, and articulate their own thoughts in relation to those of others. No reason why building student confidence can't be in multiple languages!

Together, planning for assessment *as, for,* and *of* learning solidifies the tie between curricular unit planning and instructional lesson planning. These three assessment approaches actually wrap around the components of the curricular model to create meaningful, connected, and ongoing experiences for teachers and students.

Lesson Planning in Multiple Languages Within a Unit of Learning

Now let's unpack the instructional side of the mirrored components of EL ESPEJO (steps 2a–2e) to illustrate the unfolding of teaching and learning across a set of lessons.

2. Move learning forward with feedback from assessment.

Each lesson within a unit of learning should provide insight for students and teachers to improve teaching and learning. Feedback is a daily reminder of what students and teachers have accomplished and what remains or what needs to be revamped. Research shows that feedback positively influences student achievement and suggests that meaningful feedback includes being specific, timely, and actionable, discussing the learner's advancement toward a target or goal, engaging students in the process, and motivating students to further their learning (Black & Wiliam, 1999; Hattie & Timperley, 2007).

2a. Design learning tasks and activities with multimodal communication options.

Learning tasks with multimodal communication options advantage all students by giving them access to multiple resources to make meaning. Multimodalities are different channels of information that help in scaffolding and facilitating student learning, as in:

○ Visuals: photos, diagrams, figures, and illustrations

○ Audio (e.g., podcasts)

- Video
- Speech
- Text: writing and print
- Music
- Movement
- Gestures and facial expressions
- Technology: digital representation.

Students should be given choices of expression, including use of multiple languages, so that they feel comfortable and confident in learning.

> 2b. Seek student and family resources for learning (funds of identity).

Funds of identity are personal, as each student is a unique and special human being. Ongoing recognition of an individual learner's assets spurs pride in their languages, cultures, and lived experiences. Shaped by their home life and community, multilingual learners' multilingualism and multiculturalism are to be nurtured and further developed in school through curriculum and instruction.

> 2c. Coordinate language and content standards and disciplinary practices.

There is tremendous variability in the extent to which standards and disciplinary practices are required in lesson planning across districts and schools. Our suggestion is to select your state standards and disciplinary practices identified in the unit that are applicable for each lesson.

In the unit on fairytales, we rely on language arts standards in multiple languages as well as **language development standards** in multiple languages. We could also add some social studies standards to help students understand cross-cultural customs and contexts for fairytales.

> 2d. Craft integrated objectives for content and language with cross-linguistic/cross-cultural application.

We use the term *objectives* here as it is most commonly used by educators. However, you should think about reframing objectives, which generally imply a teacher directive to meet district or school compliance, to learning targets that suggest ideas that are written for and often by students. This shift in thinking implies that students can become leaders of their own learning (Berger, Rugen, & Woodfin, 2014). Written and presented in student-friendly language (along with icons, as applicable) that are understood by all multilingual learners, learning targets should transfer ownership to students. Here's an example:

In small groups, we will ask each other to name our favorite fairytales in English and Spanish. We will tell where our fairytales are from, what they are about, and why we like them.

> 2e. Allow for student choice in oral, written, visual, tactile, and digital response to the compelling question, theme, or issue.

Students should be given opportunities to express themselves in multimodal ways as they engage in different activities throughout a unit. Over time, as multilingual learners become more metalinguistically and metaculturally aware, they will develop a better sense of when to use each language. One of the steps in the fairytale unit that leads to the final outcome and could be accomplished in a lesson or two might be:

In small groups, multilingual learners will listen to or read different versions of the same fairytale. They will compare characters and events using a graphic organizer of their choice.

WHERE DOES TRANSLANGUAGING FIT IN PLANNING ASSESSMENT?

Translanguaging, the natural interaction in two languages, is tricky to describe; just as bilingualism is often perceived as a dichotomy—either a person is bilingual or not—so too is translanguaging—either it is deemed acceptable or not. Hornberger (2003, 2004), in her description of biliteracy, draws attention to "the continuity of experiences, skills, practices, and knowledge stretching from one end of any particular continuum to the other" (2004, p. 156). The notion of a continuum also applies to translanguaging in respect to the purpose, the context, and audience when interacting with others. Figure 3.7 illustrates how translanguaging functions along a continuum of instructional and assessment practices.

We return to the language policies of the classroom and school as places for translanguaging and its role in assessment. **Cross-linguistic transfer** might be systematically incorporated into curriculum at the close of a lesson, as in the case of the Bridge (Beeman & Urow, 2012), which then becomes the logical place for assessment. Cross-linguistic transfer might also be fluid within and across lessons. If intentionally planned, then translanguaging might be included as evidence for learning; if spontaneous, translanguaging might be assessed on a case by case basis. There is no one evidence-based methodology for translanguaging to apply to curriculum, instruction, and assessment.

An easy way to be tuned into translanguaging practices and multiple language use within a classroom context is to create a pact with multilingual learners.

FIGURE 3.7 A Continuum of Classroom Translanguaging Practices in Instruction and Assessment Among Multilingual Learners Who Share a Language

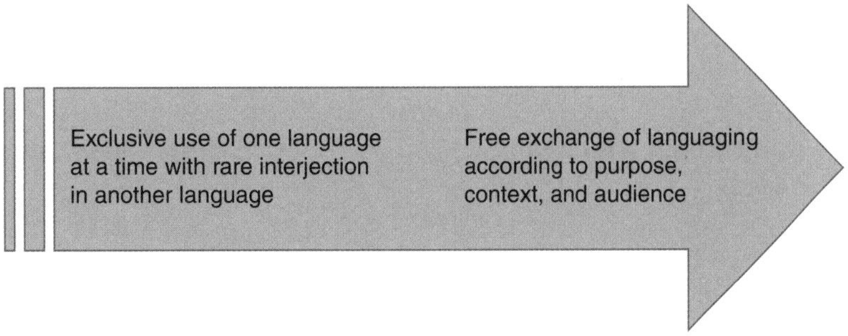

Exclusive use of one language at a time with rare interjection in another language

Free exchange of languaging according to purpose, context, and audience

In view of all students, a poster serves as a reminder of the use of multiple languages for teaching and learning. Additionally, the pact can jumpstart student self-assessment. For older multilingual learners, this pact becomes the basis for formulating a classroom language policy. Here's an example outline of a pact for young multilingual learners.

Our Classroom Pact

We, the students of Sra. Sandoval's classroom, are multilingual and are proud of our languages and cultures. We use all our languages to think and communicate.

We use English when...

We use our other language when...

We use both languages when...

HOW MIGHT WE FACE THE ISSUE? ASK QUESTIONS AND LISTEN TO YOUR STUDENTS!

Respect for multilingual learners' languages, cultures (their funds of identity), and what they have to say makes it easy for educators to dispel the myth that students are busy socializing rather than concentrating on the tasks at hand. When multilingual learners' languages and cultures are seamlessly woven into curriculum and instruction, linguistic and cultural sustainable classrooms prevail. The following questions prompt some ideas for connecting multiple languages to classroom assessment as part of curriculum and instructional design.

For Younger Multilingual Learners

- How do you feel when you have a chance to speak any language you like with a friend?

- How does knowing more than one language help you do your school work?

- How is speaking more than one language useful at home?

For Older Multilingual Learners

- How might your teachers help guide you in creating and meeting goals for learning in multiple languages?

- How do you plan which language(s) to use for different assignments and projects?

- How do you discuss upcoming projects with your peers and which language(s) do you prefer to use?

For Teachers and Other Instructional Leaders

- How do you plan for your multilingual learners' multiple language use during classroom assessment *as*, *for*, and *of* learning?

- How do multiple languages in curriculum and instruction apply to classroom assessment?

- How can you leverage your multilingual learners' identities through assessment in multiple languages?

For School Leaders

- How might you create a schoolwide advocacy plan to highlight your students', in particular your multilingual learners', strengths?

- How might you design professional learning with educators centered on assessing multilingual learners in varying classroom contexts?

- How might you plan a survey with teachers to ask students their preferences in showing what they know (e.g., quizzes, tests, projects, whether they prefer to work with peers or independently, or whether they like to display their work in multiple languages)?

HOW MIGHT WE RESOLVE THE DILEMMA? PUT TRUST IN YOUR MULTILINGUAL LEARNERS!

One of Ana's responsibilities as an instructional coach is to promote linguistic and cultural sustainability within and across classrooms in her school. One fall day she enters a middle-school social studies class and sees Julio and Mario talking to each other in the back of the room. The frustrated teacher is standing in close proximity, staring down at the pair. He then begins to tersely scold the pair, "I'm constantly having to remind you two about talking in class. Would you please tell me what's going on?" What happened next was shocking. In a small voice Julio whispers, "You talk really fast. We're making sure we understand what you say."

The boys elaborated that they were trying to translate everything said in class in order to comprehend the material, and then they worked together to formulate their responses. Furthermore, Mario said that he actually drafts his writing assignments in Spanish to better express himself and then translates his homework into English (adding substantial time and effort in the process).

Ana and the social studies teacher were amazed by the boys' grit and ingenuity. If only they had taken time to listen to the students without jumping to conclusions. The tenacity of the multilingual learners so impressed the instructional coach that she immediately shared her observation with the principal. The principal took action right away; the dilemma was presented at the next regularly scheduled school meeting. As a result, the faculty decided it was time to revisit the school's language policy and formed a committee to investigate the use of multiple languages in class (adapted from Alexander, 2019).

The resolution: In a year-long series of professional learning workshops on multicultural proficiency and sensitivity, teachers and other school leaders became aware of their own linguistic and cultural stereotypes and biases, which had led to deficit thinking about their students. Multilingual learners, by having multiple languages and cultures, were no longer perceived as having a problem. Instead, their use of other languages is now viewed as a source of strength for seeking and giving information. Teachers now put trust in their students to leverage their assets to advance learning.

Implications for assessment: When multilingual learners co-construct goals for learning in multiple languages and take the responsibility for reaching those goals, assessment should naturally flow. It should become obvious that promoting student–student interaction in the classroom in one or more languages enhances multilingual learners' opportunities to learn. Additionally, it helps nullify the myth that the students are using other languages to hide something or to socialize with each other.

Planning assessment is the first step of a multiphase process or cycle. For educators of multilingual learners, this phase always includes thinking about how to maximize linguistic and cultural equity. When multilingual learners use multiple languages to show what they know, the goals of biliteracy, biculturalism, and critical consciousness become more readily attainable.

Resources for Multilingual Learners, Teachers, and Other School Leaders

RESOURCE 3.1 FOR TEACHERS AND OTHER SCHOOL LEADERS
Purposes for Classroom Assessment

For each purpose for classroom assessment, decide its applicability to units of learning and/or individual lessons. Then choose the language(s) in which curriculum and instruction will be enacted.

PURPOSES FOR CLASSROOM ASSESSMENT IN ONE OR MORE LANGUAGES	UNITS OF LEARNING	INDIVIDUAL LESSONS	IN WHICH LANGUAGE(S)?
Provide standards-related evidence of language and content learning.			
Show growth in multilingual learners' linguistic repertoire across content areas.			
Offer evidence for translanguaging as a pedagogical and assessment practice.			
Improve teaching and learning.			
Offer immediate concrete and actionable feedback to move teaching and learning forward.			
Target learning of individual skills.			
Build multilingual learners' metacognitive, metalinguistic, and metacultural awareness.			
Guide instruction in multiple languages.			
Reflect on learning, learning goals, and integrated learning targets.			
Support decisions based on multilingual evidence.			
Facilitate student learning.			
Plan subsequent instruction in multiple languages.			
Foster student agency, identity, confidence, pride, and autonomy.			

RESOURCE 3.2 FOR TEACHERS OF MULTILINGUAL LEARNERS

Connecting Purposes for Assessment, the Final Project, and the First Week's Lessons

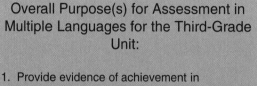

Overall Purpose(s) for Assessment in Multiple Languages for the Third-Grade Unit:

1. Provide evidence of achievement in Spanish/English.
2. Show growth in recounting through narration.
3. Identify linguistic and cultural differences in oral and written text.

Final Assessment Project for a Unit of Learning and Criteria for Success:

A multimedia exhibit or performance of multicultural versions of a fairytale including a self-assessment checklist of story elements with examples in multiple languages

Lesson 1 Assessment Idea:	Lesson 2 Assessment Idea:	Lesson 3 Assessment Idea:	Lesson 4 Assessment Idea:	Lesson 5 Assessment Idea:
Define fairytale, name its elements, and give examples.	*Summarize two versions of the same fairytale in English and your other language.*	*Compare similarities and differences in language use in the fairytales with peers.*	*Identify cultural differences in the fairytales with peers.*	*Discuss options for presenting your fairytale with peers.*

RESOURCE 3.3 FOR TEACHERS AND MULTILINGUAL LEARNERS

The Connection Among Purposes for Assessment, the Final Project, and the First Week's Lessons

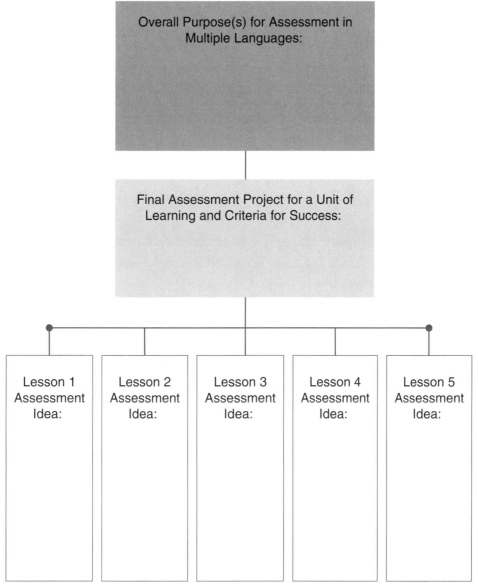

Overall Purpose(s) for Assessment in Multiple Languages:

Final Assessment Project for a Unit of Learning and Criteria for Success:

Lesson 1 Assessment Idea:

Lesson 2 Assessment Idea:

Lesson 3 Assessment Idea:

Lesson 4 Assessment Idea:

Lesson 5 Assessment Idea:

RESOURCE 3.4 FOR SCHOOL LEADERS AND TEACHERS

Evaluating the Effectiveness of Assessment in Curriculum Design for Multilingual Learners: A Rating Scale

How would you rate assessment for multilingual learners in your school's curriculum? Use this rating scale to reflect the extent to which the assessment is effective for multilingual learners.

CRITERIA FOR EFFECTIVENESS	VERY EVIDENT	EVIDENT	SOME EVIDENCE	NOT YET ON THE RADAR
1. Every learning goal sets up the context for assessment in multiple languages.				
2. Multilingual learners are afforded ample and diverse opportunities to access their full linguistic and cultural repertoires during assessment.				
3. Cross-linguistic and cross-cultural considerations are threaded throughout the unit of learning.				
4. Research-informed strategies on bilingualism and biliteracy push multilingual learners to achieve their goals through assessment.				
5. There are consistent challenging learning expectations for all multilingual learners regardless of their backgrounds and education status.				
6. The activities of each lesson build on the previous ones and contribute to form a rich culminating experience (i.e., performance, project, or product).				
7. The culminating assessment experience represents how learning goals are realized along with evidence.		.		.
8. Assessment invites student voice in multiple languages.				

RESOURCE 3.5 FOR TEACHERS AND COACHES

Planning Assessment in Multiple Languages for a Unit of Learning

As part of the planning phrase, use the following steps with colleagues to help frame your multilingual units or as a checklist to guide the development of units of learning for multilingual learners.

Step 1: Identify the overall purpose(s) for assessment in multiple languages.

Step 2: Negotiate a final product, project, or performance with students based on the theme, issue, or essential question with long-term criteria for success.

Step 3: Name community resources to contribute to the unit.

Step 4: Identify relevant content and language standards.

Step 5: Design integrated goals or targets for learning with cross-linguistic and cross-cultural considerations.

Step 6: Allow for student choice in oral, written, visual, tactile, and digital response to the compelling question, theme, or issue.

RESOURCE 3.6 FOR TEACHERS AND MULTILINGUAL LEARNERS
Planning Assessment in Multiple Languages for a Set of Lessons

As part of the planning phrase, use the following steps with colleagues to help frame your multilingual lessons or as a checklist to guide lessons for multilingual learners with assessment *as* and *for* learning.

Step 1: Use feedback from prior learning.

Step 2: Design classroom learning tasks and activities with short-term criteria for success.

Step 3: Seek student and family resources for learning (funds of identity).

Step 4: Coordinate language and content standards.

Step 5: Formulate integrated objectives (targets) for content and language with cross-linguistic and cross-cultural application.

Step 6: Allow for student choice in oral, written, visual, tactile, and digital response to everyday activities.

CHAPTER 4

Collecting and Organizing Assessment Information in Multiple Languages

Яблуко від яблуні не далеко падає

An apple never falls far from the tree.

—Ukrainian proverb

The Dilemma

But my colleagues and other school leaders simply don't understand the value of multilingualism!

As an instructional and data coach of multilingual learners, Chaido collaborates with teachers, serves on the leadership team, and is a liaison to the community. One of her personal pursuits is to promote and perpetuate a positive classroom and school culture around the value and benefits of multilingualism and multiculturalism. Yet, she often finds herself on the defense countering educators' misconceptions of multilingual learners, such as when she hears "their mere presence in schools reduces the perceived quality of education for all the students" (a racist indictment) or "the students' home language(s) interfere with their development of English" (a linguistic condemnation) (Menken & Solorza, 2014).

School leadership is constantly bombarding Chaido with questions such as, What should we do when students arrive at our school speaking languages other than English? How do we support multilingual learners who have been dually identified as English learners with Individualized Education Programs (IEPs)? How do we design a viable multilingual program when the language of power is English? Wouldn't it be best for the students just to be immersed in English?

(Continued)

(Continued)

Chaido's professional mission is to make bilingualism and biliteracy, which are increasingly visible across the nation and worldwide, commonplace across the network of schools that she serves. Having been raised in Greece, schooled in Germany, and now living in the U.S., she has witnessed first-hand the importance and benefits of being able to navigate across languages and cultures. Chaido wishes to bring legitimacy to leadership, educators, and families who endorse multilingualism. In her advocacy role, she strives to dispel the "one language, one nation" ideology that seems to be permeating some segments of society and schools and to replace it with the view that multilingualism is a resource to be cherished and nurtured.

There is general confusion among educators with whom Chaido works that multilingual learners are "semi-literate" as they are not at grade level in any language. This language-as-a-problem view has become engrained in school policies and practices (Escamilla, 2006). To dispel this misbelief, Chaido asks her colleagues during a regular staff meeting to place themselves in a line according to their perceived proficiency in an additional language. Much to the surprise of her fellow educators, no two people occupy the same place!

The point being made in this professional learning activity is that bilingualism and biliteracy, in fact, run along continua (Hornberger, 2003). Multilingual learners' proficiencies are not static; rather they are a response to particular sociocultural contexts for learning, prior experiences, and familiarity with and interest in the topic at hand. For example, some multilingual learners may be more orally proficient in some situations and more literate in particular text types or genres. Through additional hands-on activities, educators come to understand that multiliteracies, multimodal communication, and translanguaging enhance opportunities for literacy (reading and writing) and oracy (listening and speaking) development of multilingual learners.

Chaido has recently convinced her principal to form a cadre of teachers, paraprofessionals, and family members to collect and organize student data in multiple languages in order to dismiss these misunderstandings and to illustrate the value of biliteracy. She wants to have evidence of the positive connection between bilingualism and achievement to share with the educational community and district. The question is, what data best serve this purpose and how can Chaido persuade her colleagues of the merits of learning in multiple languages?

FIRST IMPRESSIONS

- In what ways does this scenario resonate with you?

- In collecting information during assessment in multiple languages, how do you ensure equity of language representation?

- What resources help provide more accurate information from multilingual learners?

- What are some of the perceived conceptions and misconceptions of translanguaging and its role in classroom assessment?

Every instructional moment in a classroom is an opportunity for assessment. More precisely, if instruction involves interaction among students, then it is deemed assessment *as* learning; if it involves teacher facilitation of student learning, then it is considered assessment *for* learning. In essence, each interaction is a potential source of information to be collected, organized, and acted upon to help move teaching and learning forward. Ultimately student learning is demonstrated in final products or projects illustrative of assessment *of* learning. The more time and careful consideration that go into the planning or co-planning phase of assessment, the easier it is to execute during the data collection phase. As shown in Figure 4.1, this chapter focuses on that phase.

Data collection in multiple languages should capture quality linguistically and culturally relevant evidence of learning for multilingual learners. Data can be qualitative (descriptive) and quantitative (numerical) in nature; both types of data, however, are essential to paint complete portraits of students. Classroom-based qualitative information, by its very nature, is intermingled with instruction. The most common form of qualitative data is observation: What are multilingual learners doing as they interpret, co-construct, and express language during learning? Quantitative data go hand-in-hand with qualitative information: For example, What kinds of learning are multilingual learners engaging in that lend themselves to tallying the number of instances of an occurrence or a particular skill? Other quantitative sources yield numerical data, such as tests, quizzes, checklists, and **rubrics**.

In this chapter, we see how purposes for assessment drive data collection. We explore how multimodal representation, **multiliteracies**, and scaffolding serve as resources for multilingual learners within the context of assessment *as*, *for*, and *of* learning. In addition, we investigate translanguaging as a strategy for generating and collecting data in multilingual contexts to increase multilingual learners' access to meaning while learning. Lastly, we share strategies for gathering and organizing oral and written data in multiple languages.

FIGURE 4.1 The `SECOND PHASE` of the Assessment Cycle: Collecting and Organizing Information in Multiple Languages

WHY MATCH DATA TO THE PURPOSES FOR ASSESSMENT?

The purpose of assessment (the why) guides the kinds of data to be collected (the what) and the manner in which the information is gathered (the how). Each purpose for assessment, introduced in the preceding chapters, requires a distinct means of presenting evidence. When multilingual learners are involved, each purpose for assessment has potential bias if not viewed through the lens of their cultures and languages.

Teachers must be vigilant and protective of their multilingual learners to ensure that data collection in multiple languages is fair and relevant. Additionally, assessment data should be representative of the students' language uses, lesson targets, and unit goals. Figure 4.2 revisits the purposes for classroom assessment and offers some ideas for embedding data collection within instruction. A blank form for duplication, Resource 4.1, is available at the close of the chapter.

FIGURE 4.2 Matching Purposes for Classroom Assessment With Ideas for Data Collection

PURPOSE FOR CLASSROOM ASSESSMENT IN ONE OR MORE LANGUAGES	IDEAS FOR CLASSROOM DATA COLLECTION FROM MULTILINGUAL LEARNERS/TEACHERS
1. Provide student evidence of language and content learning.	Oral, written, and multimodal samples in multiple languages
2. Show growth in multilingual learners' linguistic repertoire across content areas.	E-logs or blogs
3. Document translanguaging as a pedagogical and assessment practice.	Interactive academic conversations between multilingual learners and peers or teachers of shared languages; written communication
4. Improve teaching and learning.	Student journals or portfolios
5. Offer feedback to move teaching and learning forward.	Student-led interviews/conferences; oral and written work in multiple languages
6. Demonstrate learning of individual skills.	Documentation of attainment in multiple languages (e.g., through observation, checklists, annotations)
7. Build multilingual learners' cross-linguistic (metalinguistic) and cross-cultural (metacultural) awareness.	Student self-analysis and reflection
8. Guide instruction in multiple languages.	Oral interaction among multilingual learners; written samples
9. Reflect on learning based on overall learning goals/targets.	Goal setting facilitated by teachers during the year (e.g., at the end of a quarter)
10. Support decisions based on multilingual evidence.	A compendium of original student samples, such as a digital portfolio
11. Assist students in guiding their own learning.	Student learning targets with matched evidence
12. Plan instruction in multiple languages based on evidence.	Collaboration among teachers based on assessment information
13. Foster student agency, confidence, pride, and autonomy.	Student self-analysis of their multilingual multicultural identity

Relax and Reflect: How is the purpose for assessment related to data collection?

There are several themes that are interwoven throughout the book; one we often return to is the purpose for assessment. We cannot overemphasize the importance of having a clear purpose for assessment here as it sets the intent for data collection. Data gathered point to evidence that answers the question Why assess? To that end, which purposes in Figure 4.2 (or Resource 4.1) most closely match classroom assessment for your multilingual learners? What are the corresponding data that you collect?

WHAT RESOURCES ENHANCE INSTRUCTION AND ASSESSMENT IN MULTIPLE LANGUAGES?

This section introduces three related resources as part of the student learning experience (multimodal representation, translanguaging, and multiliteracies), their benefits for multilingual learners, the role of multiple languages, and some classroom examples. Figure 4.3 illustrates the close ties among these resources as expressions of meaning for multilingual learners.

These resources exemplify the aim of **Universal Design for Learning (UDL)**, a framework intended to improve teaching and learning for all students based on neuroscientific evidence. Its primary principles include (1) multiple means of representation that give students multiple entrées to learning, (2) multiple means of expression that provide learners multiple ways to demonstrate their learning, and (3) multiple means of engaging learners that reflect their multiple interests. To that end, UDL principles coupled with multilingual resources increase opportunities for multilingual learners and multilingual learners with Individualized Education Programs (IEPs) to access and achieve grade-level content. Let's take a look.

FIGURE 4.3 Resources for Multilingual Learners: Access to Meaning Through Translanguaging, Multimodal Resources, and Multiliteracies

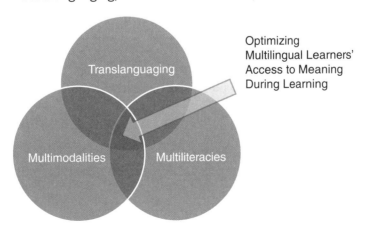

Thinking About Multimodal Resources in Data Collection for Multilingual Learners

Multimodal representation refers to the many ways (or modes) of communication, namely, the use of textual, aural, linguistic, spatial, and visual cues as sources of meaning for all students. In other words, images, graphs, symbols, charts or tables, videos, even gaze, constitute different modes that we combine with text and speech to enhance or reinforce sense-making. The blending of modes can occur simultaneously through receptive (listening, reading, and viewing) or expressive (speaking, writing, and illustrating) channels (Walsh, 2011).

Many modes for representing meaning have always existed; however, they have not always been acknowledged as socially and culturally accepted forms of expression of meaning in school. In recognition of their legitimacy, multimodal communication has become a de facto equity issue, especially for multilingual learners. For example, the use of multiple languages as a bona fide means of transmitting information, ideas, and concepts is still being contested in some educational circles, yet it is readily accepted as a multimodal resource. Thus, multimodal communication as an essential expression of learning is a naturally occurring affordance for multilingual learners.

Using Multimodal Communication During Assessment as, for, and of Learning

Multimodal communication enables students, in particular multilingual learners, to engage in learning and express their thinking and knowing in numerous ways. These resources are the tools of the disciplines, not peripheral or supplemental to teaching, but integral to the more traditional language-centric means of messaging. The following suggestions are some student-centered ideas, to be facilitated by teachers, to encourage the use of multimodal communication as part of the classroom routine that applies across content areas and disciplinary practices. To illustrate the presence of multimodal communication during assessment *as* and *for* learning, data from multilingual learners can be collected as they do the following:

- Participate in drama activities, such as role-playing or re-enactments, in multiple languages

- Express ideas through music or dance (e.g., in videos)

- Add modes, such as creating sound or movement for images or text

- Listen to just the sound in a film/video or view only its images to comprehend the big ideas (e.g., for newcomers who do not have a peer with a shared language)

- Thumb through wordless picture books or interpret visuals/graphs

- Answer compelling questions by drawing, mapping, note making, or audio recording

- Experiment with digital equipment and technologies, such as photo software or iMovie

- Network with buddies or mentors using recording equipment, such as phones or computers (as in Skyping, Zooming, or FaceTiming), in multiple languages

- Dialogue with pen pals around the globe in multiple languages through technology.

Multimodal communication can also be an expression of assessment *of* learning when wrapped into student performance at the close of a unit of learning. Extending ideas generated during assessment *as* and *for* learning, here are some products that teams of multilingual learners can work together to produce:

- A multilingual class video, such as students reporting or re-enacting events

- A grade-level assembly in multiple languages

- A multilingual schoolwide fair, such as robotics

- A multilingual gallery of murals or displays that is open to the community

- A multilingual community outreach event

- A service-learning project

- A multilingual video/radio broadcast to advertise an upcoming event

- Live multilingual performances (e.g., musicals, plays, rap) for families

- A multilingual newsletter or class website.

Another way for teachers to approach data collection is by having multilingual learners respond to imagery. Resource 4.3 offers a means of collecting data from photos or images in multiple languages. For example, multilingual learners could investigate multicultural photographs, street art, or murals as stimuli. As an assessment activity, students could analyze an image independently, such as the mural in Bogotá shown below, and then form small groups to do the following:

1. Share the image they have discovered or taken themselves, describe it in detail, and relate its meaning to them.

2. Discuss with others what they believe is happening in the image.

3. Identify the feelings the image evokes and explain why.

4. Generate questions from the image to ask others.

5. Reconcile or acknowledge the varying perceptions among group members.

▶ An Example of a Compelling Image: Street art in Bogotá, Colombia

Scaffolding Learning Using Multimodal Representation

As Gibbons (2015) states, "the regular classroom provides the best opportunity to learn a new language, because it provides an authentic context for the language most relevant to subject learning" (p. 207). **Scaffolding** is an instructional (and assessment) strategy that increases multilingual learners' access to content material as they gain proficiency in a language (Staehr Fenner, 2014). These temporary supports for students may be sensory (kinesthetic, visual, or tactile), interactive, or graphic (Gottlieb, 2013; Walqui & van Lier, 2010). Figure 4.4 illustrates some ways of scaffolding instruction and assessment for multilingual learners which are especially appropriate for newcomers but welcoming for all students.

Scaffolding learning involves teachers being intentional about reaching every student's conceptual and linguistic potential in one or more languages. An important goal of scaffolding the learning experience is to gradually transfer responsibility for learning from teacher to student. Thus, as students eventually take ownership for their own learning, they simultaneously develop agency and self-regulation (Gottlieb & Castro, 2017).

The notion of scaffolding learning is built on high expectations and challenging content for students. It is not a means of watering down an activity; rather, scaffolding learning enables teachers to gently advance multilingual learners' conceptual and language development. When scaffolding in one or more languages,

FIGURE 4.4 Example Ways of Scaffolding Learning in Multiple Languages

SENSORY	INTERACTIVE	GRAPHIC
• Seeing and touching objects to enhance and reinforce meaning • Moving around component parts (e.g., puzzles) to make sense of concepts • Co-creating diagrams, illustrations, and models to show conceptual understanding • Incorporating movement (e.g., gestures) to reinforce concepts	➢ Communicating in multiple languages with peers or teachers to clarify meaning ➢ Conversing with peers to share information in one or more languages ➢ Engaging in collaborative strategies in the language of shared choice to answer essential questions ➢ Using technology to deepen learning	❖ Representing data in tables and charts ❖ Creating or completing graphic organizers to process learning ❖ Using templates and exemplars to boost understanding ❖ Constructing or using timelines to order or sequence events

teachers are able to push multilingual learners' cognitive engagement in grade-level content, no matter what the students' language proficiency. When learning in two languages, different scaffolding strategies could be weighted for or applied to each language. Overall, scaffolding learning involves teachers or students:

- using language that expands multilingual learners' repertoire, thus moving toward greater linguistic complexity and sophistication

- modeling language that is sensitive to students' multilingual assets and resources

- stretching language use to expanded, new, and different contexts

- building on what multilingual learners know and can do in multiple languages.

To reiterate, scaffolding learning is integral to instruction and assessment as it ensures that every student is operating within a personalized **zone of proximal development**. This zone is the extent of match between what learners can do independently and what they can do when more knowledgeable adults or peers are scaffolding their learning (Vygotsky, 1978). Figure 4.5 is a checklist for teachers, with a blank one duplicated in Resource 4.2, of ways for scaffolding learning in one or more languages.

Thinking About Translanguaging in the Data Collection Phase

Translanguaging is a natural occurring phenomenon between bilinguals of the same language, so why shouldn't it extend to assessment? García and colleagues (2017) have taken on this challenge and pose a set of useful principles for translanguaging in classroom assessment. Simply stated, there must be opportunities for multilingual learners to:

1. express themselves through multiple voices and perspectives

2. show their learning in authentic performance tasks and projects

FIGURE 4.5 A Checklist for Scaffolding Instruction and Assessment in Multiple Languages

AS A TEACHER, I . . .	YES	NO
Match scaffolding strategies to the content, learning targets, and language proficiencies, cultures, and experiences of my students.		
Use a variety of modes for students to engage in the content, including visual, graphic, and interactive (e.g., translanguaging).	X	
Model oral, written, visual, and graphic exemplars for my students in multiple languages.	X	
Allow my students to select the assistance or support that suits their learning, languages, interests, and tasks.		
Am aware of the context for learning and my multilingual learners' prior experiences along with their linguistic and cultural resources.		X
Carefully push my students to challenge and advance their language and conceptual development.		
Take cues from my students as to when they wish to be more independent and take on more responsibility for their own learning.		
Give my students concrete descriptive and timely feedback to move their learning forward.	X	

ADAPTED FROM: Gottlieb and Castro (2017).

▶ A computer store in Germany that sells "everything."

3. use their interpersonal (with others, as in peers or teachers), intrapersonal (within themselves), and external resources (tools for learning) during instruction and assessment

4. represent their full linguistic repertoire without being restricted to one language or another.

While scaffolding learning may be considered a temporary support for multilingual learners until they gain autonomy, it can be coupled with translanguaging to help establish classroom norms (Daniel, Jiménez, Pray, & Pacheco, 2017). The poster shown here in English and German with visual support is an instance of translanguaging that supports the message.

Translanguaging in Assessment as, for, and of Learning

"Student learning is at the center of translanguaging pedagogy and students must be involved in assessing their own learning" (García et al., 2017, p. 92). This statement underscores one of the primary features of assessment *as* learning—multilingual learners as self-assessors. Just as important in assessment *as* learning in the translanguaging classroom is peer group assessment in which the workings of a team are evaluated along with its collective learning.

Assessment *for* learning is also evident in the translanguaging classroom. Here we see multilingual learners alongside their teachers providing input to lesson design in multiple languages. For example, translanguaging might be present in formulating learning targets and in carrying them out during instruction and assessment. As a result of student/student or student/teacher interaction, teachers can adjust their instructional course based on the different translanguaging resources and desires of their multilingual learners.

Lastly, we see how translanguaging can be incorporated into assessment *of* learning in **curriculum design,** such as in the bilingual unit of learning on multicultural fairytales described in the previous chapter. Translanguaging at a unit level is intentional and planned, often designed to build multilingual learners' metalinguistic and metacultural awareness. Therefore, there should be specific provisions for data collection in multiple languages inclusive of translanguaging based on a unit's integrated learning goals or targets.

Thinking About Multiliteracies When Assessing in Multiple Languages

Multiliteracies, rooted in local and global presence of multiculturalism, represents the shift from traditional definitions of literacy focused upon print, primarily reading and writing, to those that highlight learning through different modes of text and multiple forms of knowledge. Moving away from dependence on print media, multiliteracies is becoming central to effective pedagogical practice, especially for multilingual learners.

Multiple languages are wrapped up in multiliteracies; "effective citizenship and productive work now require that we interact effectively using multiple languages, multiple Englishes, and communication patterns that more frequently cross cultures, communities, and national boundaries" (New London Group, 1996, p. 64). As a result of this new vision, educators (especially literacy and biliteracy teachers) must be active participants along with their multilingual learners in helping to shape how multiliteracies is enacted in the classroom and beyond. If multiliteracies is becoming the new normal for students, educators must be aware of its role in assessment.

▶ Wall art in Oaxaca, México

Inspirational street art fills the landscape of Oaxaca, Mexico (e.g., the signage says "Learn from the past, live for the present, and work for the future"). It reminds us that literacy is no longer confined to books. We are stimulated and make sense of the world by extending meaning beyond print when we encounter a multiliteracy experience.

Using Multiliteracies in Assessment as, for, and of Learning

Expanding literacy to multiliteracies implies that educators must pursue more varied assessment techniques to gather the most relevant and useful data to make decisions. During assessment *as* and *for* learning, data are collected from multilingual learners, individually or in small groups, as they use multiliteracies to show how they:

- apply oral or written text to other activities, such as role-play or re-enact historical events in multiple languages

- express ideas by combining multilingual texts or videos with music, dance, or drawing

- enhance meaning of multilingual texts by creating dialogue or drawing images

- respond to hearing the sounds of a film or viewing its images by summarizing thoughts visually (such as through cartooning), orally, or written text

- explore and compare features of paper and on-screen texts considering layout and design features and how different modes add meaning

- record thoughts and responses to compelling questions through mapping, note making, and audio recording

- network with peers or mentors between schools using recording equipment, such as phones or computers in multiple languages. (Adapted from Bearne & Wolstencroft, 2007)

The use of multiliteracies in assessment *of* learning exemplifies a theoretical shift away from measuring learning in discrete ways to promoting learning more holistically as meaning-making (Buhagiar, 2007). There are a number of different types of classroom assessment that have become increasingly relevant to examining student learning over time that involve multiliteracies (Kalantzis, Cope, & Harvey, 2003).

In project-based assessment, multilingual learners could generate compelling questions, explore and research responses in the language(s) of their choice, and construct a product representing multiliteracies. In exploring the world around them, young learners curious about nature, for example, could compile a photo album of local leaves or plants that is filled with descriptive text. An example for students in upper elementary school could be comparing artifacts of Halloween with those of the Day of the Dead (El Día de los Muertos). Their final project could entail two products: (1) creating a mask of their favorite

FIGURE 4.6 Ideas for Collecting Data Using Multimodal Communication Through Multiliteracies in Assessment *as, for,* and *of* Learning in One or More Languages

	ASSESSMENT AS LEARNING IN ONE OR MORE LANGUAGES	ASSESSMENT FOR LEARNING IN ONE OR MORE LANGUAGES	ASSESSMENT OF LEARNING IN ONE OR MORE LANGUAGES
Multimodal Communication	Exchanging oral recordings and writings with peers based on cultural artifacts in multiple languages	Generating ideas for a photo album, identifying and organizing photos, and deciding on criteria for success with a teacher	Summarizing and performing content of multilingual lyrics in songs or raps
Multiliteracies	Sketching out instructions and a design for constructing a physical model for their peers	Producing multilingual multimedia segments of a presentation (e.g., with subtitles) and posting them to a class website	Co-creating museum exhibits with video recordings according to project descriptors

superhero along with an explanation and (2) producing an ofrenda (offering) in memory of a relative along with a short biography of why this person was a hero to them.

Classroom assessment *of* learning can readily incorporate multiliteracies. Students can actively participate in hands-on authentic activities that grow out of their desire to pursue answers to their research, such as investigating the amount and kinds of evidence of recycling in a school or neighborhood. Figure 4.6, duplicated as a blank figure in Resource 4.4, illustrates how multilingual learners might express their learning through multiliteracies across the three approaches to assessment.

HOW MIGHT WE COLLECT AND ORGANIZE STUDENT SAMPLES IN MULTIPLE LANGUAGES?

Students should be active participants in data collection as they are the ones producing the data. Equally important, students should be made aware of how data are used. Collecting oral, written, and multimodal language samples with scaffolding in multiple languages should be a classroom routine that is familiar to, and even initiated by, multilingual learners. At the beginning of a school year, there are several options for teachers to collect baseline data with their multilingual learners:

1. by individual language domains (listening, speaking, reading, and writing) within content area instruction

2. by combined domains or modes, namely, by receptive or interpretive (listening/reading/illustrating) and productive or expressive (speaking/writing/illustrating) language within content area instruction

3. by language (e.g., one sample in Arabic and a parallel one in English)

4. by tasks or for specific audiences, such as using translanguaging to enhance communication

5. with or without resources: scaffolding, multimodal communication, and multiliteracies.

The ways teachers choose to organize student data from these initial samples should set precedent for the rest of the year. It is important to remember that student growth can only be determined if data are collected in the same way and interpreted with the same criteria minimally twice a year.

 Stop-Think-Act-React

Relevant Research: What are the benefits of collecting data in multiple languages?

Research is clear that the stronger the literacy development in the students' home language, the greater the trajectory for English language literacy (Arellano, Liu, Stoker, & Slama, 2018; Relyea & Amendum, 2019). Such is the case of Relyea and Amendum's study, where the stronger Spanish reading group with multilingual learners with initially low levels of English oral proficiency surpassed their peers in English.

These findings highlight potential interdependence or cross-language influence of Spanish and English reading, reaffirming Cummins's 1979 hypothesis, which states that in bilingual development, language and literacy skills are readily transferred from one language to another. Do you agree with these findings? Can you cite other examples of linguistic interdependence from your multilingual learners' speaking and writing two languages? Think about conducting your own **action research** with colleagues.

Collecting Receptive Language Data: Observing Student Interaction During Content Instruction

Assessing **receptive or interpretive language** (listening/reading/viewing) centers on students' listening and reading, often in conjunction with other modes, such as in viewing, in the content classroom. It is rare that listening, reading, or viewing ever occur in isolation; rather in naturalistic situations, there is always a blending of modalities. However, for assessment purposes, at times it is important to get a pulse on multilingual learners' specific modes of communication. The most unobtrusive method of data collection is teacher observation of students participating in everyday activities within the context of instruction.

Observation may be of a student working independently, or partners interacting with each other, such as in conversations, where one student is actively listening while the other is speaking, or students engaging in small group activities. The list below is replicated in Resource 4.5 as a checklist for educators and in Resource 4.6 as an "I can" checklist for multilingual learners. During instruction, teachers may observe multilingual learners listen, read, or view in one or more languages as they. . .

Individually:

- follow oral or written directions

- sequence pictures, sentences, or paragraphs in logical order

- identify and sort information in graphs or tables

- locate information in source materials

- draw figures or charts based on oral or written instructions

- illustrate or highlight segments of oral or written discourse

- co-construct content models from oral or written instructions

- actively listen to podcasts, videos, or online presentations

- match central ideas of text to information in other modes.

Interact with peers:

- engaging in literacy tasks with different partners (e.g., reading aloud to each other; asking and answering questions)

- following written directions or instructions for playing games

- co-constructing content models, figures, or tables from videos supplemented with text

- categorizing, classifying, sorting, or sequencing visual, graphic, or digital information.

Participate in small groups:

- showing emotions or reactions during book talks or oral readings

- participating in dramatizations of text

- selecting and investigating topics that have been researched

- sharing a computer screen remotely or other digital devices to seek answers to burning questions

- producing murals or depictions of abstract constructs (e.g., social justice, democracy).

Collecting Productive Language Data: Gathering Student Samples During Content Instruction

Productive or expressive language (speaking/writing/illustrating) can readily be coupled with other modes. For assessing oral and written language, for example, teachers may wish to conference with individual or pairs of multilingual learners or have the students take the lead. Productive language can also include translanguaging and be observed as part of an instructional routine as students work in small groups or produce first drafts. Resources 4.7 and 4.8 replicate the productive activities listed below as a checklist for educators and as an "I can" checklist for older multilingual learners. In collecting classroom data in one or more languages, teachers may watch multilingual learners speak, write, and/or illustrate as they. . .

Individually or with peers:

- justify ordering of pictures, sentences, or paragraphs

- interpret and relate information in tables

- cite evidence in source materials

- describe data in figures, charts, or graphs

- recount narratives or personal experiences

- explain the relationship among concepts and ideas

- take notes or outline text in their preferred language

- apply disciplinary practices to real-life experiences in journal entries or learning logs.

Interact with peers:

- dialoguing about a topic of mutual interest or how to resolve a problem

- engaging in two-way tasks where each partner alternates

- creating or playing board or video games

- formulating and/or conducting surveys or interviews

- co-constructing and completing graphic organizers

- asking and answering questions of interest

- offering concrete feedback to peers based on preset descriptors

- brainstorming ideas in their language(s) of choice

- giving feedback on performance tasks, e.g., descriptions, stories, poetry, reports.

Discuss or act out in small groups:

- contributing to book talks

- recasting ideas in literature circles

CLASSROOM ASSESSMENT IN MULTIPLE LANGUAGES

- debating or critiquing issues

- acting in dramatizations

- re-enacting historical or literary events.

Present in front of a whole group:

- speaking spontaneously on familiar topics

- giving prepared speeches or talks (e.g., as part of capstone projects)

- creating an action plan based on research

- producing and delivering multimedia presentations

- sharing, recounting, or adding information

- retelling or summarizing experiences.

Collecting Data During Distance Learning

As we have witnessed, schooling continues during crises albeit at a distance. It is paramount that we bridge the digital divide for our multilingual learners to remain connected and growing technologically; only then can we achieve educational equity. Equally important is the sensitivity of teachers to their students' and families' social-emotional state, such as added anxiety and stress, and its impact on assessment.

With virtual learning becoming part of the educational landscape, students must become acclimated to online synchronous or asynchronous lessons. This transition from face-to-face learning has challenged teachers to provide meaningful experiences from afar, especially for multilingual learners and other marginalized students. That's where student self- and peer assessment can play a vital role for teachers in gaining insight into what might be troubling multilingual learners academically as well as emotionally during difficult times.

Online learning should provide multilingual learners opportunities to take the lead while teachers collect and organize the data to better understand their students. All the while teachers must be sensitive to the upheaval of many multilingual learners and to always provide a context for data collection. Here are some ideas for gathering information from multilingual learners as they engage in distance learning:

- Create a chat room for multilingual learners to interact in English and their other language.

- Have students submit a number of notes per week for peers or their teachers—some queries or comments generated by the students, others in response to teacher feedback, still others based on integrated targets for learning.

- Have individual conversations with students during scheduled sessions about what's working or not working in regard to technology-driven instruction.

- Flip learning so that students are listening, reading, or viewing material (as many times as needed) before coming to class.

- Build in tutorials to lessons, hyperlink resources in multiple languages, or have multilingual learners pair with peers of their partner language to discuss assignments and issues.

- Invite students to engage in a variety of digital tools that match the purpose of the lesson or the learning target.

- Have students provide feedback to each other in break-out rooms or by leaving notes, such as through padlets.

- Ask students to submit short reflective video clips based on specific criteria.

- Encourage students to use multiple modes of communication, such as uploading photos or a recording, to illustrate their conceptual understanding.

- Have students submit journal entries or learning logs in their preferred language and have teachers use Google Translate or another program to make sense of the multilingual responses (although do not rely on these programs completely).

 Stop-Think-Act-React

Relax and Reflect: How might you engage in online assessment with your multilingual learners?

With your colleagues, either virtually or in a face-to-face meeting, share ideas about assessment with multilingual learners. Then discuss how you might organize the ongoing flow of data in order to make instructional decisions.

Organizing Data in Multiple Languages

Even before collecting classroom data, teachers should think about the different ways to organize information in multiple languages from multilingual learners. One aspect of organization could be the choice of tools to be used, such as questionnaires, interviews, surveys, or notations from observations, audio, video, or yes, even worksheets. Another consideration could be the distribution of assessment tasks by languages (as in Figure 4.7 and Resource 4.9) according to classroom routines.

Still another way to organize data by mode could be by the primary stakeholders who represent the different approaches to assessment—those designed and enacted by students (assessment *as* learning), teachers and students (assessment *for* learning), and teachers in collaboration with other school leaders (assessment *of* learning). Shown in Figure 4.8, and replicated in Resource 4.10, this figure helps in the collection of information in one or more languages across assessment approaches to help create a comprehensive portrait of a student.

FIGURE 4.7 Ideas for Organizing Receptive and Productive Data in Multiple Languages

	IN ENGLISH	IN OTHER LANGUAGE	IN BOTH LANGUAGES INCLUSIVE OF TRANSLANGUAGING
Ideas for Collecting Receptive (Listening/ Reading/ Viewing) Language During Instruction	• Watching videos, TED Talks, or other media • Locating/reading print/visual resources that reinforce ideas related to a topic or theme	◆ Processing images and text from websites and other digital material ◆ Seeking information from multiple sources	❖ Attending to bilingual podcasts and other source material ❖ Interpreting different text types or genres
Ideas for Collecting Productive (Speaking/ Writing/ Illustrating) Language During Instruction	• Giving prepared speeches or talks with visual aids • Outlining ideas with others (e.g., in graphic organizers)	◆ Composing multiple genres (e.g., biographies, arguments, travelogues) ◆ Asking questions to obtain information	❖ Producing and reflecting on journal entries or learning logs ❖ Jotting down notes or sketching first drafts

FIGURE 4.8 Examples of Language Assessment *as, for*, and *of* Learning

	ASSESSMENT *AS* LEARNING IN ONE OR MORE LANGUAGES	ASSESSMENT *FOR* LEARNING IN ONE OR MORE LANGUAGES	ASSESSMENT *OF* LEARNING IN ONE OR MORE LANGUAGES
Ideas for Receptive Language (Listening/ Reading/ Viewing)	○ Research topics of personal interest ○ Share books/ materials of different genres with peers	○ Select from a list of available sources ○ Classify text-based features (e.g., by characters or places)	○ Watch multimedia produced by peers ○ Complete a checklist or rating scale based on performances
Ideas for Productive Language (Speaking/ Writing/ Illustrating)	○ Offer concrete feedback to peer/ partner to creatively express feelings ○ Keep a diary	○ Contribute to book talks ○ Take action by responding to editorials or critiques	○ Make puppets and participate in dramatizations ○ Make displays or posters for the school or community

Relax and Reflect: How might you collect and organize assessment data?

Using Resource 4.9 or 4.10, provide examples of multilingual learners' receptive (listening, reading, viewing) and productive (speaking, writing, illustrating) language use, adding other ideas from your classroom. In grade-level or department teams, decide the most appropriate cell. Then highlight the ideas and the language(s) that the team wishes to prioritize and discuss how to embed them in individual lessons or units of learning.

Another issue around data collection in multiple languages that deserves mention is, How can families of multilingual learners contribute to the conversation? How might they be engaged in their children's learning and social-emotional well-being? How might their voices be heard? How might they become empowered? Every school connects and communicates with their community in unique ways. Make sure that there is community outreach and a presence of languages and cultures that represent the multilingual families in the school.

Stretch your outreach to families, the community, and the world of your multilingual learners. Investigate additional kinds of data that can be collected in multiple languages as part of each unit of learning. Research and communicate with classrooms in countries of origin of your students. Highlight how multilingualism is alive and well wherever you are and wherever you might want to go.

HOW MIGHT WE FACE THE ISSUE? CONNECT WITH MULTILINGUAL FAMILIES, COMMUNITIES, AND OTHER EDUCATORS

Classroom assessment embodies assessment *as*, *for*, and *of* learning. For multilingual learners, it is also inclusive of scaffolding to temporarily boost their accessibility and comprehensibility, multiple modes of channels of communication, multiliteracies that extend meaning-making beyond text, and translanguaging that invites interaction in multiple languages. Teachers and multilingual learners should be aware of how multilingualism enhances their connections to others and their world view. Here are some questions to stimulate discussion among multilingual learners and between teachers and school leaders about useful resources in the collection of assessment data.

For Younger Multilingual Learners

- What does your teacher do to help you understand your work?

- Which languages do you use to do your work at home?

- When do you feel good speaking more than one language?

- In what ways do you like to show what you learn? Do you like to draw, sing, dance, talk, or draw to share your ideas?

For Older Multilingual Learners

- Translanguaging is when you use more than one language when you communicate. What does translanguaging mean to you? When do you translanguage and with whom?

- Scaffolding learning through pictures, charts, or graphic organizers should help you better understand. How does scaffolding help you?

- Do you have enough opportunities to use multiple languages when you work at school? For what kinds of assignments do you use English and your language(s) other than English?

- In what ways do you learn from family members close to you and those who live far away?

For Teachers and Other Instructional Leaders

- How do you capture your multilingual learners' full potential in collecting and organizing assessment information in multiple languages?

- How does your stance on translanguaging affect your collection of student data?

- Which kinds of scaffolding do you find most effective for maximizing instructional and assessment opportunities for multilingual learners as part of data collection?

- How do you incorporate multiliteracies and multimodal communication into instruction and assessment?

For School Leaders

- How is collecting and organizing data in multiple languages a question of equity?

- How does approval or disapproval of translanguaging as a school-wide policy affect the collection and organization of classroom data?

- What do you deem the most effective data in multiple languages for school accountability for multilingual learners, and what suggestions do you have for data collection across classrooms?

- How do you organize data in dual language or other language programs where students engage in multiple languages to form a body of evidence to demonstrate the effectiveness of the program?

HOW MIGHT WE RESOLVE THE DILEMMA? ANNOTATE DATA FROM YOUR MULTILINGUAL LEARNERS!

Assessment in multiple languages requires careful collection of data to allow for full coverage of language learning within grade-level content, but it is worth the effort! Provision should be made to capture the use of languages in a variety of contexts through available resources, including multimodal communication, multiliteracies, and translanguaging, so that multilingual learners can reach their full potential. Data collection of routine classroom activities that accumulate over time in culminating performances or projects affords educators and multilingual learners opportunities to document assessment *as*, *for*, and *of* learning.

Capturing what multilingual learners can do as they continue to grow in two or more languages should help dispel educator misconceptions and misunderstandings. Through Chaido's leadership in ongoing professional learning and collaboration among teacher teams, support for multilingualism and multiculturalism in her school begins to move from tacit acceptance to the formation of an alliance among students, educators, and the community. As multilingual principles and policies gradually become engrained in all the educators in her building, Chaido models how to gather and annotate multilingual data to prepare teachers in how to interpret information and provide actionable feedback to their students. With strong evidence, Chaido can continue her campaign for equity on behalf of her multilingual learners and their families.

Resources for Multilingual Learners, Their Teachers, and Other Instructional Leaders

RESOURCE 4.1 FOR TEACHERS AND OTHER INSTRUCTIONAL LEADERS
Matching the Purpose for Classroom Assessment With Data

Choose the most important purposes for classroom assessment in your context or prioritize the purposes provided. Then suggest data associated with that purpose and note the languages of data collection.

PURPOSES FOR CLASSROOM ASSESSMENT IN ONE OR MORE LANGUAGES	DATA AND THE LANGUAGES OF DATA COLLECTION
1. Provide student evidence of language and content learning.	
2. Show growth in multilingual learners' linguistic repertoire across content areas.	
3. Document translanguaging as a pedagogical and assessment practice.	
4. Improve teaching and learning.	
5. Offer feedback to move teaching and learning forward.	
6. Demonstrate learning of individual skills.	
7. Build multilingual learners' cross-linguistic (metalinguistic) and cross-cultural (metacultural) awareness.	
8. Guide instruction in multiple languages.	
9. Reflect on learning and learning goals/targets.	
10. Support decisions based on multilingual evidence.	
11. Assist students in guiding their own learning.	
12. Plan instruction in multiple languages based on evidence.	
13. Foster student agency, confidence, pride, and autonomy.	

RESOURCE 4.2 FOR INSTRUCTIONAL COACHES AND TEACHERS

A Checklist for Scaffolding Instruction and Assessment in Multiple Languages

Decide to what extent scaffolding assists your multilingual learners in reaching their heights in learning. Be self-reflective in answering yes or no to the different ways in which you use scaffolding to increase multilingual learners' opportunities to learn.

AS A TEACHER, WHEN SCAFFOLDING INSTRUCTION AND CLASSROOM ASSESSMENT, I . . .	YES	NO
Match ways of supporting the content, learning targets, language proficiencies, cultures, and experiences of my students.		
Use a variety of ways for students to engage in content, including visual, graphic, interactive, and linguistic (e.g., translanguaging) means.		
Model oral and written exemplars for my students in multiple languages.		
Allow my students to select the types of assistance that suit their learning style, languages of interaction, and the task at hand.		
Am aware of the context for learning and my multilingual learners' experiences along with their patterns of language use.		
Consider my students' conceptual understanding of the content and associated disciplinary practices.		
Carefully push my students to challenge and advance their language and conceptual development.		
Take cues from my students as to when they wish to be more independent and take on more responsibility for their own learning.		

ADAPTED FROM: Gottlieb and Castro (2017).

RESOURCE 4.3 FOR MULTILINGUAL LEARNERS (TO BE TRANSLATED BY PEERS INTO MULTIPLE LANGUAGES)

Using Images for Data Collection

Choose a photo or image in your community, one that you have designed, or one from a book. Make sure that it is interesting to you. Answer questions 1 and 2. Then share your photo or image with a peer and answer questions 3 and 4.

My Response: Oral or Written Language(s): _____

1. WHAT DO YOU SEE? DESCRIBE WITH DETAILS.	2. WHAT ARE YOUR FEELINGS? WRITE THEM DOWN.
3. WHAT IS HAPPENING? DISCUSS WITH OTHERS.	4. WHAT ARE YOU THINKING? SHARE YOUR THOUGHTS.

RESOURCE 4.4 FOR TEACHERS AND MULTILINGUAL LEARNERS

Categorizing Student Samples of Multimodal Communication and Multiliteracies as Assessment *as, for*, and *of* Learning

Choose from the examples of multiple modes of communication and multiliteracies in this chapter or add some of your own; then classify each one as assessment *as, for,* or *of* learning. With colleagues, discuss how you would include your multilingual learners in the process.

	ASSESSMENT *AS* LEARNING	ASSESSMENT *FOR* LEARNING	ASSESSMENT *OF* LEARNING
Multiple Modes of Communication			
Multiliteracies			

RESOURCE 4.5 FOR TEACHERS OF MULTILINGUAL LEARNERS
An Inventory of Receptive Language Activities

Based on classroom observation over time (e.g., a quarterly basis), check those receptive language activities (mainly listening, reading, viewing) in which the multilingual learner has engaged and note the language(s) of interaction.

Name of Student: _____ Date: _____

Language(s) _____

The student can:

- ☐ follow oral directions

- ☐ follow written instructions

- ☐ sequence pictures, sentences, or paragraphs

- ☐ identify information in graphs or tables

- ☐ locate information in source materials

- ☐ draw figures or charts based on oral or written instructions

- ☐ illustrate or highlight segments of oral or written narratives

- ☐ construct content models from oral or written instructions

- ☐ respond to podcasts or watch videos/online presentations

- ☐ match central ideas of text to information in other modes: visual, digital, or oral text.

When interacting with peers, the student can:

- ☐ engage in literacy tasks with different partners

- ☐ follow oral directions or instructions

- ☐ co-construct content models, figures, or tables from videos supplemented with text

- ☐ categorize, sort, or sequence visual, graphic, or digital information.

(Continued)

(Continued)

In small group activities, the student can:

- ☐ listen actively during book talks or oral readings

- ☐ participate in dramatizations or re-enactments of text

- ☐ select and investigate topics of interest

- ☐ share a computer screen remotely or other digital devices to seek answers to burning questions

- ☐ produce murals or depictions of abstract constructs (e.g., social justice, democracy).

RESOURCE 4.6 FOR MULTILINGUAL LEARNERS

When I Listen, Read, and View

This checklist shows what you can do when listening, reading, or viewing in one or more languages.

My Name:_____ Date:_____

Language(s) _____

When listening, reading, or viewing in English or my other language, I can:

- ☐ follow oral directions

- ☐ follow written directions

- ☐ sequence pictures, sentences, or paragraphs

- ☐ identify information in graphs or tables

- ☐ locate information in different materials

- ☐ draw figures or charts based on oral or written instructions

- ☐ illustrate or highlight oral or written narratives

- ☐ construct models from oral or written instructions

- ☐ respond to questions about podcasts or watch videos/online presentations

- ☐ match ideas to visual, written, or oral text.

When working with peers, I can:

- ☐ participate in different tasks

- ☐ follow oral directions in playing games

- ☐ construct models, figures, or tables from videos

- ☐ classify, sort, or sequence information.

(Continued)

(Continued)

When working in small group activities, I can:

- ☐ listen carefully during book talks or oral readings

- ☐ participate in dramas or re-enactments of text

- ☐ select and investigate topics of interest

- ☐ share a computer screen remotely or other digital devices to look for answers to questions

- ☐ draw murals that represent important ideas.

CLASSROOM ASSESSMENT IN MULTIPLE LANGUAGES

RESOURCE 4.7 FOR TEACHERS OF MULTILINGUAL LEARNERS

An Inventory of Activities for Speaking, Writing, and Illustrating

Name of Student: _____ Date: _____

Language(s) _____

Based on classroom observation over time (e.g., a quarterly basis), check those productive language activities in which the multilingual learner has engaged and note the language(s) of interaction, including translanguaging.

The student can:

☐ defend the order of pictures, sentences, or paragraphs

☐ interpret and relate information in graphs or tables

☐ name evidence in source materials

☐ describe data in figures, charts, or graphs

☐ recount narratives or personal experiences

☐ explain the relationship among concepts and ideas

☐ take notes or outline text in the language of choice

☐ apply disciplinary practices to real-life experiences in journal entries or learning logs.

When interacting with peers, the student can:

☐ dialogue on a topic of mutual interest or explain how to solve a problem

☐ engage in two-way tasks where each partner alternates turns

☐ create or play board or video games

☐ formulate and/or conduct surveys or interviews

☐ co-construct models or complete graphic organizers

☐ ask and answer questions of interest

☐ offer feedback during peer assessment based on preset descriptors

(Continued)

(Continued)

- ☐ brainstorm ideas in their language(s) of choice

- ☐ give feedback on performance tasks, e.g., descriptions, stories, poetry, reports.

When discussing or acting out in small groups, the student can:

- ☐ contribute to book talks

- ☐ recast ideas in literature circles

- ☐ debate or critique issues

- ☐ participate in dramatizations

- ☐ re-enact historical or literary events.

When presenting in front of a whole group, the student can:

- ☐ speak spontaneously on familiar topics

- ☐ give prepared speeches or talks

- ☐ create an action plan based on research

- ☐ produce and deliver multimedia presentations

- ☐ share, recount, or add information

- ☐ retell or summarize experiences.

RESOURCE 4.8 FOR OLDER MULTILINGUAL LEARNERS

When I Speak, Write, and Illustrate

This checklist shows what you can do when speaking, writing, and illustrating.

My Name:_____ Date:_____

Language(s) _____

When speaking, writing, and illustrating, I can:

- ☐ defend the order of pictures, sentences, or paragraphs

- ☐ interpret and relate information in graphs or tables

- ☐ name evidence in source materials

- ☐ describe data in figures, charts, or graphs

- ☐ recount narratives or personal experiences

- ☐ explain the relationship among concepts and ideas

- ☐ take notes or outline text in the language of choice

- ☐ produce and reflect on journal entries or learning logs.

When interacting with peers, I can:

- ☐ dialogue about a topic of mutual interest or how to solve a problem

- ☐ engage in tasks where partners alternate

- ☐ create or play board or video games

- ☐ formulate and/or conduct surveys or interviews

- ☐ co-construct and complete models or graphic organizers

- ☐ ask and answer questions of interest

- ☐ offer concrete feedback during peer assessment on preset descriptors

- ☐ brainstorm ideas in the language(s) of my choice

- ☐ create and give feedback on descriptions, letters, stories, poetry, reports.

(Continued)

(Continued)

When discussing or acting out in small groups, I can:

- ☐ contribute to book talks
- ☐ engage in literature circles
- ☐ debate or critique issues
- ☐ participate or act in dramatizations
- ☐ re-enact historical or literary events.

When presenting in front of a whole group, I can:

- ☐ speak on a topic I know about
- ☐ give prepared speeches or talks
- ☐ share reports based on research
- ☐ run multimedia shows
- ☐ share, recount, or add information
- ☐ retell or summarize experiences.

RESOURCE 4.9 FOR TEACHERS OF MULTILINGUAL LEARNERS
Collecting and Organizing Receptive and Productive Data in Multiple Languages

Based on the ideas for gathering data from multilingual learners in the body of the chapter, how might you sort them according to the language(s) of instruction and assessment? The purpose of the sort is to represent your integrated learning targets or to check on the distribution of languages across different activities.

	IN ENGLISH	IN OTHER LANGUAGE(S)	BASED ON MULTIPLE LANGUAGES INCLUSIVE OF TRANSLANGUAGING
Ideas for Collecting Receptive Language Samples During Instruction			
Ideas for Collecting Productive Language Samples During Instruction			

RESOURCE 4.10 FOR TEACHERS AND MULTILINGUAL LEARNERS

Collecting Language Samples Representing Assessment *as*, *for*, and *of* Learning

Choosing from examples of receptive and productive language activities, categorize the ideas under assessment *as*, *for*, or *of* learning. Check the distribution between modes (receptive [listening, reading, viewing] and productive [speaking, writing, illustrating]) and assessment approaches (*as*, *for*, and *of* learning).

	ASSESSMENT *AS* LEARNING	ASSESSMENT *FOR* LEARNING	ASSESSMENT *OF* LEARNING
Receptive/ Interpretive Language Ideas			
Productive/ Expressive Language Ideas			

CHAPTER 5

Interpreting Information and Providing Feedback in Multiple Languages

▶ Wall art in Oaxaca, México (Rights are not asked for, they are taken!)

Ahány nyelv, annyi ember!

*The more languages you know, the more persons
you are/human experiences you have.*
—Hungarian proverb

The Dilemma

*But learning in multiple languages confuses students and
teachers alike!*

*The fifth-grade dual language team consists of two pairs of content and
language teachers who work collaboratively to create a seamless rich learning
environment for their students. It's the close of the school year; the students
and their teachers are very busy putting together their capstone projects to*

(Continued)

(Continued)

present to school and community representatives. The team leader, Mika Morita, is responsible for setting up the student presentations, facilitating the interpretation of data from each student's presentation, and disseminating the feedback of the panel to the students, teachers, and families.

In this district, fifth grade marks the end of elementary school when students are ready to transition to middle school. The dual language teachers feel the pressure from the principal, their colleagues, and the community to show the effectiveness of multilingual learners' learning in two languages throughout their primary years. The team has studied the body of research on dual language education from Collier and Thomas (2009, 2012) and Lindholm-Leary (2012), among others, and realize that if often takes 6 years for most students to reach grade-level parity. Therefore, it is a pivotal moment for the dual language team and their multilingual learners to show evidence of growth and achievement in two languages.

*Convinced that **dual language education**, where the curriculum has been enriched with cross-cultural and cross-linguistic elements, is advantageous for all students, the team wishes to show how multilingualism has yielded cognitive, linguistic, and social-emotional benefits for the students. The strength of having artifacts of ongoing and cumulative assessment data from multilingual learners over time provides concrete proof that convinces naysayers to dispel their claim that intertwining languages is confusing to students and challenging for teachers.*

Mika and the fifth-grade teacher pairs hope that the students' capstone projects would offset the disbeliefs of faculty and administration. Together with the students, they think of options for presenting their projects along with a set of assessment descriptors to a panel of school staff and community members. To highlight becoming bilingual and bicultural, multilingual learner choices include (1) narrating an original story or play, (2) making a multimedia presentation, or (3) producing a poem, rap, mural, or poster that illustrates their identity formation over their elementary school years.

The moment has come for multilingual learners to show clear evidence of their multilingualism and multiculturalism to the doubtful teachers and the principal. The fifth-grade students are excited to show their talents and the fifth-grade teachers are united in hoping to disprove their colleagues and school leaders who doubt the benefits of dual language education. The question of the day is How might the students' presentations provide convincing evidence to help dismiss this confusion over the value of multilingualism?

FIRST IMPRESSIONS

- In what ways does this scenario resonate with you?
- How are classroom data in multiple languages interpreted in your setting?
- Why is collaboration among teachers important in data interpretation?
- How might feedback in multiple languages positively and negatively affect student performance and identity formation?

FIGURE 5.1 The **THIRD PHASE** of the Assessment Cycle: Interpreting Assessment Information and Providing Feedback in Multiple Languages

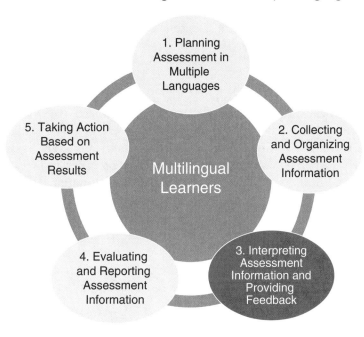

With movement toward greater acceptance of multilingualism and its teaching in school by scholars and practitioners alike, the need for linguistically and culturally sound evidence from classroom assessment is more important than ever (Basterra, Trumbull, & Solano-Flores, 2011; Leung & Valdés, 2019; López, Turkan, & Guzman-Orth, 2017). That's what we are trying to show throughout the assessment cycle in multiple languages. Having multilingual data from our multilingual learners in hand, we turn to phase 3: how educators determine the meaning of the information that has been collected and organized from assessment in multiple languages. Figure 5.1 highlights this phase of the assessment cycle.

There is a tremendous amount of information available from student assessment, more so in the classroom than any place else. Teachers have to be strategic in how to present, analyze, and interpret data to inform decision-making, whether for an individual student, a class, a grade level, or an entire school. This chapter examines a variety of strategies, resources, and tools for capturing and interpreting multilingual data with the understanding that at the heart of the shift toward more student-centered approaches of learning and assessment is a socially embedded consciousness of schooling. Simply stated, when interpreting data, educators should recognize the context of the broader communities in which students interact that are ingrained in their identities (Kaul, 2019). As part of data interpretation, we also see how effective feedback enhances teaching and learning in the moment and over time. Additionally, the chapter addresses the importance of collaboration between teachers as well as between teachers and students during this phase of assessment.

HOW MIGHT WE INTERPRET EVERYDAY CLASSROOM DATA IN MULTIPLE LANGUAGES?

As multilingual learners have increasing freedom to express themselves in multiple languages, teachers should be ready to interpret a lot of data. Generating classroom data where multilingual learners have had access to resources (i.e., multiliteracies, multimodal communication, and translanguaging) makes interpretation a truer depiction of multilingual learners' potential. As a result, students are able to show the broadest extent of their language, conceptual, and social-emotional development.

Generating and Interpreting Data From Classroom Observation

Classroom observation provides a direct and naturalistic way for teachers and students alike to assess what multilingual learners do with language while engaging in content learning. In bilingual and dual language classrooms that have relatively restrictive language policies or rely on strict models of language allocation (e.g., 90/10, 50/50, alternate days for each language), teachers rarely have opportunities to gauge students' full linguistic and conceptual understandings. Why not? In these settings, the two languages of instruction are not programmed to come in contact; therefore, multilingual learners are not translanguaging to access their full linguistic repertoire. In contrast, in those multilingual instructional settings where there is a less restrictive language allocation, languages tend to flow more freely as multilingual learners interact with each other and their teachers.

Observation is an authentic assessment method that captures the social nature of learning during instruction. For multilingual learners, classroom observation entails noting their development in two languages, including the metalinguistic and metacultural nuances they are picking up by having the availability of two languages. In addition, through follow-up conversations, teachers have a window into the students' interpretations of their actions and reactions to learning.

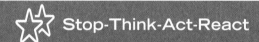

Stop-Think-Act-React

Relax and Reflect: How do you use classroom observation as an assessment tool?

Think about how you might observe your multilingual learners during learning and ponder the following questions: (1) What are you looking for—language, conceptual, or emotional development? (2) How many students do you plan to observe at one time? (3) Will the students be aware that you are observing them, or might you shadow them without their knowledge? (4) Do you have a form, such as a checklist, or do you jot down anecdotal notes? (5) Do you give your students concrete actionable feedback; if so, in what form and when?

Figure 5.2 offers ideas for collecting information (shown in the first, third, and fourth columns) from classroom observation as students interact orally or engage in literacy practices in one or more languages during learning. Columns 2 and 5 suggest ways of recording and interpreting the data. Resource 5.1 replicates the figure for instructional leaders, including coaches, to contemplate how to codify the recording of observations across classrooms, for co-teachers to use for co-assessment, and for teacher use in individual classrooms.

FIGURE 5.2 Collecting, Recording, and Interpreting Information on Multilingual Learners' Language and Literacy Practices

Language(s) _____ Date: _____

Data Collection, Recording, and Interpretation of _____

COLLECTING INFORMATION ON ORAL LANGUAGE PRACTICES DURING CONTENT LEARNING	RECORDING AND INTERPRETING ORAL LANGUAGE PRACTICES	COLLECTING INFORMATION ON TRANSLANGUAGING PRACTICES	COLLECTING INFORMATION ON LITERACY PRACTICES ACROSS CONTENT AREAS	RECORDING AND INTERPRETING LITERACY PRACTICES
Observing student interaction by: • engaging in academic conversations • participating in debates, literature circles, Socratic seminars • relating personal experiences, events, readings, or stories • asking and answering questions • role-playing • rehearsing responses • using technology	Documenting and interpreting student interaction with or by: • checklists of classroom norms • integrated content and language rubrics • criteria for success • self- and peer assessment • anecdotal notes • videotaping • audiotaping	Observing and documenting student interaction in two languages: • oral language/ writing practices • learning strategies (e.g., clarifying, extending, restating) • goal-oriented exchanges • conceptual understanding • metalinguistic awareness • metacultural awareness	Student products: • learning logs • interactive journals • multimedia projects • interactive writing • essays • research reports • editorials/critiques • responses to open-ended questions • tables, charts, graphs • illustrations or diagrams • content-based writing • movies and videos	Interpreting student products with: • teacher or student feedback • student self-reflection • project descriptors • process checklists • 3-, 4-, or 5-point rubrics • oral descriptions • genre-specific rubrics • agreed upon success criteria • evidence from videotaping • evidence from audiotaping

FIGURE 5.3 Observational Notes: Recording and Interpreting Milestones of Student Development

Student: **Manny**   Quarter: **Third**

Composite Language Proficiency Level in English: **3 out of 5**

Language Proficiency Level in Spanish: **4 out of 5**

DATE	LANGUAGE DEVELOPMENT IN ENGLISH	LANGUAGE DEVELOPMENT IN SPANISH (OR ANOTHER LANGUAGE)	DEVELOPMENT THROUGH TRANSLANGUAGING	CONCEPTUAL DEVELOPMENT (WITHIN OR ACROSS CONTENT AREAS)	SOCIAL-EMOTIONAL DEVELOPMENT
1–15	Exchanged information with a peer on a step-by-step process for the first time!		"Wow, 'steps' en este caso quiere decir 'pasos' in Spanish. No se usa 'medida' ni 'escalón.'" *Note the student's metalinguistic awareness!*		
2–18		Contributed to a literature circle providing detailed character development		Illustrated how multiplication is repeated groups of addition using cubes	
3–22			*Note the student's empathy in offering a helping hand, a sign of social-emotional learning!*		Initiated clarifying instructions for a classroom routine to a new student

Observational data offer a wealth of information on individual multilingual learners as well as their interaction with others. Figure 5.3 (duplicated as a worksheet in Resource 5.2) provides one of many ways of mapping a multilingual learner's language, conceptual, and social-emotional development in a classroom context. Here teachers or paraprofessionals can jot down instances of student insights, accomplishments, milestones, or even challenges. In this example, the clouds are illustrative of specific student breakthroughs. Students from middle and high school could also this format to self-reflect.

In addition to being qualified through note taking, information from classroom observation can be also be quantified. For example, teachers may keep a tally of the number of times and the contexts in which multilingual learners use their other language, English, or translanguage when interacting with peers. Class meetings or small group discussions, when students generally have more freedom of expression, might be an excellent time to take notice of their oral language use. Notes could also be taken from multilingual learners' writing samples. Teachers may choose to transfer the information onto a class spreadsheet with columns devoted to developmental milestones for each student.

 Stop-Think-Act-React

Relax and Reflect: How do you interpret observational data on your students?

The teacher in Figure 5.3 keeps ongoing anecdotal notes of the actions of each student that contribute to overall development. Other teachers may prefer to be more quantitative by prepopulating the cells with learning targets and then evaluating each student's movement toward attainment of the target with check marks (as in check -, check, or check +). Which is your preferred method of interpreting observational data? Exchange your ideas with colleagues to help gain insight into the many ways you can document what students do day by day.

Generating and Interpreting Data From Multimodal Communication and Multiliteracies

As introduced in Chapter 4, multimodal communication and multiliteracies are cousins that are integral to the learning experience. While modes of communication are descriptive of the types of resources accessible to students during learning, literacies deal with how readers or viewers make sense of the world around them. Multimodal literacy implies that meaning is communicated through combinations of two or more modes; in addition to text, multimodal multilingual texts, for example, might convey meaning through gestural, audio, and visual modes.

Traditionally, language learning has been parsed into four domains: listening, speaking, reading, and writing. However, with the introduction of multiliteracies in the mid-1990s, the notion of literacy has expanded beyond written text to encompass interaction of the reader with digital technologies (New London Group, 1996). Literacies have become inclusive of linguistic and cultural diversity,

FIGURE 5.4 Multimodal Resources for Generating Meaning

VISUAL RESOURCES	GESTURAL RESOURCES	DIGITAL RESOURCES	AURAL RESOURCES
• Illustrations • Photographs • Diagrams • Graphic organizers • Emojis or icons • Charts • Tables • Videos • Animations • Painting • Drawing • Symbols • Infographics • Picture books	• Facial expressions • Hand expressions • Body language • Dance • Movement	• Social media • Software • Computer programs • Online tools • Mobile apps • E-books • Video streaming • Animation • Web pages • Font choice	• Audiobooks • Podcasts • Music • Dialogue/ Conversations • Discussions • Oral story telling

multimodal forms of linguistic expression, and representation to include visual, digital, textual, and aural materials. Even the International Literacy Association (2017) has broadened its definition of literacy and literacy assessment, stating "literacy assessment needs to reflect the multiple dimensions of reading and writing and the various purposes for assessment as well as the diversity of the students being assessed" (p. 2).

Multilingual learners should be able to access multimodalities and use multiliteracies as means of expressing their understanding while having language choices during learning. If in fact multilingual learners are using multimodal communication resources in multiple languages to maximize their ability to make meaning outside of or in conjunction with text, how can assessment capture it? By having multilingual learners self-report the modalities they prefer as they engage in learning, teachers could more readily include those modalities in instruction and classroom assessment. Figure 5.4 (with a blank form in Resource 5.3) can serve as a starting point for identifying multimodal resources that enhance multilingual learners' accessibility to meaning.

Generating and Interpreting Data From Translanguaging

Translanguaging is a positive attribute of bilingualism, not a deficiency in the ability of a person to manage two or more languages (Schissel, De Korne, & López-Gopar, 2018). In classrooms where translanguaging is an accepted practice and languages are not isolated, multilingual learners' linguistic repertoires are on display all day long. Thus, teachers can more accurately assess students' language use through observation and other means across content and contexts (Sánchez, García, & Solorza, 2017). Figure 5.5 illustrates how translanguaging among multilingual learners draws from the bilingual practices of the home/community and the school/classroom.

FIGURE 5.5 An Ecology of Translanguaging Through the Lens of Multilingual Learners

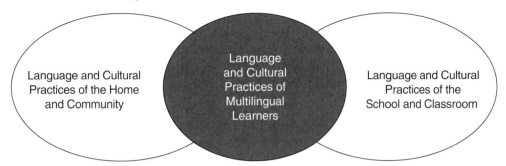

Stop-Think-Act-React

Relax and Reflect: How do you envision translanguaging?

The language education community has not reached consensus on the definition and the many roles of translanguaging. There is general agreement that it is an assets-based approach that honors multilingual learners' full linguistic repertoires. Additionally, translanguaging promotes student agency while it enhances metalinguistic, metacultural, and metacognitive awareness by drawing on multilingual learners' life experiences with family and the community. What does translanguaging mean to you? How might you represent it in classroom assessment?

We have seen how translanguaging has become a vehicle for liberating multilingual learners from their monolingual shackles. By having the advantage of being able to interact in multiple languages, multilingual learners have the potential of using their full linguistic repertoire. In doing so, these students become empowered, confident, and proud of their multilingualism and multiculturalism. As multilingual learners are developing language in conjunction with content, they are making meaning from print and other resources. Here is a Grade 2 writing sample from a Chilean student who translanguages to explain how to make cookies.

The mom and Max is making cockies.

The mom and Max they go to the congelador (refrigerator) and see they

haven't got eggs.

And they walking to the house of the neighbor.

The neighbor les presto eggs. (They borrow eggs from their neighbor.)

And next they make the cockies.

Finally they put the cockies en el horno (in the oven).

Relax and Reflect: How do you interpret evidence of translanguaging?

In interpreting work of multilingual learners, remember to consider various problem-solving strategies, including those from other cultures (Solano-Flores & Nelson-Barber, 2001). Think about these questions to help guide the interpretation of your multilingual learners' use of translanguaging in written expression.

➤ Through what lens would you interpret this language sample? Would you focus on the student's messaging in one language at a time or both languages simultaneously?

➤ What can this multilingual learner do in English?

➤ What can this multilingual learner do in Spanish?

➤ How does this multilingual learner translanguage? What does it reveal?

➤ Does this child appear confused? How can you use the context to point out what the student is saying?

➤ How would you explain translanguaging and its usefulness in language learning to a colleague who is not bilingual?

WHAT ARE SOME STRATEGIES FOR INTERPRETING LITERACY DATA?

Although sociocultural context plays an important role in interpreting data, multilingual learners generally are identified and described according to their language proficiencies that are derived from large-scale language proficiency tests. Scaffolding instruction and classroom assessment within each student's zone of proximal development (Vygotsky, 1978) can help boost multilingual learners' language proficiency.

In interpreting reading passages in one or more languages, multilingual learners should choose among multiliteracies to express themselves. For example, graphic organizers could serve as a visual means of summarizing information. Textual information could also be displayed in charts, and students could respond by indicating their extent of agreement with issues or actions. Diagrams could illustrate the relationship among ideas and photos, or pictures could show detail. Multilingual learners and their teachers should become aware of the many ways to interpret literacies in multiple languages. Figure 5.6 is a self-reported rating scale that lists literacy strategies for multilingual learners.

Interpreting Literacy Through Content

Introduced in the 1980s, the principle of language and content integration has become a mainstay in the education of multilingual learners as more and more educators realize that in school, it is through language that content is taught and through content that language is understood. Nowhere is the connection more

FIGURE 5.6 A Rating Scale for Older Multilingual Learners: Interpreting Literacy in Multiple Languages

	ALL THE TIME	SOMETIMES	NEVER
1. I translate the ideas on the page in my head from one language to another language.			
2. I use both my languages to comprehend what's on the page.			
3. I rely on one language and check with my other language.			
4. I use diagrams and illustrations on the page or screen to help me make sense of print.			
5. I try to understand the message even though I skip words or phrases I don't know.			
6. I interpret what I read by outlining the information, taking notes, or using graphic organizers.			
7. I use digital tools (like Google Translate) to help me better understand the message.			
8. I ask my peers of my partner language what something means or to explain what to do.			
9. I ask my teacher for extra time so I can use both my languages to figure out the meaning.			
10. I try to find sources of information in my other language to help me understand.			

evident than in literacy instruction, as content provides the context for making meaning from text.

Multiliteracies encompasses writing and represents ideas textually, visually, and digitally that can be assessed in a variety of ways. Expectations for learning can be displayed numerous ways, such as in a series of descriptors, a checklist, or, as in Figure 5.7, a rubric with levels of language proficiency. No matter what the criteria, students should be invited to engage in self- and peer assessment.

In Figure 5.7 the integrated target for learning and the rubric show how language data are to be interpreted in a science class. The language for science instruction is the lens through which the content is interpreted. It is based on different genres or purposes for communication (i.e., explain, argue, and recount) that are focal points for organizing and promoting student interaction with science content and with one another (Gottlieb & Castro, 2017).

FIGURE 5.7 A Science Rubric Across Levels of Language Proficiency for Multiple Languages

Integrated Target of Learning: Multilingual learners will recount, explain, and argue their position; verify claims; provide evidence and reasons using multiple modes of communication in one or more languages, from language proficiency level 1 (the lowest) to level 5 (the highest).

Student: _____ Date:_____ Language(s): _____

Mode(s): __ Speaking ____ Writing ___ Visualizing ___ Illustrating ____

LANGUAGE PROFICIENCY LEVEL	PURPOSES FOR USING SCIENTIFIC LANGUAGE
Level 5 In English In another language	○ Explain how the results of scientific experimentation along with the sequence of steps relate to the "why" of the research questions. ○ Recount the experiment or investigation in descriptive scientific reports using illustrations. ○ Argue the extent of impact of claims under varying conditions (e.g., if, then) matched to evidence and reasons.
Level 4 **In English** In another language	○ Explain with details how the research questions and sequence of steps relate to the conclusions. ✓ Recount the experiment or investigation in short descriptive reports using illustrations. ○ Argue results of scientific experimentation using claims matched to evidence and reasons.
Level 3 In English **In another language**	✓ Explain how research questions and sequence of steps lead to conclusions. ○ Recount research questions and a description for conducting scientific experimentation from illustrations. ○ Argue pros and cons of claims with some evidence and reasons.
Level 2 In English **In another language**	○ Explain by stating research questions, naming steps, and conclusions. ○ Recount research questions and a general description of what to do from illustrations. ✓ Argue by making claims along with sparse evidence and reasons.
Level 1 In English In another language	○ Explain by showing how the language of claims is different from the language of evidence. ○ Recount from illustrations that are descriptive of research questions and what to do. ○ Argue by asking questions to form claims and choose from evidence and reasons.

ADAPTED FROM: Gottlieb (2016).

Student Self-Assessment of Character Traits: Interpreting Social-Emotional Learning

The age of the novel COVID-19 virus has made **social-emotional learning** more important to the health and well-being of students than ever before. Re-entry into a unique and perhaps even unfamiliar school environment takes time. For multilingual learners, the emotional adjustment is often stark as students have to become reacclimated to different languages and cultures in addition to common stressors.

Part of social-emotional learning is character development; for multilingual learners, it is an expression of their growing sense of identity. When working with multilingual learners, teachers must realize that the students' languages, cultures, and experiences help shape their character. In essence, Figure 5.8 is both a reminder and a checklist of character traits that can be nurtured (and self-assessed, in the case of older students) in the classroom.

FIGURE 5.8 A Checklist of Character Traits Inclusive of Multiple Languages and Cultures

	MY CHARACTER TRAITS
	I can present multiple perspectives on issues and respect those that differ from mine.
	I appreciate languages and cultures from around the world.
	I can change how I use my language(s) depending on who I am speaking with.
	I take responsibility for my actions and I do what is culturally appropriate.
	I appreciate being challenged in school as it pushes my thinking.
	I care about the quality of my work and can defend it against criteria I have agreed to.
	I can freely express my ideas to others in one or more languages.
	I like to share my cultural traditions with others and actively listen to theirs.
	I share my evidence for learning with others and engage in discussions about it.

ADAPTED FROM: Gottlieb and Noel (2019).

HOW MIGHT WE INTERPRET LONG-TERM PROJECTS IN MULTIPLE LANGUAGES?

In the classroom, data may be accumulated and folded into more long-term projects. A capstone project, generally for middle school and high school students, is an expression of assessment of *as, for,* and *of* learning all rolled into one as it represents learning at critical moments and over time. This **performance assessment** occurs at the conclusion of a semester or even an entire year during which students research in depth a topic that they are passionate about. For younger students, portfolio assessment, where the portfolio is deemed a project unto itself, is also long term in nature and a venue for representing growth in multiple languages.

Specific descriptions and specifications of activities along with a timetable mark the milestones of assignments. Feedback from participating teachers and peers along the way helps move student learning toward its final product. Ultimately students make a live report of their research findings and its influence on their final product to a panel, often with an audience of teachers, school leaders, community members, and family members. The panel has an analytic rubric of the major components (e.g., content, organization, style) to thoroughly interpret the presentation.

Culminating projects, often a schoolwide graduation requirement, entail learning in action where students engage in service learning, volunteer in the community, or conduct field work to deepen their personal and academic experiences. Capstone projects afford multilingual learners opportunities to reveal their inner feelings about being bilingual while expressing themselves in multiple languages. An example comes from a multilingual learner from Guatemala attending Holbrook Junior-Senior High School in Massachusetts who chose to research the role of culture on language development and author an illustrated bilingual children's book (https://www.holbrook.k12.ma.us/userfiles/38/my%20files/capstonehandbook2016-17.pdf?id=3939). Thus, in a project of this magnitude that spans assessment *as*, *for*, and *of* learning, multilingual learners hopefully have the opportunity to explore what has influenced them and who have helped shape their identities to define their goals for the future.

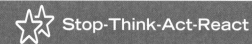
Stop-Think-Act-React

Relax and Reflect: How might you imagine capstone projects in multiple languages in your setting?

What makes a capstone project an expression of assessment of *as*, *for*, and *of* learning in your school? How might it incorporate multilingual learners' accomplishments in multiple languages? How might a fifth-grade team of teachers, such as those in the opening scenario (assuming students will be going to middle school), along with other school leaders or high school departments in preparation of student graduation, sketch out some viable projects with their students and guide them through the process?

WHAT IS THE ROLE OF FEEDBACK IN CLASSROOM ASSESSMENT IN MULTIPLE LANGUAGES?

Feedback is a teacher's or student's oral or written response to student work or performance with the intent of stimulating learning. It has been described as in-the-moment (or contingent) teaching, an assessment strategy that invites multilingual learners to share their understanding, or a resource to help students advance or redirect learning (Heritage, Walqui, & Linquanti, 2013, 2015). Other forms of feedback include helpful remarks on a draft research paper, personal comments added to a rubric, or encouraging words specific to a student's action.

Feedback from classroom assessment must be understandable to the user who needs to take action; therefore, if possible, it should be given in the multilingual learner's preferred language(s). In middle school and high school settings where teachers may have more than 150 students, it is most practical to rely on peer feedback during learning (Matlick, 2020). Not only does it ease the burden on teachers, it allows students to be more comfortable interacting with peers in their shared language(s).

Relevant Research: Why is feedback so important?

Giving students ongoing concrete, yet descriptive, feedback within the context of instruction is an effective strategy for raising student achievement and improving teaching (Black & Wiliam, 1998). In his series of meta-analyses, Hattie (2012) found that feedback has an effect size of 0.7 (beyond the average effect size of 0.4), meaning that it significantly impacts student learning. Simply stated, teachers are able to "see learning through the eyes of their students to help students become their own teachers" (p. 6).

FIGURE 5.9 Defining Feedback by Its Features and Non-Features

WHAT FEEDBACK IS	WHAT FEEDBACK ISN'T
• Descriptive targeted information, preferably in the language most understood by the student	• Evaluative information that speaks to the quality of a performance
• Based on mutually agreed upon criteria for success or clear learning goals	• Based on numbers, scores, percentages, or grades
• Close to or infused into instruction	• Distant or removed from instruction
• Focused on building student self-efficacy	• Focused on destroying student self-esteem
• A means to relate what students are to do next	• A means to relate what students did in the past
• A strategy for building trust between teachers and students	• A strategy for legitimizing criticism
• An objective response to student behavior or performance	• An emotional response to student behavior or performance
• The modeling of language, content, or behavior in context	• Correction of language or content errors or behavioral issues
• Attainable and actionable, with specific next steps for learning	• A negative experience that stifles learning
• Practical and sensible, personalized for the student	• Unrealistic expectations
• A positive experience that sparks learning	• Punitive in nature, centered on what students have not accomplished

The use of effective feedback has proven to support achievement (Heritage, 2010; Moss & Brookhart, 2009). However, there has to be sufficient detail to the feedback to guide the learner's actions; single test scores or grades, for example, do not suffice (Stiggins, 2006). Another feature of feedback is that it should be part of a system (Wiliam & Leahy, 2015), as in the classroom assessment cycle illustrated throughout this book. Figure 5.9 provides contrasting features as to what feedback is and what it is not.

In the words of Dylan Wiliam (2017), "feedback should cause thinking" (p.127). For that reason, for multilingual learners feedback has the benefit of supporting not only their metacognition, or how they are thinking, but also their metalinguistic awareness, or how they are using language (any language) intentionally and strategically. Teacher feedback that is given to small groups or individual students in one or more languages should also be a stimulus for making instructional decisions in multicultural classrooms.

There are generally two sources of feedback, that of teachers and students who have a unified goal: to trigger new learning in classrooms within a culture of trust. Timely and descriptive oral or written feedback from teachers serves as instructional scaffolding, offering linguistic or conceptual support for multilingual learners in the form of examples, samples, models, elaborations, clarifications, or explanations. In student-directed feedback, students can critique their own work or give, receive, or thoughtfully use feedback to deepen their learning. For students to provide effective actionable feedback to each other, the feedback must be clear and center on the specific aspect of the work that is being assessed, and the students must have criteria for success and time to deliver the feedback (Berger et al., 2014).

In addition, feedback should be:

- sensitive to the individual needs and personality of the student

- educative, focusing on positive next steps

- referenced to standards or specific criteria

- geared to helping students meet their learning target

- given in the mode favored by the student—oral, written, or visual

- to the extent feasible, given in the language the student best understands.

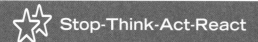

Stop-Think-Act-React

Relax and Reflect: What does feedback mean to you?

The Frayer model, shown below, is a useful resource for multilingual learners and educators alike. As feedback is central to interpreting assessment information to move teaching and learning to the next step, it might be mutually beneficial to complete this graphic together.

Significado (What It Means)	Comentarios (Feedback)	Ilustración (What It Looks Like)
Ejemplo (An Example)		No Ejemplo (A Non-example)

Giving Content-Related Feedback

In classrooms with multilingual learners, content and language are intertwined as students engage in learning. Although learning targets and the activities themselves are integrated, at times, feedback might be directed at either the students' conceptual or the students' language understanding. The following example illustrates how multilingual learners can demonstrate map skills as articulated in state standards for social studies. The use of multiliteracies (in this case, maps and their associated tools) provides concrete visual and kinesthetic referents to assist students in gaining conceptual insight through language.

Peer assessment for this elementary school task echoes Grant Wiggins's (2012) advice on the usefulness of descriptive actionable feedback. Notice how students are asked to engage in content by making maps to scale of familiar community locations and then have peers assess the authenticity and usability of the tools.

> After a series of hands-on activities involving directionality and map interpretation, pairs of students choose a floor (or a wing) of their school to make a map. Success in navigating the map is based on their peers' ability to find a location or a treasure, using the key and a compass rose.
>
> After each team has had others use their map, the pairs engage in peer assessment; criteria for success include the clarity of the map, the accuracy of the map, and the helpfulness of the tools in finding specified locations. Peers respond to a few prompts: (1) Did you find the different locations? (2) How did the compass rose help you find them? (3) How did the key help you know where to go?

Giving Language-Related Feedback

Feedback by teachers or peers on a multilingual learner's language use offers information or scaffolding that furthers language development. Feedback can be in the form of multimodal communication; it might be nonverbal, such as in gestures of approval (e.g., a smile, thumbs up, high five, nod), verbal, written, visual (e.g., through symbols), or a combination of modes. Multilingual learners new to a language are going to make mistakes (it's part of the learning process). Teachers should be patient by:

- allowing more wait time

- paraphrasing the intended message

- providing an example

- recasting idiomatic expressions

- clarifying the intended meaning in context (especially for words with multiple meanings)

- accepting translanguaging as meaningful communication.

As a teacher or a peer, you may ask a multilingual learner to describe or explain in one language or another. Another strategy would be to seamlessly recast what the students say incorporating challenging language (e.g., "'He's trailing in the polls' means he is behind the other candidate"). There is also metalinguistic feedback, where a student discovers a language pattern or a cognate that links one language to another (e.g., "wow, *animal* is spelled the same and means the same in English and Spanish"). Above all, acknowledge that the student is making strides in making meaning. Avoid giving negative feedback because it has a social-emotional impact on students—it discourages student effort and reduces their motivation.

Oral Language Feedback

Let's take the same map activity and now think about the language side of learning. Language-related feedback by peers deals with how well they understood their friend, the clarity of the directions, and whether their friend could rephrase or give additional information.

Following a series of hands-on activities involving directionality and map interpretation, pairs of students choose a floor (or a wing) of their school to make a map. Success in the activity is dependent, in part, on their peers' ability to find a location or a treasure based on *oral directions*.

After each team has had others use their map, the pairs engage in peer assessment. Criteria for success include following directions of peers, giving directions to peers, and redirecting peers to find specific locations. Peer feedback might include responding to a few questions: (1) Did you understand your friend's directions? (2) What could you ask your friend to better understand where to go? (3) What else could your friend say to help you find the place on the map?

Written Language Feedback

Together, teachers and students might craft a writing code sheet for giving feedback that, when adopted by the class as a whole, offers an abbreviated, yet meaningful, way of communication. The code could readily be a reminder posted on a classroom wall, saved on a computer, or laminated for students. Of course, feedback on written language within content learning is going to vary according to grade level and subject matter. Some general suggestions to help students improve their written expression might include giving them instructions such as the following:

1. Expand your thought.

2. Say it another way.

3. Ask a friend for help.

4. Check another source.

5. Use both languages to think about what you want to write.

6. Reread what you write to make sure it is what you want to say.

WHAT IS THE ROLE OF COLLABORATION IN INTERPRETING ASSESSMENT INFORMATION?

Collaboration between students, teachers and students, and teachers contributes to sound practices throughout the assessment cycle. Through partnering, students and teachers can engage in purposeful instructional and assessment experiences that can be readily documented and interpreted. In working together, decisions around evidence collected on learning goals and targets can be validated. Indeed, professional collaboration is a powerful tool in shaping student performance and in teacher learning.

Additionally, collaboration affords the building of consensus from disparate points of view or perspectives and contributes a sense of ownership of the assessment process. Collaboration between teachers and between teachers and other school leaders is a necessary partnership to ensure that assessment practices are congruent within a grade or department and, preferably, aligned across grades. When there are disruptions to brick and mortar teaching, such as when experiencing long lapses of remote learning during a global pandemic, relying on teacher collaboration to use technology to share protocols for assessing students and interpreting data is a tremendous source of support.

With teacher guidance, multilingual learners can engage in collaborative discourse to check for understanding, analyze, and interpret their work whether in class or at home. If the students have a shared language, they have the bonus of being able to communicate in multiple languages. Having conversations is productive whether in person or online! Through thoughtful and collaborative conversations, students can become adept at examining their own and each other's work.

Co-teaching and co-assessing give multilingual learners space to grow and learn. Together they can:

- apply criteria for success to their work samples and defend their interpretation

- self- and peer-assess drafts, such as writing pieces, oral language samples, or visual displays, leading to the final project or product

- revise drafts based on self, peer, and teacher feedback

- prepare for and practice **student-led conferences** or presentations for peers, teachers, and family members. (Gottlieb & Honigsfeld, 2020)

HOW MIGHT WE FACE THE ISSUE? CREATE AN INTERNATIONAL NETWORK OF EDUCATORS

To probe deeper into the beliefs of multilingualism and multiculturalism, ask your students and colleagues to share their experiences. Watch videos of teachers instructing in languages other than English, explore international teacher organizations, or use social media to connect with other educators worldwide. To dispel some of the negative thinking and replace it with a positive mindset, think about how classroom data can be interpreted to accentuate what multilingual learners can do in multiple languages.

Learning together and from each other can dispel confusion. The following questions personalize some of the topics we have addressed in this chapter.

For Younger Multilingual Learners

- What is best about knowing two languages?

- How do you use both your languages to learn?

- How do pictures, videos, and charts help you better understand?

- How do your friends help you learn?

For Older Multilingual Learners

- What kinds of feedback are helpful from your teachers and peers?

- What opportunities do you have to self-assess?

- How is your identity tied to knowing and using more than one language?

- How is being bilingual and bicultural helpful in learning?

For Teachers and Other Instructional Leaders

- How might you organize data in a capstone project or an assessment portfolio for your grade with students and teachers?

- In what ways might you reconsider providing feedback to your students?

- How might you best bring out your multilingual learners' multilingualism in instruction and assessment?

- How might you use multimodal communication to improve multilingual learners' opportunities to learn?

For School Leaders

- How might you expand teacher engagement in interpreting data in multiple languages?

- How can you ensure that data interpretation is fair and equitable for all students?

- How might you provide joint free time for co-teachers or grade-level teams to interpret their students' data?

- How do you deal with families who believe that learning in two languages is confusing for their children?

HOW MIGHT WE RESOLVE THE DILEMMA?
BELIEVE IN YOUR STUDENTS AS LEARNERS!

Although there may be some adults who remain dubious as to the strengths of bilingualism, for the most part, there is no doubt in the minds of multilingual learners, especially those who have opportunities to use their languages and cultures to grow in school. Watching multilingual students seamlessly interact in multiple languages as they learn should cast away any doubt that they are confused. As the fifth graders in the opening scenario, think about how your students, including your multilingual learners, can express their inner feelings about personal issues, such as what it means to be bilingual and bicultural, in the design of a project that extends learning into action that can be taken to the community.

Resources for Multilingual Learners, Their Teachers, and Other Instructional Leaders

RESOURCE 5.1 FOR TEACHERS AND OTHER INSTRUCTIONAL LEADERS
Collecting and Recording Information on Multilingual Learners' Language, Literacy, and Translanguaging Practices

You may wish to dive deeper into classroom assessment by examining multilingual learners' oral language and literacy development by each instructional activity and how the data are recorded. Use the suggestions from Figure 5.2 as a starting point. Think about how your multilingual learners' language use and classroom activities impact your interpretation of the information.

Language(s) _____ Date: _____

Data Collection, Recording, and Interpretation of _____

COLLECTING INFORMATION ON ORAL LANGUAGE PRACTICES DURING CONTENT LEARNING	WAYS OF RECORDING ORAL LANGUAGE PRACTICES	COLLECTING INFORMATION ON TRANSLANGUAGING PRACTICES	COLLECTING INFORMATION ON LITERACY PRACTICES ACROSS CONTENT AREAS	WAYS OF RECORDING LITERACY PRACTICES
Observing student interaction by:	Documenting and interpreting student interaction with or by:	Observing and documenting student interaction in two languages	Student products:	Interpreting student products with:

RESOURCE 5.2 FOR INSTRUCTIONAL LEADERS AND OLDER MULTILINGUAL LEARNERS

Student Milestones Based on Observational Notes

For those of you who are not tech savvy, here is a sheet that you are welcome to copy and use to note how your multilingual learners are developing month by month or quarter by quarter. If preferred, you can transfer the information onto a device or create a spreadsheet on your computer to record and interpret observational data.

You may wish to convert the columns to student-friendly terms for your older multilingual learners who are accustomed to self-assessment. You also may wish to use the information you gather for teacher–student conferences.

Student: _____ Quarter: _____ Language Proficiency Level: ___

DATE	LANGUAGE DEVELOPMENT IN ENGLISH	LANGUAGE DEVELOPMENT IN OTHER LANGUAGE(S)	DEVELOPMENT THROUGH TRANSLANGUAGING	CONCEPTUAL DEVELOPMENT	SOCIAL-EMOTIONAL DEVELOPMENT

RESOURCE 5.3 FOR MULTILINGUAL LEARNERS

A Rating Scale for Interpreting Text in Multiple Languages

What do you do when you open a book or the computer screen and begin to read? How often do you do it? Put a check in the column whether you do it all the time, sometimes, or never.

WHEN I READ....	ALL THE TIME	SOMETIMES	NEVER
1. I translate the ideas on the page in my head from one language to another language.			
2. I use both my languages to comprehend what's on the page or the screen.			
3. I rely on one language and check with my other language.			
4. I use diagrams and illustrations to help me make sense of the print.			
5. I try to make sense of the message even though I skip words or phrases that I don't know.			
6. I interpret what I read by outlining the information or using graphic organizers.			
7. I use digital tools (like Google Translate) to help me better understand the message.			
8. I ask my peers who share my other language what something means or to help me understand.			
9. I ask my teacher for extra time so I can use both my languages to figure out the meaning.			
10. I try to find another source of information in my other language to enhance my understanding.			

RESOURCE 5.4 FOR MULTILINGUAL LEARNERS

How I Learn

What do you use to help you learn? How do you interpret information? Put a circle around what you *look at*. Next, put a circle around how you *move* to communicate with others. Then put a circle around what *technology* you find useful. Finally, put a circle around what you *listen to* to understand.

WHAT YOU *LOOK AT* TO UNDERSTAND	WHAT YOU *MOVE* TO EXPRESS YOURSELF	WHICH *TECHNOLOGY* YOU USE	WHAT YOU *LISTEN TO* TO UNDERSTAND
• Pictures	• Your face	• Social media	• Audiobooks
• Photographs	• Your hands	• Software	• Podcasts
• Diagrams	• Your body	• Computer programs	• Music
• Graphic organizers	• Through dance	• Online tools	• Dialogue/ conversations
• Emojis or icons		• Mobile apps	• Discussions
• Charts		• E-books	• Oral story telling
• Videos		• Video streaming	
• Animations		• Animation	
• Paintings		• Web pages	
• Drawings			
• Symbols (e.g., <, >, +, =)			
• Objects			

CHAPTER 6

Evaluating and Reporting Assessment Information in Multiple Languages

▶ A sign in a department store in London, England

Una lingua diversa è una diversa vision della vita.

A different language is a different vision of life.

—Federico Fellini

The Dilemma

But the same grading policy for all students, including multilingual learners, just doesn't make sense!

As the opening sign illustrates, we live in a world of multiple Englishes; we also live in a world of multiple Spanishes, dialects, indigenous, creole, and thousands of other languages. No one language has more status than another; they are all legitimate, of equal worth, and signs of one's identity. So, when one language appears to be devalued, the situation has to be rectified. Such is often the case when assessment information is converted into grades for multilingual learners.

Second grade is the first time that students receive grades in O'Keefe School. Until that time, teachers provide individual narratives that speak to each area of learning and multilingual learners' use of dual languages. As the majority of the multilingual learners have been participating in dual language programs since kindergarten, the narrative reports have addressed multilingual learners' growth in two languages, achievement, and social-emotional development. However, now is the time for multilingual learners and their teachers to transition to more traditional report cards.

The second-grade team is faced with a two-pronged dilemma as inequity seems to rear its ugly head in regard to grading multilingual learners. First, the district report card just does not have enough room for the necessary information for multilingual learners who are participating in language education programs. There is no devoted space to note their English language development let alone their development in their additional language and their interaction between their two languages. It's not enough to simply squeeze in some grades without providing a description or context (it also appears rather unprofessional and an add-on).

The second issue is how to counter the biased grading policy of the school, which mirrors that of the district. The multilingual learners who are English learners are being held to the identical criteria as their proficient English peers when it comes to grading, thus promoting equal over equitable treatment. By virtue of their categorical label, these multilingual learners are being punished for not having reached linguistic parity in English whether knowledgeable of grade-level concepts or not.

Additionally, the second-grade team is worried about a handful of second graders who are recent arrivals from war-torn countries whose families have been traumatized with lingering emotional scars. Then there is the related issue of how to evaluate students who are returning to school after a long hiatus, such as that due to a global pandemic and social unrest. Yet the school, for fear of "discrimination," requires a uniform grading policy irrespective of any extenuating circumstances. The team feels strongly that grading based on testing, the primary form of evaluation and reporting, especially for young multilingual learners, is inappropriate. What should they say to their principal?

- In what ways does this scenario resonate with you?

- What are the grading policies for multilingual learners in your school?

- How does metalinguistic, metacultural, and metacognitive awareness provide insight into the evaluation of multilingual learners?

- How can multilingual learners contribute to classroom evaluation and reporting efforts?

FIGURE 6.1 The **FOURTH PHASE** of the Assessment Cycle: Evaluating and Reporting Assessment Information

Assessing multilingual learners' knowledge and development from a monolingual lens represents only a fractional view of students' ability (Grosjean, 1989). Over the last chapters we have seen how classroom assessment should consider the complexity of students' bilingualism, biliteracy, and their ways of languaging in the classroom, school, home, and community. As shown in Figure 6.1, we now turn our attention to the fourth phase of the assessment cycle, evaluating and reporting information in multiple languages.

In this phase of the cycle, we take assessment information that has been interpreted and assign a value, or judgment of its worth, to be shared with stakeholders. In classroom assessment with multiple languages, teachers know their multilingual learners (the primary stakeholders) best. Evaluation of assessment data in multiple languages should always provide accessible and actionable information that supports further learning (Calkins et al., 2018).

This chapter explores different ways to evaluate and report classroom data that make sense for learning in multiple languages. It suggests how to change the grading paradigm for multilingual learners by looking to the student as an informant in evaluation and reporting associated with assessment *as, for,* and *of* learning, We see how assessment *as* learning can grow metacognitive, metalinguistic, and metacultural awareness for multilingual learners and assessment *for* and *of* learning can promote the crafting of classroom tools and rubrics by students and teachers. Finally, we attempt to cast away the monolingual bias inherent in grading, still the most commonplace form of student evaluation, and look to reconsider current grading practices in light of what multilingual learners can do in multiple languages.

WHAT IS THE BASIS FOR EVALUATING INFORMATION FROM ASSESSMENT IN MULTIPLE LANGUAGES?

Students are going to be judged, it's just part of school and life. Too often, tests or exams are seen as the end goal of teaching and the basis for evaluating learning, especially in middle and high schools. Evaluation of assessment data doesn't necessarily mean attaching a grade to it. Let's revisit our framework from Chapter 1 (Figure 1.4) to see where we have been and where we are as we evaluate and report information from assessment in multiple languages.

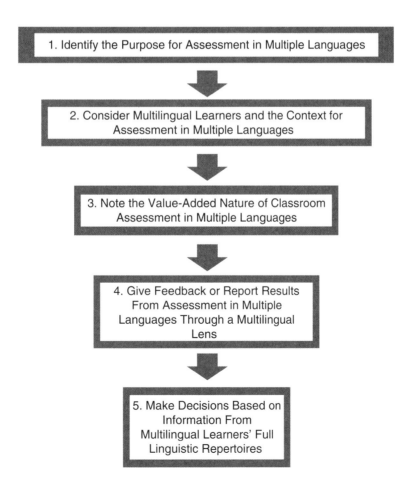

1. Identify the Purpose for Assessment in Multiple Languages

2. Consider Multilingual Learners and the Context for Assessment in Multiple Languages

3. Note the Value-Added Nature of Classroom Assessment in Multiple Languages

4. Give Feedback or Report Results From Assessment in Multiple Languages Through a Multilingual Lens

5. Make Decisions Based on Information From Multilingual Learners' Full Linguistic Repertoires

Relax and Reflect: What are some initial thoughts on reporting and evaluating assessment results?

As you can see in the framework, reporting assessment data is step 4; it follows the purpose for assessment, the characteristics of the multilingual learners, and the context for multiple language use. How might you take steps 1 through 3 into account when evaluating and reporting assessment information on multilingual learners in multiple languages?

RETHINKING EVALUATING AND REPORTING BASED ON ASSESSMENT IN MULTIPLE LANGUAGES

Even if testing reigns supreme in your setting, we can still push multilingual learners and other students to be agents of their own learning. Teacher guidance can and should encourage student voice throughout the assessment cycle. In this phase, students can readily engage in reflective thinking in evaluating a performance assessment task or test and provide feedback in one or more languages to each other and their teacher.

To increase the role of students in evaluating assessment information, teachers or other instructional leaders should facilitate an analysis of a performance task or test questions with their class. After an initial discussion, a set of questions, such as those suggested below, could spark reflection on an assessment task or test in one or more multiple languages. Individual questions from this list could then be distributed to partners or small groups to tackle. These questions can be revisited throughout the school year. For older multilingual learners, these and other questions have been converted to a rating scale in Resource 6.1.

- How easy or difficult do you think the assessment (or test) was? What made it easy or difficult?

- Do you think that the assessment (or test) represented what had been taught? Give an example.

- How were you able to show what you have learned? Give an example.

- Did you know ahead of time which languages you could use? How did that help you?

- Did you use more than one language during the assessment (or test)? If so, in what ways?

- Did you use resources other than text, such as graphs or illustrations? How were they helpful or not helpful?

- What could you have done better? What could your teacher have done better?

- Did you think that the assessment (or test) was fair? Why or why not?

With these types of questions, teachers should see that inviting multilingual learners to reflect on their assessment experience helps ease their apprehension, allows them to interact with each other in multiple languages, and enhances their opportunities to become more vested in learning. Although these reflective questions are evaluative in nature, hopefully they stimulate thinking about what and how students are learning rather than just getting the results. In essence, students' critique of assessment gives them insight and useful information for improving both teaching and learning.

HOW MIGHT WE REPORT ASSESSMENT RESULTS?

How do you provide your students results from assessment? Do you give them a happy face, a check mark, or a grade of some sort, such as in the form of a numeral, letter, or percent correct? Is there a shared understanding between students and teachers of what the results mean? To what extent does the current kind of reporting show what students can do and how they might be able to improve?

Although these quick-fire ways of evaluating students are expedient, there are an array of alternative ways of reporting results from classroom assessment that are more meaningful. Here are some ideas to consider when brainstorming options or extensions of traditional reporting. Instead of, or in addition to, what is currently in place, consider these options which can be made available in multiple languages:

- offering personalized **descriptive feedback** to individual students either orally or in writing

- co-creating classroom criteria for success with students based on learning targets

- using a classroom devised system for scoring tied to what students can do

- summarizing information from learner portraits and suggesting actions to take

- giving interpretive summaries on projects of what students have accomplished

- graphing progress within and across languages along with precise narratives

- creating progress reports that describe where students are and where they are going

- referencing the road toward meeting language and content standards, how to get there, and how far students have gone.

Relax and Reflect: What are some ideas for reporting assessment results for multilingual learners?

In grade-level teams, review the pros and cons of different ways of reporting results from classroom assessment in multiple languages. Prioritize the top three to five most effective ways for the team. Then, based on your selection, think about how you might reform ways of reporting classroom assessment practices to be more inclusive of students, their languages, and their cultures.

FIGURE 6.2 Reporting Assessment Results for Multilingual Learners to Various Stakeholders

STAKEHOLDER GROUP	CONTEXTS FOR REPORTING ASSESSMENT RESULTS IN ONE OR MORE LANGUAGES
Multilingual Learners	• In oral discussion groups or in student–student interaction • As written feedback from peers or teachers • In individual student–teacher conferences • As part of individual student goal setting
Family Members	• On the school website, presented in multiple languages • In information flyers in multiple languages • In meetings held at school, in homes, or public places in multiple languages • In the presence of a translator or community liaison
Teachers and Other School Leaders (e.g., Coaches, Principals)	• At grade-level or department meetings • During collaboration time between co-teachers • During faculty meetings • In professional learning communities
The Community	• At local meeting points, such as a library or community center • Through newsletters, infographics, and bulletins in multiple languages • Through a dedicated school website in multiple languages • Through a network of neighborhood organizations

There are many forms for reporting information generated from assessment. At the same time, we must be sensitive to the needs of each stakeholder group. Figure 6.2 identifies the most prominent groups that use student data at the classroom and school levels and suggests contexts for reporting the results.

STUDENT SELF-REFLECTION AND SELF-REPORTS: ASSESSMENT *AS* LEARNING

Assessment *as* learning may be initiated or facilitated by teachers; however, it is driven by students. This student-centered approach is an everyday occurrence that is wrapped in instruction. Self-reflection gives multilingual learners opportunities to think critically about what and how they learn. At the same time, it allows multilingual learners to make sense of the interplay of their languages, cultures, content, and the learning process.

One strategy to promote multilingual learners' self-reflection is for teachers to pose open-ended questions about a policy, practice, or procedure, such as "How does knowing two languages help you solve today's problem?" Multilingual learners can translate or paraphrase the question in the shared languages of other students. Students can then silently answer the question to themselves with the option of responding orally or writing in their journals.

For evaluation and reporting purposes, assessment *as* learning for multilingual learners is multifaceted and personalized, and it encompasses metacognitive, metalinguistic, and metacultural awareness. These data provide insight into learning that is specific to multilingual learners and their perceptions of multi-lingualism and multiculturalism.

Metacognitive Awareness

Metcognitive awareness (also called metacognition), reflection on one's own thought processes, is the foundation for building self-confidence and courage for learning. Being metacognitively aware helps students connect their background knowledge to new information. For example, at the beginning of a unit, students may be asked to reflect on what they already know about the topic or theme and how they might apply that knowledge. Multilingual learners often rely on multiple languages in their thinking process and should become aware of how they utilize both of their languages to make sense of the world. By becoming more assured in tackling new challenging content and taking on language risks, multilingual learners simultaneously engage in cognitive and social-emotional development.

Prompting students to monitor their thinking, such as in a think-aloud strategy, aids in building their self-awareness. Generally associated with comprehension of reading material, this strategy can readily be applied to writing or oral language activities in one or more languages. First, teachers model the process by asking a series of questions, and then have students take over by practicing in pairs or small groups before taking on the strategy independently. Here are some typical questions that can be asked during a think-aloud activity to prompt metacognitive awareness; they are repeated (and translated into Spanish) in Resource 6.2 to share with multilingual learners.

1. What do I know about this topic?

2. What in my home or community helps me know about this topic?

3. What information do I know in each of my languages about the topic?

4. What does what I just read or heard mean to me?

5. How might I use this information?

6. Do I have a picture in my head about information I just read or what I plan to write or talk about?

7. How might I use illustrations or graphs to help me understand?

8. What are the most important ideas about what I just read or heard?

9. What new information did I learn?

10. How do I connect this new information with what I already know?

Metalinguistic Awareness

Metalinguistic awareness is the understanding of the nuances and uses of language. It includes examining the similarities and differences in the features and forms of languages. Boosting students' metalinguistic awareness has significant impact on their reading comprehension (Zipke, 2007). Additionally, research indicates that simultaneous bilinguals, those multilingual learners developing two or more languages at the same time, are advantaged over their monolingual peers in their metalinguistic awareness (Bialystok & Barac, 2012).

Teachers with a multilingual mindset tend to encourage **cross-linguistic transfer,** applying linguistic features from one language to a related one, along with the development of general language awareness (Cummins, 2005). Having gained a more **assets-based orientation,** they are able to cast away monolingual instructional assumptions that essentially deny students access to multiple languages as resources for learning. Through metalinguistic awareness, multilingual learners acquire insight into the relationships between their languages, such as similarities and differences in meaning from **genres** (specific purposes for language uses that are defined by a set of characteristics), idiomatic expressions, and **cognates** (words from different languages with similar meaning that are derived from the same word family). One example of cognates is the resemblance of word families in Spanish and English, such as those illustrated in Figure 6.3.

FIGURE 6.3 Becoming Metalinguistically Aware: Similarities in Word Groups in Spanish and English

NOMBRES— NOUNS	ADJETIVOS— ADJECTIVES	VERBOS—VERBS	ADVERBIOS— ADVERBS
-ción = -tion	*-oso/a = -ous*	*-ar = -ate*	*-mente = -ly*
revolución = revolution	fabuloso = fabulous	contemplar = contemplate	actualmente = actually
emoción = emotion	lujoso = luxurious	participar = participate	exactamente = exactly
transición = transition	generoso = generous	evaluar = evaluate (also assess)	generalmente = generally
edición = edition	estudioso = studious	relatar = tell (relate)	diariamente = daily

ADAPTED FROM: Minaya-Rowe (2014).

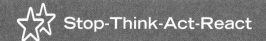

Relax and Reflect: How metalinguistically aware are your multilingual learners?

It is a fun learning activity for literate multilingual learners who speak any of the romance languages (i.e., Spanish, Portuguese, French, Italian, and Romanian) to dive into a grade-level text to see how many words in English are connected to their other language. Show them how cognates give clues to meaning and how, in the future, they might predict what the word might mean, not only by the context, but by knowing another language. See to what extent your multilingual learners can also apply this strategy to an assessment task.

Metacultural Awareness

Metacultural awareness is related to multilingual learners' sensitivity to and knowledge of their own culture(s) and its norms in relation to other cultures. In regard to assessment, it applies to the ability to detect cultural nuances (often hidden or implied) and their influence in comprehending and carrying out an activity, task, or project. Ideally, in evaluating assessment results for multilingual learners, teachers should be aware of the cultural context in which the activity had been situated.

Here is a fourth-grade English language arts passage that at one time was a sample for a testing consortium. Read the story with a metacultural lens; note the number of instances in which cultural knowledge or insight affects the comprehension of the narrative and compare them with those of a colleague.

GRANDMA RUTH

Last night I learned that my grandma was named after Babe Ruth, the greatest baseball player of all time. I learned this six hours too late.

Yesterday I wanted to work on throwing a baseball. I needed a baseball, since my brother wouldn't let me borrow his. Unfortunately, I knew right where one was.

I tiptoed into my grandma's bedroom. Sunlight from the late morning sun filtered in through the leaves of the dogwood tree outside the open window. I moved slowly through my favorite room in the house, which belonged to my favorite person in the world, my grandma.

I reached into the back of her closet and pulled out a shoebox full of old baseballs wrapped in tissue paper. I shoved my hand in and grabbed the first one I touched. I threw off the paper and ran out into the yard with our dog, Bowie, who would always play a game of catch with me.

We had a spectacular game of catch. By the end of our session I was throwing straight as an arrow and Bowie was bringing it back as fast as he could. It was perfect.

(Continued)

(Continued)

I went back into my grandma's room and wrapped the ball back up in paper, just like I'd found it. Except now it looked dirty and used, like a good baseball should. At dinner, though, I heard the story.

"Have I ever told you that I'm named after the greatest baseball player who ever lived?" Grandma asked suddenly.

James and I shook our heads. We leaned forward to listen. It isn't often we hear new stories from her.

My grandmother stood up and walked into her bedroom. She came back with the shoebox in her hands. She sat down and started her story.

"So, your great-grandfather was the dentist for the Detroit Tigers back in the 1920s. His favorite player was Ty Cobb, the best player the Tigers have ever had. When Ty found out that your great-grandparents were going to have a baby, he brought your great-grandfather a big package full of baseballs signed by the best-known players of the time. He said, 'Doc, you can have these under one condition: name your daughter Tyrina. After me.' And my father, too excited to say no, agreed.

"When my mother heard about this she told my father to go to Ty Cobb and give him back the baseballs, because she had her own ideas for names. Ty just laughed when he heard this. He said to my father, 'Doc, I'll tell you what: keep the baseballs but name her after my good friend Babe Ruth.'

"My father smiled and said, 'I'll see what I can do. Keep these for me until then.'

"It turned out my mother loved the name Ruth. That's how I got my name and how my father got these: he let Ty Cobb name me after Babe Ruth."

I tried to swallow but couldn't. I hoped that she wasn't going to say what I thought she was going to say. Then she said it.

"In this shoebox are the ten baseballs Ty Cobb gave my father. They are signed by some of the most famous ballplayers in history, including one that has one single signature on it: Babe Ruth's."

My grandma pulled the ball out, unwrapped it, and held it out for us to see. The ball was scarred almost beyond recognition. It had dog bite marks, dirt scuffs, and fraying seams. Right in the middle was a big signature in black ink that I had somehow overlooked. It was smudged now and faded, but it still clearly said "Babe Ruth." I began to shake inside.

But my grandma just looked at the ball and smiled sweetly. She said softly, "Even though it doesn't look like much, this ball has brought our family a lot of joy in its time. I remember when I was your age, Naomi, I almost rubbed the signature right off from tossing it up and down all the time. You see, I've always felt that a baseball should be used for a lot more than looking. My dad, your great-grandfather, used to say the same thing."

She lowered her hand and gently tossed the ball toward Bowie, sleeping by the door. It rolled in a perfectly straight line and came to rest softly between the dog's paws. A perfect throw.

....

Reproduced from Gottlieb (2016), pp. 208–209.

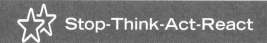 **Stop-Think-Act-React**

Relax and Reflect: To what extent are you culturally aware?

Classrooms are enriched by the cultural perspectives of multilingual learners. In contrast, multilingual learners' unfamiliarity with the dominant U.S. culture often places them in a compromised position. Read the following questions about Grandma Ruth to become more sensitive to multicultural nuances.

1. To what extent do you consider this story to be culturally biased?

2. What are the cultural assumptions of this story? Here are the most obvious ones:

   - Baseball is a sport considered to be a favorite U.S. pastime.

   - Baseballs can be thrown "straight as an arrow" when playing "catch."

   - The Detroit Tigers is a baseball team from the city of Detroit, Michigan.

   - Babe Ruth and Ty Cobb were famous baseball players.

   - Old baseballs that have been signed by famous players are valuable.

   - People make collections of valuable things and their monetary value generally increases if left unused.

   - Some people are named after famous athletes.

3. Do you see any connections of these cultural assumptions to other cultures?

4. How might some of these cultural assumptions be understood by multilingual learners? For example, to help build metacultural awareness for this story, you might ask your students, "Are you named after anyone? Who? Is it based on a cultural tradition in your family?" "Tell me about it."

Becoming multiculturally aware is a learning experience. Consider taking a short story that typifies your grade and determine how metacultural awareness (or cultural dissonance) impacts its significance for multilingual learners, especially newcomers, or multilingual learners with disabilities. Then select a cross-cultural story or one with translanguaging and think about how cultural harmony with that of multilingual learners helps their understanding of the story's nuances.

CLASSROOM-GENERATED REPORTS: ASSESSMENT *FOR* LEARNING

Evaluating and reporting classroom information as an expression of assessment *for* learning is a combined effort by teachers and students. Teachers however, when evaluating work with multilingual learners in multiple languages, must be sensitive to the students' levels of language proficiency in each language and the scaffolding provided for learning. Here are some ideas for classroom teachers, co-teachers, dual language teachers, or content and language teachers working with multilingual learners in one or more languages.

FIGURE 6.4 A Self-Evaluation Tool for Oral or Written Arguments

Our learning target: _____

What is your stance or position? _____

EVIDENCE THAT I MET THE CRITERION	CRITERIA FOR SUCCESS BASED ON OUR LEARNING TARGET FOR CONSTRUCTING AN ARGUMENT	WHAT ELSE I NEED TO DO
	Criterion 1: State your claim.	
	Criterion 2: Provide evidence to support your claim.	
	Criterion 3: Pose a counterclaim.	
	Criterion 4: Provide evidence to support your counterclaim.	
	Criterion 5: Share your reasoning.	
	Criterion 6: Paraphrase or summarize your position.	
	Criterion 7: Produce a strong conclusion.	

- Use the criteria for success based on agreed upon learning targets as the basis for reporting.

- Model learning expectations with samples of what meeting the learning targets looks like.

- Facilitate students to engage in self- and peer reflection using samples of student work.

- Guide students to self-evaluate, provide evidence, and discuss any discrepancy with teacher judgment.

- Coach students in suggesting ways to improve (e.g., their strategies) based on their self-evaluation or in identifying areas they would like to investigate more in depth.

Figure 6.4 is an example self-evaluation tool for students. This one specifically addresses criteria related to argumentation; Resource 6.3 is a blank form for you and students in upper elementary and high school to use.

UNIT-LEVEL REPORTS: ASSESSMENT *OF* LEARNING

In classrooms, assessment *of* learning is equated with more long-term products, performances, or projects, where reporting generally corresponds to the extent to which students are meeting shared learning goals or standards. Learning goals become real for students through project descriptors or **rubrics**, which are guides for evaluating the quality of student work.

FIGURE 6.5 A Sample Rubric for Evaluating Multilingual Learners' Language, Conceptual, and Social-Emotional Development for a Unit of Learning

	4 ARRIVING	3 ADVANCING	2 ACCELERATING	1 APPRENTICING
Development in English	I use precise language needed for the situation, task, and audience.	I use language for the situation, task, and audience.	I use, and at times elaborate, language asked of me.	I am beginning to use language asked of me.
Development in My Other Language	I use precise language needed for the situation, task, and audience.	I use language for the situation, task, and audience.	I use, and at times elaborate, language asked of me.	I am beginning to use language asked of me.
Conceptual Development	I thoroughly understand what I need to do and am able to teach others.	I understand what I need to do and I do it.	I mostly understand what I need to do but sometimes I ask others to help me.	I am beginning to understand what I need to do and I try to do it with help.
Social-Emotional Development	I am very confident and sometimes take risks in the work I do.	I am confident in the work I do.	I am quite certain about the work I do.	I am a bit unsure about the work I do.

For every extended assessment task, multilingual learners and their teachers could evaluate and report different levels of language proficiency and conceptual understanding for each language. This variability is attributed to the different contexts in which the assessment occurs. Figure 6.5 is an example of an "I can" rubric where multilingual learners evaluate what they can do at the close of a unit of learning. These broad dimensions of learning are applicable across a variety of projects and languages; Resource 6.4 is a blank rubric.

One other useful tool associated with assessment *of* learning that can be shared by multilingual learners and teachers are standards-based rubrics. Figure 6.6 is a generalized rubric that has broad applicability across languages; it illustrates how reporting for students can parallel that of teachers. Teachers are welcome to insert specific standards into it to meet their classroom goals.

HOW IS GRADING A FORM OF EVALUATION?

Grading is an action that occurs daily, activity by activity; weekly, task by task; or for longer stretches of time, such as for projects. Historically, the variability and subjectivity of grading across classrooms, especially when more than one language is involved, has remained an issue of teacher power and control. The following is a series of short scenarios that accentuate some of the many ways

FIGURE 6.6 A Sample Standards-Referenced Rubric for Teachers and Students

Standards Addressed: _____

LEVEL OF EXPERTISE		STANDARDS-REFERENCED LANGUAGE	STUDENT-FRIENDLY LANGUAGE	LANGUAGE(S)
Expert ☐	6	Exemplary demonstration of understanding of standards	"Your evidence shows you could teach the standards!"	
	5	Strong demonstration of understanding of standards	"Your evidence shows you have a strong understanding of the standards!"	
Experienced ☐	4	Reasonable demonstration of understanding of standards	"Your evidence shows a good understanding of the standards."	
	3	Borderline acceptable demonstration of standards	"Your evidence shows that you understand the standards."	
Apprentice ☐	2	Minimal understanding of standards	"Your evidence shows that you are beginning to understand the standards."	
	1	Unsure of understanding of standards	"Your evidence makes it difficult to know your understanding."	

ADAPTED FROM: Dueck (2020).

teachers tend to grade multilingual learners in multiple languages; see which one(s) resonate with you.

1. Sra. Sánchez grades her Latinx students in Spanish, and her cooperating teacher uses the same report card to grade the students in English. Although they both use letter grades to indicate student achievement, one teacher also includes motivation and effort while the other teacher uses attendance and timeliness as factors.

2. Mr. Cho and his co-teacher meet to determine one set of grades for each content area and then specify multilingual learners' language development in English and Mandarin separately.

3. Multilingual learners in Ms. Jackson's room have opportunities to put their own grades alongside those of their teacher's according to criteria for success that they have agreed upon for that marking period in both their languages.

4. Habib's teacher averages his homework and test scores, based on percent correct, then adds a sprinkle for work habits and effort to determine grades. She marks the content areas taught in English and those in Arabic, the other language, using the identical criteria for evaluating both languages.

5. The eighth-grade team decides to purposely give low grades at the beginning of the school year in both languages to motivate students to work hard up to graduation day.

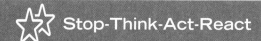

Stop-Think-Act-React

Relax and Reflect: What is the best form of grading in multiple languages?

Do you believe that your grading policy is equitable for your multilingual learners? Have your students had any input in its formation? How might you make it more inclusive of multiple languages? Refer to Resource 6.5 where the scenarios are duplicated if you wish to explore these ideas more in depth with your colleagues.

Here is another scenario about the use of feedback for evaluative purposes in response to grading. A teary-eyed multilingual learner named Ambra approached her teacher after class and timidly asked about why she received the grade she did. Together the two spent the next few minutes combing through the report and discussing what the student specifically could do to improve it. The positive oral feedback from the teacher boosted Ambra's confidence in herself; subsequently, she felt more able and motivated to tackle writing tasks.

Grading Multilingual Learners

Grading is typically the last area of focus in addressing education reform efforts. We all have been at its receiving end and have opinions on how best to report assessment results. Because there is so much variability on this topic, the literature urges us to adopt grading policies and practices that are based on research evidence rather than personal experience (McTighe & Brookhart, 2019).

Grading associated with report cards is a time-honored tradition of schooling. It is a summative marker of student performance that generally occurs on a quarterly basis. A comprehensive review of grading reveals that K–12 teachers use a mix of factors, both academic (for each subject area) and nonacademic (such as attendance, effort, participation, timeliness, behavior, or improvement) to determine grades (Brookhart et al., 2016). Traditionally, grading is considered a type of normative feedback (Marzano, 2010), where scores are distributed on a curve—that is, one student's performance is graded in reference to others in the class. Grading confined to performance in English disadvantages English learners are who, by definition, have not reached academic parity with their proficient English peers. Today most schools and districts have been moving to criterion-referenced or standards-based grading systems.

Admittedly there is a rationale for changing grading practices and policies. It has been shown that grades tend to (1) demotivate learning, (2) stifle creativity, and (3) inhibit habits for students in becoming life-long learners (Percell, 2019). There are signs that this tradition is starting to break down; some reform efforts include the following:

- inclusion of technology, where districts or schools have chosen different online programs to expedite the process of student evaluation and reporting

- conversion from grades to a standards-referenced system, where standards serve as the criteria against which students are evaluated categorically, such as approaching, meeting, or succeeding

- reliance on student feedback, placing more emphasis on assessment *as* and *for* learning as a motivator to equalize assessment sources in making evaluative decisions (Gottlieb & Honigsfeld, 2020)

- acknowledgment of any one of the choices above within a dual system that gives equal weight to each language or one system that seamlessly integrates two languages.

There are many other considerations for multilingual learners who use multiple languages during instruction and assessment. Here are a couple of more options: (1) a composite grade for both languages of instruction, let's say for language arts; (2) grades assigned to each language by content area; or (3) a grade for evaluating the interaction between languages that recognizes translanguaging as a mode of communication. In the case of dual language or bilingual instructional models, should grades be a function of the amount of time devoted to instruction in each language or should grades reflect language use as multilingual learners engage in learning?

And there are still more questions to contemplate. What do grades mean for English learners and other multilingual learners who may not be participating in dual language programs? What about grades for recent arrivals who are just becoming acclimated to the U.S. classroom and school culture? What about students who have been labeled SIFE (students with interrupted formal education), **long-term English learners** who historically have not succeeded in school, or English learners who have been dually identified whose IEP may not even recognize the need or type of language support? Where is the equity in grading practices for multilingual learners? According to Feldman (2019), "the ways we grade disproportionately favor students with privilege and harm students with less privilege: students of color, from low-income families, who receive special education services, and English learners" (p. xxii).

Although there has been a cry for alternatives to grading, it remains a mainstay of our educational system. That said, we must try to ameliorate the situation for the sake of our multilingual learners. Here are some tips for how to apply or update grading policies in one or more languages.

1. Grades should be meaningful to students and not be represented as a numeral, such as in an average of test scores; student evaluation and reporting should reveal valued information on the students' overall performance based on specified criteria.

2. Grading should be a time of reflection for students and a time for teachers to be supportive, provide concrete actionable feedback, and focus on how students can grow.

3. Grades, if required, should be negotiated between students and teachers during student-led conferences and should be based on mutually agreed upon learning goals, multilingual learners' language choices, and student evidence for learning.

4. Multilingual learners' language proficiency in English and their other languages should be considered in light of their achievement; their language proficiency should never mask the evaluation and grading of their content knowledge.

5. Multilingual learners' choice in language use should be a context for evaluation that then can be converted into grades, as necessary.

6. Students should have multiple opportunities to show what they know and can do in multiple ways about a specific issue or topic before being formally evaluated.

7. Students should be evaluated based on multiple resources (scaffolding, using multiliteracies, or in multimodal ways using textual, aural, linguistic, spatial, and visual cues) that have been incorporated into instruction and assessment.

8. Social-emotional development, including students' work ethic (e.g., persistence on a task, effort), interaction with others, and motivation should be reported separately from academic performance.

☆ Stop-Think-Act-React

Relax and Reflect: What are your grading practices, in general, and for multilingual learners, in particular?

Do you consider your grading practices equitable for all your students? Do you think that any one group of students is unduly favored over another? Reread the tips for grading practices for multilingual learners. Are there one or two tips that you might adopt or adapt for your classroom? How might you discuss these tips at a grade or school level to create a grading policy? How might your multilingual learners contribute to the conversation?

HOW MIGHT WE RESOLVE THE DILEMMA? MAKE SURE MULTILINGUAL LEARNERS ARE REPRESENTED IN GRADING PRACTICES!

The issue of how to evaluate assessment information and report it in equitable ways will remain unresolved until educators are able to devote time and energy to reassessing their current grading policies with multilingual learners in mind. For reporting purposes, special attention and dedicated space must be allocated for content delivered in multiple languages so that its status is as prominent as all other subject areas. Multilingual learners and their teachers should be empowered by all the activities in their classrooms, and if grading is the form of delivering those accomplishments, then it has to be positioned to ensure student success.

If grading is still alive and well in your school, like that in O'Keefe School, and you feel that data from assessment of your multilingual learners in multiple languages are not fairly represented, ask your principal to investigate changing the policy, just like the second-grade dual language team. Perhaps your school could form a committee or task force to design a new, or amend the current, report card or narrative report. If so, make sure to include both multilingual learners and family member representatives in the decision-making process. And last, but not least, whatever is produced to evaluate and report student performance, make sure that it is available in multiple languages for multilingual learners.

GRADING MULTILINGUAL LEARNERS IN TIMES OF STRESS AND HARDSHIP

Most multilingual learners, even those who have been born and raised here, have encountered hardships, trauma, anxiety, or are living in stress. That's not to say that all students must adjust to school and life on one level, but it is exacerbated for multilingual learners. Given what the US has witnessed in the last years and compounded by what multilingual learners and their families have dealt with, there should be some flexibility when it comes to evaluating or grading. Figure 6.6 provides some background information that could affect multilingual learners, their schools/ communities, and domestic/ international experiences to help contextualize local grading practices and policies.

FIGURE 6.6 Social-Emotional Distress: Hardships That Multilingual Learners May Encounter

PERSONAL	SCHOOL/ COMMUNITY	DOMESTIC/ INTERNATIONAL
• Is separated from parents or close relatives • Fears deportation of a family member	• Aware of/ witnessed shootings • Inequality of available services	• Witnessed natural disasters (e.g., tsunami, hurricane, earthquake)

(Continued)

(Continued)

PERSONAL	SCHOOL/ COMMUNITY	DOMESTIC/ INTERNATIONAL
• Faces gang pressure • Is vulnerable (e.g., an undocumented or unaccompanied minor) • Endures physical or emotional abuse • Faces discrimination • Serves as translator/ spokesperson for the family • Works a full-time job • Is transient • Has a loss of belonging and self-worth	• Rejection of multiculturalism • Blame cast on marginalized groups • Dread of immigration raids • Impact of poverty or homelessness • Restrictive language policies	• Affected by global pandemics • Labeled a transnational or a 'retornado/a'

HOW CAN TEACHER COLLABORATION IMPROVE GRADING PRACTICES?

A culture of collaboration does not permeate all schools. In fact, there are still silos where language and content teachers are isolated from each other and have precious little time, if at all, to co-plan. When evaluating multiple languages, the issue is that teachers, as well as multilingual learners, may represent different cultures with varied grading practices. For example, Mexico uses a numerical system from 1 to 9 as a means of student evaluation, in Korea, high school grading is divided into 9 ranks.

Grading is challenging and often nerve racking in the best of situations. When multiple languages are involved in instruction of different content areas, teachers should share information about their students' performance and should try to coordinate ways for grading. In that way, there is:

- consistency for students in terms of expectations and how to meet them

- reliability between or among teachers in their feedback

- an established, mutually understood set of criteria on which to base grading

- a shared understanding of the consequences of grading for students (e.g., regrouping, eligibility for or dismissal from specialized services).

Teachers who work with multilingual learners should carve out some time to sit together and pour over student work. With learning targets in mind, the teachers can point out to each other what students can do and areas of improvement, discuss any discrepancies in their thinking, and provide timely feedback to students.

Relax and Reflect: How might content and language teachers work together to evaluate multilingual learners?

Language and content co-teachers bring unique perspectives regarding the evaluation (or grading as the case may be) of multilingual learners. With opportunities to co-plan, think about how you might reach consensus on grading policies.

As a *content teacher*, what is your policy on grading and its specific applicability to multilingual learners? How can you benefit from co-planning and co-assessing with a language expert?	As a *language teacher*, what is your policy on grading multilingual learners? What might be your contribution to co-evaluating multilingual learners? How might a content expert offer insight?

Let's revisit the grade 2 writing sample, this time with an eye on grading. Where would you begin to consider evaluating multilingual learners who maximize their expression of meaning through translanguaging? Before you even contemplate how to assign a grade, first is to go back and ask yourself, 'What is the purpose of this activity?' Obviously, here the multilingual learner is explaining how he made cookies step by step. There are several ways of thinking about how to evaluate this sample. For example, teachers could:

- specifically note how the multilingual learner used translanguaging to communicate

- give an overall grade for combined language use

- assign a separate grade for each language and then 'average' them

- not give any grade at all, but gave feedback regarding the multilingual learner's overall description of the event

- consider how well the multilingual learner was able to retell an experience.

Which idea for evaluation do you prefer for this second grader's writing? Why?

The mom and Max is making cockies.

The mom and Max they go to the congelador (refrigerator) and see they haven't got eggs.

And they walking to the house of the neighbor.

The neighbor les presto eggs. (Their neighbor lends them eggs.)

And next they make the cockies.

Finally they put the cockies en el horno (in the oven)

HOW MIGHT WE FACE THE ISSUE? EVALUATE MULTILINGUAL LEARNERS AND MULTILINGUAL LEARNERS WITH DISABILITIES IN THE CONTEXT OF THEIR GOALS FOR LEARNING

Evaluating and reporting classroom assessment results is a sensitive topic as judgement is involved, often without taking context into consideration. When it comes to grading, some educators feel that the same policy should apply to all students. Other educators are of the belief that the grades of multilingual learners, in particular English learners, should be influenced by their overall level of English language proficiency or their lived experiences (as in Figure 6.6). Still others insist on different configurations for assigning grades according to the language allocation of their dual language program, such as 90/10 or 50/50. Finally, there are some educators who simply do not believe that grading should occur at all, especially in primary school. Here are some questions to ask different stakeholders:

For Younger Multilingual Learners

- Do you think getting a grade for your work is important? Why?

- What does a happy or sad face on your paper tell you?

- Do you like to grade yourself? Why or why not?

- What do you do best in school? How do you know?

For Older Multilingual Learners

- Do you think that grading shows what you know and can do in your different languages? Why or why not?

- How should you or your teacher evaluate work when you use two languages to communicate, as when you translanguage?

- What suggestions might you have to improve your classroom's grading practices? Should grades not be used at all?

- Do grades motivate you to do better? Why or why not?

For Teachers and Other Instructional Leaders

- How best can you report your multilingual learners' multilingualism?

- What do you do in your classroom to equalize the presence and importance of multiple languages in reporting assessment information?

- How might you give some responsibility for evaluation to your multilingual learners?

- What strategies might you try for building your multilingual learners' metacognitive, metalinguistic, and metacultural awareness?

For School Leaders

- How might you be more inclusive of family members and students in formulating a school-wide grading policy?

- Should criteria for grading be the same for all instructional languages in the school?

- How might you move away from relying on grading for student evaluation? How might you complement current grading practices?

- How might you dabble in digital reporting for assessment *of* learning on a class by class basis?

HOW MIGHT WE RESOLVE THE DILEMMA? MAKE SURE GRADING PRACTICES ARE GEARED FOR MULTILINGUAL LEARNERS

The issue of how to evaluate assessment information and report it in equitable ways will remain unresolved until educators are able to devote time and energy to re-assessing their current grading policies with multilingual learners in mind. For reporting purposes, special attention and dedicated space must be allocated for content delivered in multiple languages so that its status is as prominent as all other subject areas. Multilingual learners and their teachers should be empowered by all the accomplishments in their classrooms, and if grading is the form of delivery, then it has to be positioned for student success.

If grading is still alive and well in your school, and you feel that data from assessment of your multilingual learners in multiple languages is not fairly represented, form a committee to design a new or amend the current report card or student report. Be sure to include both student and family member representatives in the decision-making process. Take action by sending your recommendations straight to the district. And last, but not least, whatever is produced, make sure that it is available in multiple languages.

Resources for Multilingual Learners, Their Teachers, and Other Instructional Leaders

RESOURCE 6.1 FOR MULTILINGUAL LEARNERS
A Rating Scale for Evaluating Assessment Tasks and Tests

Fill out this form after you have taken a test or have completed an assessment task. For each question, put a number from 1 to 10, with 1 being the lowest (No, not at all.) and 10 the highest (Absolutely.). At the bottom or the page, you may add comments about what you would change about the assessment.

Name:_____ Date: _____ Class: _____

FROM 1 TO 10	WHAT DID YOU THINK OF THE ASSESSMENT TASK OR TEST? TO WHAT EXTENT . . .
	was it difficult?
	did it represent what was taught?
	were you able to show what you had learned?
	were you able to choose your preferred language?
	were you able to use more than one language?
	did you find illustrations, graphs, and diagrams useful?
	did you understand what to do?
	did you find it fair?
	did you do your best?

My Comments: What would you change about the test or assessment task?

RESOURCE 6.2 FOR TEACHERS AND OTHER SCHOOL LEADERS
Analyzing Grading Practices and Policies of Multilingual Learners in Multiple Languages

In teams or as a professional learning community, analyze each of the mini scenarios in terms of its feasibility and applicability to your setting. Jot down what you consider to be the positive and negative points of each. Then decide which one or combination of scenarios would work best for evaluating your multilingual learners in multiple languages.

MINI SCENARIO	POSITIVE POINTS	NEGATIVE POINTS
Sra. Sánchez grades her Latinx students in Spanish and her cooperating teacher uses the same report card to grade these students in English. Although they both use letter grades to indicate student achievement, one teacher also includes motivation and effort while the other teacher uses attendance and timeliness as factors.		
Mr. Cho and his co-teacher meet to determine one set of grades for each content area and then specify multilingual learners' language development in English and Mandarin separately.		
Multilingual learners in Ms. Jackson's room have opportunities to put their own grades alongside those of their teacher's according to criteria for success that they have agreed upon for that marking period in both their languages.		
Habib's teacher averages his homework and test scores based on percent correct, then adds a sprinkle for work habits and effort to determine grades. She marks the content areas taught in English and those in Arabic, the other language, using the identical criteria for evaluating both languages.		
The eighth-grade team decides to purposely give low grades at the beginning of the school year in both languages to motivate students to work hard up to graduation day.		

RESOURCE 6.3 FOR TEACHERS AND MULTILINGUAL LEARNERS
Think-Aloud Questions for Building Metacognitive Awareness

Choose from the following list of questions in English or Spanish to think about how you learn, in which languages you prefer to learn, and who or what helps you learn.

1. What do I know about this topic? ¿Qué sé yo sobre este tema?

2. What in my home or community helps me know about the topic? ¿Qué hay en mi casa o en mi comunidad que me ayuda a explorar este tema?

3. What information do I know in each of my languages about the topic? ¿Qué información sé en cada uno de mis idiomas sobre este tema?

4. What does what I just read or heard mean to me? ¿Qué significa lo que acabo de leer o escuchar a mi?

5. How might I use this information? ¿Cómo pudiera usar esta información?

6. Do I have a picture in my head about this information I just read or plan to write or talk about? ¿Tengo una imagen en mi mente de esta información que acabo de leer o planeo escribir o hablar?

7. How might I use illustrations and graphics to help me understand? ¿Cómo podría usar ilustraciones y gráficos para ayudarme a comprender?

8. What are the most important ideas about what I just read, heard, or wrote? ¿Qué son las ideas más importantes que acabo de leer, escuchar, o escribir?

9. What new information did I learn? ¿Qué información nueva aprendí?

10. How did I connect this new information with what I already knew? ¿Cómo conecté esta nueva información con lo que ya sabía?

RESOURCE 6.4 FOR MULTILINGUAL LEARNERS

A Self-Evaluation Tool

Write down what you need to do to meet your learning target (the criteria) in the middle column. Then put the evidence for meeting each criterion on the left. Lastly, write what else you need to do to meet that criterion on the right.

EVIDENCE THAT I MET THE CRITERION	CRITERIA FOR SUCCESS BASED ON OUR LEARNING TARGETS	WHAT ELSE I NEED TO DO
	Criterion 1:	
	Criterion 2:	
	Criterion 3:	
	Criterion 4:	
	Criterion 5:	
	Criterion 6:	
	Criterion 7:	

RESOURCE 6.5 FOR MULTILINGUAL LEARNERS

Language, Conceptual, and Social-Emotional Development for a Unit of Learning

With your teacher, fill in the boxes for each unit of learning (or use those in Figure 6.5). Have your teacher describe what's in each box. Use the rubric as a guide. When you finish each unit, mark the cell in each row that best describes what you have done to grow in English, your other language, in what you understand, and in how you feel.

Unit of Learning: _____ Date: _____

	APPRENTICING	ADVANCING	ACCELERATING	ARRIVING
My Development in English				
Development in My Other Language				
My Development of Concepts				
My Social-Emotional Development				

CHAPTER 7

Taking Action Based on Assessment Results in Multiple Languages

Empowering Language Professionals

Valoriser les Professionnels en Langues

Sprachlehrende in ihrer Rolle stärken
—European Centre for Modern Languages (2011)

The Dilemma

But assessment for multilingual learners is only in one language; what can we do to know who our students really are and what they can do?

For many multilingual learners, kindergarten is their first encounter with school. The majority have been born in the U.S. and are simultaneously developing two or more languages. Some, however, live in isolated linguistic enclaves and have had little exposure to English. Others may use English with their older siblings but also communicate in the languages of their parents and other family members.

Then there are those multilingual learners who have had the opportunity to attend preschool. These youngsters have participated in neighborhood programs, such as Head Start in local community centers. They come to kindergarten having been deemed dual language learners, although they may or may not have had interaction in languages other than English. In recent years, more and more of these multilingual learners have had early literacy experiences in two languages and have been encouraged to grow in multiple languages.

(Continued)

(Continued)

The kindergarten teachers at Washington School are joining forces to insist on furthering the language development of their multilingual learners in multiple languages. This school year they have planned on establishing multilingual language–rich classrooms in preparation for launching more formal dual language services in the upcoming year. They wish to dedicate time in building school and community resources while instilling pride in their multilingual learners' languages and cultures.

The teachers have already taken action to build relations with the community and to persuade the faculty of the benefits of establishing linguistically and culturally sustainable classrooms. The kindergarten team has had meetings with the media specialist to ensure that the school's center is packed with accessible and stimulating books, murals, and computer software in multiple languages. They have had families create posters in multiple languages with pictures of their homelands to display in the hallways. In their classrooms, the teachers have matched the kindergartners' languages and cultures with pen pals from around the world and have set up face-to-face online get-togethers to share their favorite story books.

No matter how much the kindergarten teachers have tried, they are stymied in one area—assessment. All incoming kindergartners in the school are required to take a "readiness test" in English and a kindergarten language proficiency screener in English without any attempt on the school's part to ascertain the multilingual learners' overall development across languages. Results from those tests in English are the primary pieces of information that determine initial identification as English learners, classroom placement, and eligibility for language services.

With community and faculty support, the teachers are trying to push for a schoolwide language policy that recognizes the importance and value of multiple languages and cultures to be the gateway for multilingual education from the early grades on up. By planning, collecting, interpreting, and evaluating assessment data in multiple languages, it is the sincere hope of this teacher team that their combined efforts and actions will make dual language at Washington School a reality. What other actions should the teachers take to push their agenda forward?

FIRST IMPRESSIONS

- In what ways does this scenario resonate with you?
- How might you take action at a classroom level based on inadequate or inequitable assessment information?
- How might you join forces with other educators to take action at a program or school level?
- How might you, in conjunction with family members and the community, take action to insist on assessment in multiple languages for multilingual learners?
- How might your multilingual learners take action to advocate on their own behalf?

Improving teaching and learning relies on the actions of educational stakeholders. It is teachers and other school leaders who are going to make the difference in enhancing opportunities for multilingual learners to learn and apply their learning in meaningful ways. At the same time, as educators become more aware of the strengths of multilingual learners and their many assets from which to draw from in their classrooms, their pedagogy improves. Having a school take on a linguistic and cultural sustainable stance allows multilingual learners to thrive. As we are nearing the end of this book and are better understanding the role of assessment in multiple languages, let's renew our commitment to multilingual education and the benefits it reaps.

 Stop-Think-Act-React

Relax and Reflect: Taking Action on Behalf of Multilingual Learners and Their Families

How can teachers bolster multilingual learners' confidence in their students' use of multiple languages whether instruction is in two languages or not? How can teachers encourage family members to use their language(s) to introduce and reinforce learning as well as provide stability in multilingual learners' social-emotional development? How can teachers advocate for multilingual learners in and out of school?

At grade-level meetings or through professional learning, take time to brainstorm ideas with colleagues as to how to be more inclusive of the languages and cultures of the school and community. Then bring your ideas to a faculty meeting. Prioritize those that are considered most important to you and your team as well as the school as a whole. Then create a short- and long-term action plan for advancing multilingualism and multiculturalism.

This chapter recaps how assessment in multiple languages will help realize the mission of leveraging and building on the linguistic repertoires of multilingual learners. It is the strength of the data in multiple languages coupled with the convictions and passions of multilingual learners, their families, and teachers that will push stakeholders to take action to eventually reshape our educational landscape. Through assessment *as*, *for*, and *of* learning, we invite multilingual learners and their teachers to reflect on teaching and learning to devise an action plan that makes a difference for acting on and reacting to multilingual data. And so, as shown in Figure 7.1, we enter the last phase of the assessment cycle, taking action based on assessment results.

Classroom assessment that is seamlessly embedded in instruction should ultimately embody student learning. However, we also want students to take their learning outside classroom walls. The questions thus become: (1) How can we facilitate and capture enduring learning of content and language for our multilingual learners that extends to other spaces? (2) How can we instill in our students that language and culture are expressions of their agency and identity? (3) How can we engage multilingual learners in self- and peer assessment in multiple languages that yields lasting and meaningful effects?

FIGURE 7.1 Completing the Cycle: Using Assessment Results to Take Action

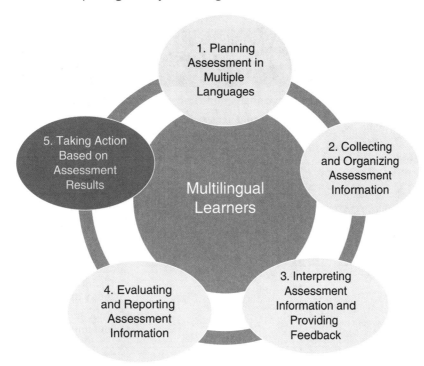

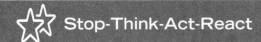

Stop-Think-Act-React

Relax and Reflect: How does the assessment cycle provide for a built-in action plan?

Each phase of the assessment cycle has a distinct purpose. Referring to Resource 7.1, think back and review what has stood out in your mind, phase by phase. What is the cumulative effect of the contribution of each phase to assessment in multiple languages? What steps have you taken along the way, and what remains to be done? How might your actions make a difference for your multilingual learners whether you are monolingual, bilingual, or multilingual?

WHAT ARE THE ASSETS THAT MULTILINGUAL LEARNERS BRING TO CLASSROOM ASSESSMENT?

Knowing and using two or more languages is a worldwide phenomenon and its power is enormous. Throughout the book we have seen how to leverage multilingual learners' languages and cultures in classroom assessment in elementary and secondary school settings. Figure 7.2 is a recap of the benefits of instruction and assessment in multiple languages for multilingual learners as a starting point for advocacy, equity, and for taking action.

FIGURE 7.2 A Summary of the Benefits of Instruction and Assessment in Multiple Languages for Multilingual Learners

ACADEMIC (COGNITIVE) DEVELOPMENT	LANGUAGE DEVELOPMENT	SOCIAL-EMOTIONAL DEVELOPMENT
• Inclusion of funds of knowledge from home and community • Access to multilingual and multicultural resources • Increased conceptual knowledge • Cognitive flexibility • More varied perspective-taking • Creativity in problem-solving • Understanding of multiple perspectives	• Growth in biliteracy • Use and acceptance of translanguaging • Increased opportunities for student interaction • Greater array of modes of communication to draw from • Exposure to cross-linguistic and cross-cultural connections • Increase reach in audiences	• Identity formation • Metalinguistic, metacognitive, and metacultural awareness • Self-efficacy and agency • Autonomy and self-regulation • Positive self-image and self-confidence • Strong connection to family and community • Greater effort and motivation to learn • Pride in multilingualism and multiculturalism

 Stop-Think-Act-React

Relax and Reflect: How can we reach out to others to take action on behalf of multilingual learners?

How might you take a sampling of benefits listed in Figure 7.2 to design an action plan with your multilingual learners to advance their thinking and learning in two or more languages? For example, using evidence from assessment, in what ways do the students show cognitive flexibility? To what extent does assessment in multiple languages capture multilingual learners' full breadth of bilingualism?

Teachers Taking Action on Behalf of Their Multilingual Learners (Even If Only Knowledgeable in English)

Not everyone has the fortune of being bilingual. With the current rise in the numbers of multilingual learners and the decrease in the number of qualified teachers and university teacher education programs, every educator should be aware of how to optimize multilingual learners' opportunities to succeed in school and beyond. There is no reason why teachers of multilingual learners can't be effective if they are only knowledgeable in one language, English. Equally important, there is no reason why multilingual learners cannot further their learning in the language(s) of their choice. Therefore, it is critical that monolingual teachers are aware of how to support multilingual learners in their classrooms in multiple languages as the students simultaneously navigate language and grade-level content.

In this age where multilingual learners' languages and cultures are resources for furthering learning, to the extent that students feel comfortable, they should utilize those assets during instruction and classroom assessment. Figure 7.3 catalogs some ways in which monolingual teachers can work with multilingual learners in their use of more than one language as part of the instructional and assessment flow of the classroom.

Ultimately, monolingual teachers can team with bilingual teachers or bilingual paraprofessionals to help each other and their multilingual learners gain greater access to learning content. Even if co-teaching is not in the realm of possibilities, teachers can still pair or work together to generate ideas for promoting their multilingual learners' development in multiple languages. Teachers can also form an online network among themselves and generate/share documents. Having a partner or small group of colleagues with whom to take action steps will most likely increase the potential of enacting a plan for furthering multilingual learners' multilingual development.

FIGURE 7.3 What Monolingual Teachers and Multilingual Learners Can Do to Optimize Multiple Language Use in Instruction and Classroom Assessment

HOW MONOLINGUAL TEACHERS CAN TAKE ACTION TO ENCOURAGE MULTILINGUAL LEARNERS' MULTIPLE LANGUAGE USE	HOW MULTILINGUAL LEARNERS CAN TAKE ACTION USING MULTIPLE LANGUAGES
<ul><li>Ask thought-provoking questions.</li><li>Recruit family and community members as volunteers and role models.</li><li>Provide access to multimodal communication.</li><li>Maximize multilingual learners' opportunities to engage in rigorous content.</li><li>Support multilingual learners' language choice(s).</li><li>Incorporate others' languages, cultures, and perspectives into instruction and assessment,</li><li>Provide opportunities for multilingual learners to connect content to their families and community.</li><li>Encourage multilingual learners to show evidence of learning through multimodal communication.</li><li>Nurture multilingual learners' social-emotional development.</li><li>Teach in linguistically and culturally sustainable ways.</li><li>Bring in multilingual speakers (e.g., form a speaker's bureau) and mentors.</li><li>Provide multilingual and multicultural resources.</li></ul>	<ul><li>Engage in partner work in shared languages.</li><li>Collaborate with peers before, during, and after school on meeting learning targets.</li><li>Engage in problem-solving or negotiate issues.</li><li>Explore multilingual resources, including technology.</li><li>Investigate or pursue topics of interest.</li><li>Brainstorm, outline, and draft essays or reports.</li><li>Paraphrase or summarize information (e.g., directions).</li><li>Respect peers' languages, cultures, and perspectives.</li><li>Clarify misunderstandings of peers.</li><li>Probe deeper into content.</li><li>Use multimodal communication to increase access to and understanding of content (e.g., podcasts or videos).</li><li>Be mentors and teachers to others.</li><li>Connect to each other's lives and the community.</li><li>Provide descriptive feedback to each other.</li><li>Reflect on learning orally, in writing, or graphically.</li><li>Engage in self- and peer assessment.</li></ul>

Relax and Reflect: How can monolingual teachers take action on behalf of their multilingual learners?

When co-teaching multilingual learners, more often than not, one of the teachers is monolingual. Another common situation is having a language teacher (e.g., English language development or English as an additional language teacher) or paraprofessional work in an array of content classrooms. Whether you are monolingual or multilingual, what can you do to further your multilingual learners' language development in multiple languages? Use Figure 7.3 to jumpstart some ideas for your classroom or your team.

HOW MIGHT WE STRENGTHEN YOUR STANCE FOR TAKING ACTION THROUGH ASSESSMENT *AS*, *FOR*, AND *OF* LEARNING?

Taking action should be a collaborative adventure for students or students and teachers after they have had opportunities to evaluate results from assessment. Teachers and other school leaders should think about how assessment *as*, *for*, and *of* learning in multiple languages can make a difference for their classrooms and school. Figure 7.4 describes the roles of stakeholders and their investment in assessment results by suggesting ways for applying data in one or more languages from classroom assessment to new situations.

FIGURE 7.4 Taking Action Based on Results From Assessment *as*, *for*, and *of* Learning

ASSESSMENT *AS* LEARNING... STUDENTS SHARE WITH EACH OTHER:	ASSESSMENT *FOR* LEARNING... STUDENTS AND TEACHERS WORK ON:	ASSESSMENT *OF* LEARNING... TEACHERS, OTHER SCHOOL LEADERS, AND STUDENTS STRIVE TO:
• Ideas during discussions in multiple languages to decide a course of action • Presentation of assessment data in multiple languages to other audiences as evidence of success • Personal reflections of their work and planning for what to do next • Options for leading with data; taking initiatives and risks based on assessment results	• Setting individualized action plans in one or more languages based on agreed upon goals • Involving the community in the design of new projects in multiple languages • Providing actionable feedback or agreeing on criteria of success for moving learning forward • Figuring next steps based on assessment results in relation to learning targets	• Become assessment literate on behalf of multilingual communities • Apply assessment results to multimodal models in multiple languages • Value and use assessment information in multiple languages to set new goals for learning • Determine the impact of students' projects on their lives and learning

Our commitment to equity for multilingual learners is illustrated throughout the book through assessment *as*, *for*, and *of* learning. This comprehensive approach values the roles of students, teachers, and other school leaders in the assessment process. It begins with co-planning when teachers and students co-construct learning goals and targets from language and content standards to match their essential questions. They then set criteria for success for those goals that are illustrated by models or examples of exemplary student work. Classroom assessment, an ongoing activity, is marked by interaction among students as well as between teachers and students with frequent actionable feedback to improve teaching and learning.

Figure 7.5 offers some guidance for teachers as seen through the lens of assessment *as*, *for*, and *of* learning for multilingual learners for each phase of the cycle. This synopsis offers a balance of assessment approaches in multiple languages that can be enacted in classrooms throughout the year. Resource 7.2 is a blank figure for you or your team to address how the assessment process can unfold in multiple languages for your multilingual learners.

FIGURE 7.5 Ideas for Assessment *as, for,* and *of* Learning for Each Phase of the Cycle With Considerations for Multiple Languages

PHASE	IN ASSESSMENT *AS* LEARNING	IN ASSESSMENT *FOR* LEARNING	IN ASSESSMENT *OF* LEARNING
1. Planning Assessment	• Think about how to directly involve multilingual learners. • Introduce and maintain student choice in language use.	• Think about how to include language-rich activities for instruction and assessment. • Design a classroom policy for multiple language use.	• Think about how to use multiple languages in final projects. • Pair assessment with the languages of instruction.
2. Collecting and Organizing Information	• Facilitate students' co-construction of learning experiences with peers in their preferred languages.	• Decide on types of evidence for learning with students in one or more languages.	• Ensure reliability of student work for the given purpose for assessment.
3. Analyzing and Interpreting Information	• Allow for student voice in the sharing of their linguistic and cultural perspectives.	• Match student performance against mutually agreed upon **success criteria**.	• Determine student growth (in multiple languages) based on descriptors (e.g., rubrics).
4. Evaluating and Reporting Information	• Let students have input in evaluation-related decisions across languages (e.g., grading).	• Exchange information with students (e.g., through conferencing and feedback).	• Revisit learning goals and learning targets with students in relation to standards and associated evidence.

(Continued)

FIGURE 7.5 (Continued)

PHASE	IN ASSESSMENT *AS* LEARNING	IN ASSESSMENT *FOR* LEARNING	IN ASSESSMENT *OF* LEARNING
5. Taking Action	Engage students in authentic meaningful activities that potentially make a difference in their lives and impact their community.	Use assessment data to enhance learning experiences for students and share results with other stakeholders to make joint decisions.	Conduct action research sparked by assessment results.

Assessment *as* Learning

In assessment *as* learning, students own the assessment process. In taking action, multilingual learners must be able to articulate their learning targets and their plans to accomplish them. In their classrooms, multilingual learners articulate what success looks like (in multiple languages), use oral or written feedback to discover where they are in relation to where they want to be, and determine what they need to do next. As multilingual learners become increasingly proficient in language, literacy, and content, they learn to generate and give concrete descriptive feedback or co-construct and set goals with peers to steer their learning adventure.

Self-assessment is a powerful tool in that it serves as an indicator of understanding which is a precursor to the transfer of learning to new and novel situations (Wiggins & McTighe, 2005). Along the way, students gain confidence in who they are and are able to take action on their own behalf. Multilingual learners hopefully have opportunities on a regular basis to engage in self-assessment in the language(s) of their choice. As part of their social-emotional development and identify formation, multilingual learners are mindful that there is value in their use of multiple languages, including translanguaging or other multimodal representations, to express their feelings. Equally important, students are gaining access to an increasing number of resources and strategies to reflect and act on their academic endeavors.

Assessment *for* Learning

In assessment *for* learning, teachers and students are partners. When dealing with multiple languages, there also must be a shared understanding of the appropriateness of language use such as where and when translanguaging fits into instruction and assessment. Assessment *for* learning is often dialogic, meaning it enables students and teachers to share information interactively. Therefore, it is an approach whereby both participants can immediately use feedback to take action to improve teaching and learning in specific ways.

To enable all students to become more productive and engaged learners, educators need to move from reliance on assessment that verifies or documents learning to assessment that supports learning (in multiple languages)—in essence, assessment *for* learning (Stiggins, 2007). By having students become consumers of assessment information, that is, understanding the implications for what they say and do, they tend to become proactive in taking on responsibility for their own actions. In the context of school, multilingual learners must be mindful of the interplay between their languages and cultures, in essence, how to further their overall development within and across languages.

Assessment *of* Learning

Student products, performances, or projects at the culmination of units of learning demonstrate the extent to which multilingual learners have reached their goal(s) or learning targets. That information yields how students might take a concrete action step for new learning. Many schools rely on **backward design** or **Understanding by Design** (Wiggins & McTighe, 2005) for crafting and enacting curriculum. This framework jumpstarts assessment *of* learning by placing long-term desired results or expectations as the first stage in the process. In essence, curriculum development flows into classroom assessment, which produces the evidence, which, in turn, informs a learning plan.

Having teachers and other school leaders plan an evidence-based course of action and carry it out through curriculum is quite a demanding undertaking. Whenever multilingual learners are members of the student body, there must be specific time devoted to ensuring equity, that is, fair representation of their languages, cultures, and experiences to optimize opportunities for their participation in school and classroom activities. If multilingual learners' "funds of identity" and "funds of knowledge" are neither considered relevant to curriculum nor connected to school life, it will be a challenge for students to act proactively.

 Stop-Think-Act-React

Relax and Reflect: How does assessment *as*, *for*, and *of* learning strengthen your position for taking action?

Taken together, data from assessment *as, for,* and *of* learning can provide a strong body of evidence for taking next steps for curriculum and instruction. How might you pool assessment results from these three approaches with your team to make recommendations or substantiate a multilingual position? As a group, jot down the role that each assessment approach plays in making classroom-related decisions, with special attention to your multilingual learners.

HOW MIGHT WE TAKE ACTION THROUGH REFLECTIVE PRACTICE?

Do you ever sit back and think about your students' reaction to an activity or a lesson? If you are like me, you have even awakened in the middle of the night with thoughts for how your teaching might have been more effective. How can teachers improve their craft, especially when it comes to assessment of multilingual learners in multiple languages? What can they do individually and collectively to create an alliance that promotes multilingualism and multiculturalism in classrooms and throughout a school?

Reflective Practices of Teachers and Multilingual Learners

The notion of evidence-based reflective practice goes back to the early thinking of John Dewey almost a century ago. As part of his progressive education ideology, Dewey (1933) stated that "reflection is something that is believed in, not on its own account, but through something else which stands as evidence" (p. 8). Traditionally, reflective practice in education has been a space for allowing teachers and other school leaders to respond in writing to a variety of issues. However, Mann and Walsh (2017) expand that notion to be more data-driven collaboration between teachers that is an interactive and dialogic "reflection in action."

Another example of prompting reflective practice of teachers and other school leaders of multilingual learners is through action statements that spark teacher planning, enacting, and evaluating language learning (Gottlieb, 2013; Robertson, 2014). It is a call to take action and collaborate in the design and enactment of standards-referenced curriculum, instruction, and assessment. This resource (with the Actions in Resource 7.4) is intended to help individual teachers and teacher teams evaluate instructional practices for all students, including multilingual learners, according to research-based principles.

Encouraging reflective practice of multilingual learners and other students as a form of self-assessment is a rather recent occurrence. Reflective practice might be represented by students' thinking themselves as mathematicians, scientists, historians, or writers while engaged in instruction and assessment (Murphy, 2011). For multilingual learners, reflective practice also encompasses investigation of their growing metalinguistic and metacultural awareness as an avenue to forming their identities and informing their social-emotional development.

Reflective practice that centers on multiple language use enables multilingual learners to think deeply about which language they use, with whom, and when or under which circumstances (as in the language surveys in Chapter 2). Once multilingual learners have a stronger sense of how they language, then they might be introspective and probe more deeply by:

- summarizing My Language Portrait in Chapter 2 at the beginning and end of a semester and comparing instances of language use

- analyzing ongoing diaries of their language practices

- crafting multimedia memoirs or creating a memoir of the class

- producing videos or photo albums of everyday life

- reflecting on the impact of language use throughout the neighborhood or with family members

- writing an autobiography from a language use perspective or from a perspective of feelings toward use of languages stemming from pivotal events in their lives.

Relax and Reflect: How can you best capture multilingual learners' reflections?

Reflective practices of multilingual learners stimulate their thinking about their linguistic repertoire, their language choices in communicating with others, and self-assessment of their language practices. How might the ideas in the previous bulleted list be useful for documenting multilingual learners' social-emotional development in addition to their language development?

Action Research by Teachers Throughout the Assessment Cycle

More and more, teachers and students are being recognized as leaders in their own right and are relying on a more actionable model for classroom assessment. One area in which these stakeholders shine is showing their creativity in action research. **Action research** is a reflective process that revolves around inquiry of a self-identified question or a group's pressing issue. The question is of immediate concern to teaching or assessment, and its resolution serves as a means for instilling change and improvement in everyday practices.

Action research follows a series of phases, much like those in the assessment cycle. As outlined in Resource 7.3 for teachers to explore, action research includes:

1. selecting an issue for investigation and identifying its potential impact

2. posing relevant questions of personal importance

3. identifying sources of information and gathering data

4. analyzing and interpreting the information

5. giving feedback, drawing conclusions, and reporting results

6. acting on evidence and deciding on a course of action.

While a teacher may work independently on personal dilemmas or perhaps as a member of a professional learning community, teachers may also collaborate in their research. For example, when it comes to assessment in multiple languages, it would be ideal for dual language teachers to work together or for language and content teachers to be thinking partners. There are a number of resources that can also be tapped as part of action research, including the support of administrators, the guidance of teacher educators or researchers, the advice of test developers, and the expertise of community members. By investing in the power of inquiry, teachers are able to take action to steer their own course for improving their craft.

Teachers could center their action research on issues that directly impact the treatment and achievement of multilingual learners. In that way, the entire educational community could benefit from the findings. Here are some questions that teachers of multilingual learners might pose for action research:

- To what extent do our multilingual learners feel connected to the languages and cultures of their families? To what extent does learning in two languages help strengthen that bond?

- What actions can we take to support our multilingual multicultural community, and what are areas of expertise of our students' families?

- How can we document translanguaging as it occurs among multilingual learners? How can it lead to empowering multilingual learners and in what ways?

- How can we become a more effective dual language teacher team?

- What are some strategies for assessing in two languages that yield the most useful information about our multilingual learners?

- How can assessment in multiple languages strengthen evidence of student learning?

- How can multilingual learners play a more active role in classroom assessment?

- What are the pros and cons of partnerships or **co-teaching** between content and language teachers when it comes to assessment in multiple languages?

- How might we improve the educational equity of multilingual learners in our school? How might it bring about social justice?

☆ Stop-Think-Act-React

Relax and Reflect: How can older multilingual learners pursue action research?

Older multilingual learners' perceptions of equity or inequity, their feelings toward their multiple languages and cultures, their relationships with peers and family members, and their growing identities are ripe for action research. Chances are that student vestment in this multistep process will build their self-esteem, self-confidence, and social-emotional development. Take time with your students to devise questions of personal interest, assist them in pursuing a plan for conducting their research and deciding on a mode of communication for presenting the results to others.

Questioning by Students in Multiple Languages

As we have seen in both academic content standards and action research, inquiry is at the heart of teaching and learning. For teachers of multilingual learners, questioning might center on policy and practice of instruction and assessment in multiple languages. Older multilingual learners may wish to delve into identity formation or relationship building through personal reflection and action. On the front end, questioning can jumpstart investigation into a unit of learning, but it also can be at the back end when it's time to evaluate the extent to which the question has been answered.

Because questioning at the planning phase of the assessment cycle should be revisited at the close of the assessment process, here are some examples of how a dual language (Spanish–English) school in Colorado employs questioning to stimulate investigation of different themes.

> Students are generating their own questions about beavers in first grade (see Figure 7.6), *esfuerzo y moción* in second grade, author's craft in third grade, multiplying large numbers in fourth grade, European colonization in fifth grade, *las complejidades de las ecuaciones lineales* in sixth grade, *la tabla periódica de elementos* in seventh grade, and the Constitution of the United States in eighth grade. (Rewold, 2019, pp. 2–3)

If themes of this nature were adopted by your class to explore in depth, how might you and your students evaluate their impact at the close of the unit? What

FIGURE 7.6 A Sample First-Grade Unit of Learning Following the Phases of the Assessment Cycle

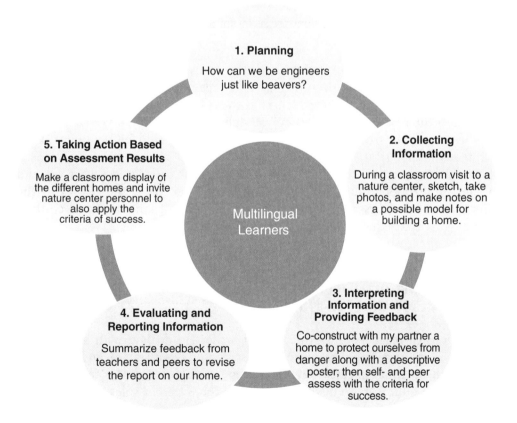

kinds of projects, performances, or products would you design to answer their questions? What would you be your criteria of success?

Let's take the unit about beavers for first graders and follow it through the assessment cycle (see Figure 7.6) using the source material https://www.readworks.org/article/All-About-Beavers/b689a464-b811-4bb2-9730-e4b5e839e47e#! articleTab: content/, which includes a video and short text in English.

Essential Questions, one of the hallmarks by Understanding by Design, help organize curriculum around big ideas. Essential Questions are thought-provoking, inquiry-based, and intended to spark more questions in order for students to develop a plan or course of action, make a decision, or direct a course of research (McTighe & Wiggins, 2013). In the world of multilingual education, however, more attention needs to be paid to the roles of language and culture in learning. Example Essential Questions might include the following: How can I describe peoples and cultures without stereotyping them? How can knowing more than one language be beneficial to me when I graduate? What are some examples of translanguaging in children's books?

BECOMING ASSESSMENT LITERATE: A SCHOOLWIDE ACTION

Assessment literacy is an individual's understanding of the fundamental concepts and procedures of assessment that most likely influence educational decisions (Popham, 2018). In our context, it includes the knowledge of how to gather and analyze information on what students know and can do in multiple languages, interpret and report the results in equitable ways, and apply the results to improve the quality and effectiveness of multilingual education. The set of beliefs, knowledge, and practices associated with assessment literacy has become so integral to schooling that there are assessment literacy standards (Michigan Assessment Consortium, 2020).

"If language teachers are to understand the forces that impact upon the institutions for which they work and their daily teaching practices, and to have a measure of control over the effects that these have, it is important for them to develop their assessment literacy" (Fulcher, 2012, p.114). Given the contexts in which classroom assessment operates, we would be negligent if we didn't acknowledge the role of assessment in the educational system as a whole (at least at the school level) and the impact of related directives and policies on teachers. One area we have not touched on is the reality of the other side of the assessment *of* learning coin—annual language and content testing—one that educators face, often with trepidation.

STRENGTH IN ACTION FOR LARGE-SCALE ASSESSMENT *OF* LEARNING

The tensions of teachers and other school leaders in dealing with all facets of assessment are unmistakable, especially for those tests that are high stakes in nature with potential negative consequences for students and/or teachers. It is important for educators to distinguish among the different roles, purposes, and audiences of classroom assessment aimed at improving teaching and learning while simultaneously abiding by often contradictory accountability requirements of their school, district, and state (Gottlieb & Honigsfeld, 2020). Imagine the added pressure on teachers when instruction is in two languages and assessment is expected to follow suit, yet state and local accountability tends to be one-sided and in one language—English.

Federal policy stemming from legislation and second language acquisition theory have historically leaned toward the use of one language, English, for assessing multilingual learners in K–12 settings on an annual basis. In general, the field of large-scale language testing across the globe has been built from a monolingual (English) perspective and construct. Rather than embracing the use of multiple languages, test developers and psychometricians alike have feared that an English language test could be potentially contaminated by another language, resulting in diminishing the **validity** of test claims.

However, it's a new era. Demographic shifts (including mobility of student populations worldwide), changing theoretical perspectives, and emerging research-based pedagogies have introduced multiple language use as an accepted occurrence in testing. In addition, there is a real-world demand that standardized language testing considers multilingual constructs and the inclusion of languages other than English to facilitate improved assessment of content and language use. The time has come to expand the theoretical foundations of language assessment to welcome and be inclusive of integrated multilingual testing constructs and translanguaging pedagogies (Chalhoub-Deville, 2019).

We must dispel the notion that the sole means of accountability for learning in typical dual language classrooms with multilingual learners still rests only in English. By definition, the "other" language is of equal value and should contribute its equal share for how we measure language development and achievement. That's where assessment *of* learning in large-scale contexts can make a difference. If we could use measures in multiple languages as the yardstick for multilingual growth, we would have a more accurate portrait of our students now and over time.

HOW CAN STAKEHOLDERS TAKE ACTION BASED ON ASSESSMENT RESULTS?

Each stakeholder group is going to use assessment results, in English, in other languages, or through translanguaging, in different ways for different purposes. Figure 7.7, along with Resources 7.5 and 7.6, names the closest stakeholders who can make a difference in the education of multilingual learners and provides space for thinking how to take action based on classroom assessment in multiple languages.

Resource 7.7 allows for combining results from multiple measures—**large-scale assessment** of language proficiency and achievement with classroom assessment *as, for,* and *of* learning—to yield a student snapshot. The information from various sources allows for more comprehensive and appropriate actions by teachers and other school leaders.

FIGURE 7.7 How Different Stakeholder Groups Can Take Action Based on Assessment Results

WHAT MULTILINGUAL LEARNERS CAN DO	WHAT FAMILY MEMBERS AND COMMUNITIES CAN DO	WHAT TEACHERS AND OTHER SCHOOL LEADERS CAN DO
• Form a pact with teachers to move learning forward using multiple languages • Use feedback to reset goals for learning • Commit to community service based on personal and academic interests • Connect family assets and community resources to school • Partner with shared language peers to work together toward learning goals	• Share their expertise, languages, and cultures in classrooms • Use one or more languages every day to be models for and teach their children • Give their children social-emotional support • Understand the role of language development in learning • Be language and cultural ambassadors • Advocate on behalf of the languages and cultures of multilingual learners	• Set multilingual learners up for success by respecting multiple language use • Create a classroom/school environment that allows students to take risks with language • Encourage students to pursue their dreams • Create professional learning communities around multilingual issues • Form networks with teachers around the world to discuss multilingual multicultural issues of interest

Stop-Think-Act-React

Relax and Reflect: How can we better connect assessment results to action?

As an educator, how might you enact one of the suggested actions in Figure 7.7? Brainstorm with others as to how to equitably deal with classroom or large-scale assessment results when discussing them with multilingual learners, their families, or even colleagues. How might you engage other stakeholders in taking action to improve educational opportunities for multilingual learners based on assessment results? For example, how might you revisit classroom assessment policies or form committees to investigate specific issues?

Taking Action: Infusing Multilingualism and Multiculturalism in Curriculum, Instruction, and Classroom Assessment

Schools have evolved substantially to respond to the changing demographic trends (Stiggins, 2007) while teachers and other school leaders are becoming more sensitive to the research on language learning. Findings substantiate the benefits of multilingualism and urge multilingual learners to continue their development in multiple languages; at the same time teachers must encourage the use of languages other than English as an effective scaffolding device for learning (Billings & Walqui, 2017).

The education of multilingual learners is heavily influenced by politics that, more often than not, attempts to perpetuate these students' minoritized status. In addition, misunderstandings (some of which have been underscored in the opening vignettes) tend to discredit multiple language use as a threat to the power of English. As a result of these and other factors, in many places, multilingual learners have been discouraged, if not banned, from using additional languages.

Throughout the world of preK–12 education in the U.S. and beyond, we are slowing creeping from a credo of monolingualism to multilingualism (Soto & Gottlieb, 2020). The renewed interest in this ideology, although long in our history, is sparking acceptance and development of curriculum, instruction, and assessment in multiple languages. In some small way, it has taken a global pandemic for us to realize how interconnected the world and we truly are.

Teachers and school leaders alike are examining the notion of equity, realizing that language can be a leverage point for instilling social justice. As a result, multilingual learners are being afforded opportunities to continue fostering simultaneous development of multiple languages as part of schooling. It is our joint responsibility to continue to promote full participation of multilingual learners in one or more languages in classrooms, schools, homes, the community, and society at large.

HOW MIGHT WE FACE THE ISSUE? TAKE ACTION TO MAKE ASSESSMENT EQUITABLE FOR MULTILINGUAL LEARNERS!

As we close out the assessment cycle before starting it anew, let's recount the ways in which our major stakeholder groups can be ongoing participants in the process and carry it forward. When we now think about assessment in multiple languages, hopefully it conjures up myriad ideas for how to enhance and sustain multilingual development of our multilingual learners through evidence-based practices. Equity should be a tenet that permeates the assessment cycle. It is especially important when it's time for evaluating and reporting data on multilingual learners as that is when monolingual bias or an anglo-centric perspective can come creeping through. Here are some final questions to ponder.

For Younger Multilingual Learners

- What can you do to show how you learn in different ways?

- How does knowing more than one language help you learn?

- Why is knowing more than one language important to you?

- How does knowing more than one language make you proud? How do you show it?

For Older Multilingual Learners

- How might you use what you have learned in more than one language to further your learning?

- How does using English and your other language help you plan for the future?

- What can you and your classmates do to increase the acceptance of multiple languages and cultures in your school?

- What suggestions do you have to improve assessment in multiple languages in your classroom?

For Teachers and Other Instructional Leaders

- How can you build on the assets of your multilingual learners, in particular, their languages, cultures, and experiences during instruction and assessment?

- What checks and balances have you put into place that ensure representation of multiple languages in assessment *as*, *for*, and *of* learning?

- What does equity mean to you for assessment in multiple languages?

- How might you engage in reflective practice independently and with colleagues so that you are always growing professionally?

For School Leaders

- How can you facilitate teachers taking action to improve their pedagogical and assessment practices for multilingual learners in one or more languages?

- How can you coordinate an action plan that involves changing assessment practices for students and teachers?

- What steps can you take to ensure that your action plan becomes operationalized?

- How can you sustain linguistically and culturally responsive assessment throughout your school?

HOW MIGHT WE RESOLVE THE DILEMMA? ASSESS MULTILINGUAL LEARNERS IN MULTIPLE LANGUAGES!

Multilingual learners, by virtue of housing multiple languages and cultures in their souls, are very special people with tremendous potential. As educators, it is our responsibility to elicit and nurture multilingual learners' unique linguistic and cultural qualities whether instruction is in their languages or not. This principle extends to classroom assessment—allow multilingual learners choices in their language use even though teachers may not have that linguistic flexibility.

Returning to the opening vignette of this chapter, we see a kindergarten team that is knowledgeable of the importance of building on multilingual learners' cognitive, linguistic, cultural, and social-emotional foundations at a young age to further the students' overall development. As teachers and other school leaders create an alliance to instill multilingualism and multiculturalism through sound instructional and assessment practices, we can inspire multilingual learners, help shape their identities, and let their voices be heard.

▶ Taking action in São Paulo, Brazil: Preserve nature's smile: recycle!

In this book, we have illustrated an assessment cycle for ensuring equity for multilingual learners by optimizing their use of multiple languages as a leverage for learning. We have sought to have more learner-centered classroom assessment that showcases multilingual learners' assets and encourages them to lead through agency and authority. In addition, we have shared the urgency, literature, and evidence for endorsing multimodal approaches of communication and languages as central to classroom assessment to offset the one language (English), one form (**standardized testing**) norm that has dominated K–12 education. Just as in the photo where São Paulo urges its citizens to take action to conserve its natural resources, so, too, can we transform education through our actions to safeguard our most precious resources—the languages and cultures of our multilingual learners.

Resources for Multilingual Learners, Teachers, and Other School Leaders

RESOURCE 7.1 FOR TEACHERS AND OTHER INSTRUCTIONAL LEADERS
Making Assessment Plans for Assessment in Multiple Languages

How might you envision the assessment cycle through the lens of multiple languages? Think about how you might enact each phase with your multilingual learners in mind.

PHASE OF THE ASSESSMENT CYCLE	MY (OUR) INITIAL REACTION AND PROPOSED ACTIONS FOR CHANGING ASSESSMENT PRACTICES FOR MULTILINGUAL LEARNERS IN ONE OR MORE LANGUAGES
1. Planning Assessment	
2. Collecting and Organizing Information	
3. Analyzing and Interpreting Information	
4. Evaluating and Reporting Information	
5. Taking Action	

RESOURCE 7.2 FOR TEACHERS AND OTHER INSTRUCTIONAL LEADERS

Assessment *as, for,* and *of* Learning in Multiple Languages Throughout the Assessment Cycle

How can you incorporate multiple languages in the assessment cycle? For each phase, write down some ideas to apply assessment *as, for,* and *of* learning in one or multiple languages.

PHASE OF THE ASSESSMENT CYCLE	IN ASSESSMENT *AS* LEARNING	IN ASSESSMENT *FOR* LEARNING	IN ASSESSMENT *OF* LEARNING
1. Planning Assessment			
2. Collecting and Organizing Information			
3. Analyzing and Interpreting Information			
4. Evaluating and Reporting Information			
5. Taking Action			

RESOURCE 7.3 FOR TEACHERS AND OTHER SCHOOL LEADERS

Engaging in Action Research

Independently, with a partner, a grade-level team, or professional learning community, decide on an important issue related to multilingual education that you wish to pursue. Here are the steps you may wish to follow over the course of a semester to conduct action research.

STEPS FOR ACTION RESEARCH	WHAT I (WE) PLAN TO DO	TIME FRAME
1. Identify an issue or a focus for investigation and its potential impact.		
2. Pose questions to explore.		
3. Gather relevant data.		
4. Analyze and interpret the information.		
5. Give feedback and report results.		
6. Act on evidence and decide on a course of action.		

RESOURCE 7.4 FOR TEACHERS AND OTHER SCHOOL LEADERS

Taking Action Classroom by Classroom

WIDA Essential Actions (Gottlieb, 2013)

Think about the implications of these essential actions for instruction and assessment in multiple languages and how you might enact change in your grade, department, or school.

ACTION 1	ACTION 2	ACTION 3
Capitalize on the resources and experiences that ELLs bring to school to build and enrich their academic language.	Analyze the academic language demands involved in grade-level teaching and learning.	Plan differentiated language instruction around the conceptual knowledge and language development of ELLs.
ACTION 4	ACTION 5	ACTION 6
Connect language and content to make learning relevant and meaningful for ELLs.	Focus on the developmental nature of language learning within grade-level curriculum.	Reference content standards and language development standards in planning for language learning.
ACTION 7	ACTION 8	ACTION 9
Design language teaching and learning with attention to the sociocultural context.	Provide opportunities for all ELLs to engage in higher-order thinking.	Create language-rich classroom environments with ample time for language practice and use.
ACTION 10	ACTION 11	ACTION 12
Identify the language needed for functional use in teaching and learning.	Plan for language teaching and learning around discipline-specific topics.	Use instructional supports to help scaffold language learning.
ACTION 13	ACTION 14	ACTION 15
Integrate language domains to provide rich, authentic instruction.	Coordinate and collaborate in planning for language and content teaching and learning.	Share responsibility so that all teachers are language teachers and support one another within communities of practice.

RESOURCE 7.5 FOR MULTILINGUAL LEARNERS

What Students Can Do: Taking Action Based on Classroom Assessment Results

Use this form as a learning log every time you start a new unit of learning. Write down (1) the date and the name of the unit, (2) the theme or essential question, and (3) your learning goal. As you work through your unit, make note of (4) the evidence you are collecting and (5) the feedback from your teacher or peers. Finally, think about (6) what you plan to do based on the feedback.

DATE: UNIT:	THEME OR ESSENTIAL QUESTION:		
My Learning Goal	My Evidence of Learning	Feedback From Teachers or Peers	What I Plan to Do Next

DATE: UNIT:	THEME OR ESSENTIAL QUESTION:		
My Learning Goal	My Evidence of Learning	Feedback From Teachers or Peers	What I Plan to Do Next

RESOURCE 7.6 FOR TEACHERS AND OTHER SCHOOL LEADERS

Taking Action on Behalf of Multilingual Learners

Stakeholders can make a difference in the education and lives of students. For each group, generate some ideas for how assessment results in multiple languages can enhance opportunities for multilingual learners to succeed in school.

STAKEHOLDER GROUP	POTENTIAL ACTION BASED ON ASSESSMENT RESULTS IN MULTIPLE LANGUAGES
Content Teachers	
Language Teachers	
Other School Leaders (e.g., Coaches)	
Administrators (e.g., principals)	
The Community	

RESOURCE 7.7 FOR TEACHERS AND OTHER SCHOOL LEADERS

Taking Action Based on Assessment Results

Ideally schools have digital platforms to store and use annual student, interim, and classroom data. Six Parts (I-VI) provide an overview of the kinds of information from various data sources that may be useful to input and store from year to year.

School Year: _____ Grade Level: _____

Part I. Annual English Language Proficiency Testing:

Results for _____ Overall Composite: _____

LANGUAGE DOMAIN(S)	SCALE SCORE	LANGUAGE PROFICIENCY LEVEL	ACTION STEP
Listening			
Speaking			
Reading			
Writing			
Oral Language			
Literacy			

CLASSROOM ASSESSMENT IN MULTIPLE LANGUAGES

Part II. Action Steps for Classroom Assessment *as*, *for*, and *of* Learning of Language Development in One or More Languages

ASSESSMENT *AS* LEARNING	ASSESSMENT *FOR* LEARNING	ASSESSMENT *OF* LEARNING
Activities:	Activities/ Tasks:	Projects:
Evidence and Next Steps:	Evidence and Next Steps:	Evidence and Next Steps:

Part III. Annual Achievement Testing in Grades 3–8 and Once in High School: Classroom Results

CONTENT AREA	SCALE SCORE	PROFICIENCY LEVEL	ACTION STEP
English Language Arts/Reading			
Mathematics			
Science			

Part IV. Interim or Annual Achievement Testing in Languages Other Than English

Date: _____ Language: _____

CONTENT AREA	RESULTS	ACTION STEP
Language Arts/ Reading		
Mathematics		
Science		

V. Action Steps for Classroom Assessment *as*, *for*, and *of* Learning of Conceptual Development in One or More Language

ASSESSMENT *AS* LEARNING	ASSESSMENT *FOR* LEARNING	ASSESSMENT *OF* LEARNING
Activities:	Activities/ Tasks:	Projects:
Evidence and Next Steps:	Evidence and Next Steps:	Evidence and Next Steps:

VI. Overall Summary of Data and Recommendations:

CLASSROOM ASSESSMENT IN MULTIPLE LANGUAGES

Glossary

Academic content standards: the skills and knowledge descriptive of student expectations in school, generally for each grade, such as for English language arts/reading, mathematics, science, and social studies

Accountability: holding educational stakeholders responsible for the performance of students, teachers, programs, schools, or districts

Achievement testing: measuring students' level of knowledge, skills, and concepts in the content areas

Action research: a reflective process involving inquiry and discussion of pressing issues experienced in school as a means for instilling change and improvement in everyday practices

Assessment *as* learning: an approach in which students are agents of their own learning shown through self-reflection to show evidence against personal goals and criteria for success and communication of their learning to others

Assessment *for* learning: an approach in which teachers, along with students, plan and use evidence that is internal to their classroom and provide one another descriptive, criterion-referenced feedback to improve teaching and learning

Assessment literacy: the knowledge about how to assess what students know and can do, interpret the results of these measures, and apply results to enhance student learning and program effectiveness

Assessment *of* learning (summative assessment): (1) an approach in which school leaders and administrators use data external to the classroom, such as that from high-stakes tests, to report on students' language growth and achievement; and (2) an approach in which teachers and students design end-of-unit products, performances, and projects along with acceptable evidence based on criteria for success

Assets-based orientation: a strength-based mindset where multilingual learners' languages, cultures, and resources are viewed in a positive light

Backward design: a three-part curriculum framework that begins with the end in mind, meaning, (1) identify the goals for learning, (2) determine the evidence for meeting the goals, and (3) craft matching instructional activities

Classroom assessment: an iterative process that is part of curriculum and instruction where there is an ongoing dynamic interaction among stakeholders in the gathering, analysis, interpretation, and reporting of information from multiple sources over time based on standards, learning targets, or goals

Cognates: words from different languages with similar meaning that is derived from the same word family (e.g., appreciate–apreciar)

Co-teaching: two or more educators working together and sharing the responsibility for planning, instructing, and assessing students

Cross-cultural considerations: the application of cultural assumptions from one language and culture to another one

Cross-linguistic transfer: the analysis and application of features from one language to a related one by multilinguals (e.g., cognates, discourse structures)

Curriculum design: a way of organizing learning experiences that are relevant, meaningful, and inclusive of students and their resources

Deficit ideology: a negative mindset, often referred to as a medical model, where multilingual learners' languages, cultures, and resources are viewed as barriers to their educational success

Descriptive feedback: a formative assessment strategy whereby students gain understanding of their performance in relation to integrated learning targets or criteria for success by teachers or peers

Digital mode of communication: making meaning by navigating, collecting, and evaluating information using a range of technologies, including computers, the internet, educational software, and cell phones

Dual language education: an enrichment or additive educational model in which multilingual learners are learning in English and a partner language for minimally half a day, generally through elementary school grades

Dual language learners: multilingual learners who are participating in dual language education programs in kindergarten through Grade 8 or any and all multilingual learners participating in early childhood education during prekindergarten years

Emergent bilinguals: persons who have the potential of becoming knowledgeable in two languages; also known as English learners or multilingual learners

English learners (ELs): the legal term for a heterogeneous group of multilingual learners who are exposed to multiple languages and cultures, have not reached academic parity with their English-proficient peers, and through assessment, qualify for language support services; also known as English language learners

English learners with disabilities: multilingual learners who have been dually identified and qualify for language support and also have an Individualized Education Program (IEP)

Equity: the provision for each and every student to have access to personalized educational resources, regardless of race, gender, sexual orientation, disability, ethnicity, language, religion, family background, or family income

Every Student Succeeds Act (ESSA): the U.S. Department of Education 2015 reauthorization of the Elementary and Secondary Education Act whereby states or consortia are to have content standards, minimally in reading/language arts, mathematics, and science, with corresponding English language proficiency/

development standards that are aligned to annual state testing of language proficiency in Grades K–12 and achievement in Grades 3–8 and once in high school. For the first time, a state's accountability plan under Title I accounts for multilingual learners' English language proficiency and achievement.

Feedback: descriptive concrete timely information about the performance of students or teachers to help improve teaching and learning

Formative assessment (or assessment *as* and *for* learning): providing timely, concrete, and relevant feedback and support to students related to their progress toward meeting integrated learning targets or objectives; the gathering of information during the instructional cycle for teachers to ascertain the effectiveness of their instruction

Genres: specific purposes for language use that are defined by a set of characteristics

Gifted and talented English learners: dually identified multilingual learners whose assessment of their creativity, cognitive abilities, and achievement yield exceptional results

Grading: rating or evaluation of student work, often referenced to standards or learning goals

Heritage language learners: students who come from home backgrounds with connections to multiple languages and cultures although the students themselves may not be proficient in a language other than English

Heteroglossic language ideology: one that embraces the presence and contexts of multiple language use by multilingual learners

High-stakes testing: measures that are part of accountability systems and have consequences for individual test takers (e.g., grade retention) and, at times, for teachers

Home language: preferred term over "native language" to describe multilingual learners who have been exposed to various languages in their home environment

Individualized Education Program (IEP): a legal contract between educators and family members that spells out the school's responsibility in ensuring that students with special needs receive the maximum amount of accessibility and accommodations permitted under federal law

Integrated goals for learning: combined content and language targets for long-term learning

Language development standards: grade-level cluster expectations descriptive of what multilingual learners are to do with language as part of multimodal communication

Language proficiency testing: demonstration of an English learner's competence in processing (through listening and reading) and using (through speaking and writing) language at a point in time, such as on an annual basis

Large-scale assessment: testing student progress/attainment with the same measure at the same time at the local, state, or national level

Learning goals: forms of student learning, thinking, and engagement, mutually agreed upon by students and teachers, that provide long-term pathways to academic success

Learning targets (or objectives): short-term expectations of student learning, thinking, and engagement (usually for lessons), crafted by students and teachers, that delineate pathways to academic success

Linguistic and cultural sustainability: the leveraging and preservation of languages, literacies, and other cultural practices of students and communities throughout schooling

Long-term English learners (LTELs): multilingual learners who are most likely in middle and high schools who have attended school for more than six years without attaining a threshold of academic language proficiency; generally transnational students who move back and forth between the U.S. and their family's country of origin or have received inconsistent schooling in the U.S.

Metacognitive awareness: the ability to think and reflect on one's own thinking; regulating one's own thoughts

Metacultural awareness: multilingual learners' sensitivity to and knowledge of their own culture(s), its norms, practices, and traditions in relation to other cultures

Metalinguistic awareness: understanding, comparing, and expressing the nuances and uses of language, including the process of reflecting on the features and forms of language(s)

Minoritized students: those who are considered marginalized, stemming from the desire to establish one nation, one language status for education, commerce, and government

Monoglossic language ideology: one that looks through the lens of monolingualism ignoring the presence and contexts of multiple language use by multilingual learners

Multilingual education: a comprehensive school reform effort that has at its core a critical pedagogy that represents social justice within a sociocultural context

Multilingual learners: an assets-based term that describes a wide range of students who are or have been exposed to multiple languages and cultures on a consistent basis inside or outside of school, including English learners, English learners with disabilities, heritage language learners, students with interrupted formal education, long-term English learners, and students participating in dual language or two-way immersion programs

Multilingualism: in a school context, the use of multilingual learners' (as well as educators') multiple languages and cultures as resources for curriculum, instruction, and assessment

Multiliteracies: in response to the globalization of education, relying on increased linguistic diversity and multimodal ways for learners to make sense of the world (e.g., through oral genres, visual literacies, information literacy, digital literacy) and subsequently communicating and connecting with each other

Multimodal communication: also referred to as multiple modes of communication; the many ways of communicating, including the resources available to students—namely, through the use of textual, aural, linguistic, spatial, and visual materials—to relate meaningfully to one another and to show their learning

Newcomers: students who are recent arrivals to the United States (generally within the past two to four years) whose conceptual understanding and communicative skills, in large part, are in a language other than English

Peer assessment: descriptive feedback on student work based on specified criteria given by fellow grade-level students

Performance assessment: the planning, collection, and analysis of original hands-on authentic activities, such as curriculum-related projects, that are interpreted and reported based on specified criteria

Productive or expressive language: ways associated with language use, generally referring to oral and written communication

Proficient English speakers: multilingual learners who are former English language learners or students who have always been fully functional in English

Rating scales: a type of rubric where traits, language functions, skills, strategies, or behaviors are defined by their frequency of occurrence (how often) or quality (how well)

Receptive or interpretive language: ways associated with the processing of language, generally referring to listening, reading, and viewing

Reliability: the internal cohesiveness of a measure, the amount of agreement or uniformity of interpretation from rater to rater, or the consistency of results

Rubrics: criterion-referenced tools that enable teachers and students to interpret or evaluate student work using a uniform set of descriptors

Scaffolding: temporary supports for learners to maximize their access to grade-level content material as they are gaining proficiency in a language

Self-assessment: students' application of performance criteria or descriptors to monitor and interpret their own work as a means of reflecting on their learning

Social-emotional learning: a process by which students acquire and apply the knowledge, attitudes, and skills necessary to understand and manage their emotions, set and achieve positive goals, feel and show empathy for others, establish and maintain positive relationships and make responsible decisions (see http://www.rodel-foundationde.org/wp-content/uploads/2018/06/SEL-Brief-2-_-final.pdf)

Standardized testing: any exam applied to achievement testing, generally large-scale in nature, that is administered, scored, and reported in predetermined standard ways

Students with interrupted formal education (SIFE): a label that serves as a classification scheme for multilingual learners who have not had consistent schooling (due to mobility, refugee status, or trauma)

Student-led conferences: meetings with family members or with teachers in which students take the initiative to engage in a discussion of their work based on established learning goals

Success criteria: statements or descriptions of what students should know, understand, and be able to do at the end of a lesson or a unit of learning that serve as the basis for interpreting student work

Summative assessment (or assessment *of* learning): the "sum" of evidence of learning gathered over time, such as at the culmination of a unit of study at the classroom level, or an interim or annual test at a school or district level, that is generally used for accountability purposes

Test: a systematic procedure for collecting a sample of student behavior or performance at one point in time

Translanguaging: an interchange between multilingual learners who use their full linguistic resources of two shared languages; in school, the interaction of students in two or more languages in naturally occurring or specified learning situations

Transnationals: students who move back and forth between the U.S. and their family's country of origin, sometimes referred to as "transtornados"

Understanding by Design: a three-stage curricular framework and planning process (conceptualized by Grant Wiggins & Jay McTighe) that involves (1) identifying desired results, (2) determining assessment evidence, and (3) planning learning experiences with clear alignment of the stages to each other and with standards

Universal Design for Learning (UDL): a set of neuroscience principles that includes (1) multiple means of representation to give students multiple entries to learning, (2) multiple means of expression to provide learners with additional means to demonstrate their learning, and (3) multiple means of engaging learners to include their interests

Validity: the extent to which an assessment and data generated from it are appropriate for the decisions to be made; the extent to which a test matches its stated purpose

Zone of proximal development: a Vygotskyan theory that proposes that there is a difference between what learners can do independently and what they can do when their learning is supported through scaffolding by more knowledgeable adults or peers

References

Alexander, C. (2019, September). Learning to see students' deficits as strengths. *Edutopia*. Retrieved from https://www.edutopia.org/article/learning-see-students-deficits-strengths

Arellano, B., Liu, F., Stoker, G., & Slama, R. (2018). *Initial Spanish proficiency and English language development among Spanish-speaking English learner students in New Mexico* (REL2018-286). Washington, DC: U.S. Department of Education, Institute of Education Sciences, National Center for Education Evaluation and Regional Assistance, Regional Educational Laboratory Southwest. Retrieved from http://ies.ed.gov/ncee.edlabs

Bachman, L. F., & Damböck, B. (2017). *Language assessment for classroom teachers*. Oxford, UK: Oxford University Press.

Basterra, M. del R., Trumbull, E., & Solano-Flores, G. (Eds.). (2011). *Cultural validity in assessment: Addressing linguistic and cultural diversity*. New York, NY: Routledge.

Bearne, E. & Wolstencroft, H. (2007). *Visual approaches to teaching writing*. London, UK: Paul Chapman.

Beeman, K., & Urow, C. (2012). *Teaching for biliteracy: Strengthening bridges between languages*. Philadelphia, PA: Caslon.

Berger, R., Rugen, L., & Woodfin, L. (2014). *Leaders of their own learning: Transforming schools through student-engaged assessment*. San Francisco, CA: Jossey-Bass.

Bialystok, E., & Barac, R. (2012). Emerging bilingualism: Dissociating advantages for metalinguistic awareness and executive control. *Cognition, 122*(1), 67–73.

Billings, E., & Walqui, A. (2017). *Dispelling the myth of "English only": Understanding the importance of the first language in second language learning*. Albany: New York State Education Department. Retrieved from https://www.wested.org/resources/dispelling-the-myth-of-english-only/

Black, P., & Wiliam, D. (1998). *Assessment for learning: Beyond the black box*. Cambridge, UK: University of Cambridge.

Brenda. (2018). Brenda's story: La historia de Brenda. In *Voces sin fronteras: Our stories our truth* (pp. 152–153). Washington, DC: Shout Mouse Press.

Brookhart, S. M., Guskey, T. R., Bowers, A. J., McMillan, J. H., Smith, J. K., Smith, L. F., . . . Welsh, M. E. (2016). A century of grading research: Meaning and value in the most common educational measure. *Review of Educational Research, 86*(4), 803–848.

Buhagiar, M. A. (2007). Classroom assessment within the alternative assessment paradigm: Revisiting the territory. *Curriculum Journal, 18*(1), 39–56.

Burris, M. (2020). When closing schools during COVID-19, always remember the marginalized. *The Century Foundation.* Retrieved from https://tcf.org/content/commentary/closing-schools-covid-19-always-remember-marginalized/?session=1

Calkins, A., Conley, D., Heritage, M., Merino, N., Pecheone, R., Pittenger, L., . . . Wells, J. (2018). *Five elements for assessment design and use to support student autonomy.* Lexington, KY: Center for Innovation in Education.

Celic, C., & Seltzer, K. (2011). *Translanguaging: A CUNY-NYSIEB guide for educators.* New York: City University of New York.

Cenoz, J., & Gorter, D. (Eds.). (2015). *Multilingual education: Between language learning and translanguaging.* Cambridge, UK: Cambridge University Press.

Chalhoub-Deville, M. R. (2019). Multilingual testing constructs: Theoretical foundations. *Language Assessment Quarterly, 16*(4–5), 472–480.

Cheuk, T. (2016). Discourse practices in the new standards: The role of argumentation in common-core era next generation science standards classrooms for English language learners. *Electronic Journal of Science Education, 20*(3), 92–111. Retrieved from http://ejse.southwestern.edu

Christenson, S. L., Reschly, A. L., & Wylie, C. (Eds.). (2012). *Handbook of research on student engagement.* New York, NY: Springer.

Collier, V. P., & Thomas, W. P. (2009). *Educating English learners for a transformed world.* Albuquerque, NM: Dual Language Education of New Mexico, Fuente Press.

Collier, V. P., & Thomas, W. P. (2012). What really works for English language learners: Research-based practices for principals. In G. Theoharis & J. Brooks (Eds.), *What every principal needs to know to create equitable and excellent schools* (pp. 155–173). New York, NY: Teachers College.

Council of Chief State School Officers (CCSSO). (2018). *Revising the definition of formative assessment.* Washington, DC: Author. Retrieved from https://ccsso.org/sites/default/files/2018-06/Revising%20the%20Definition%20of%20Formative%20Assessment.pdf

Cuéllar, D. (2019). *Celebrate your child's multilingualism!* Washington, DC: NAEYC. Retrieved from https://www.naeyc.org/our-work/families/celebrate-childs-multilingualism

Cumming, A. (2009). What needs to be developed to facilitate classroom-based assessment? *TESOL Quarterly, 43*(3), 515–519.

Cummins, J. (2005). Teaching for cross-language transfer in dual language education: Possibilities and pitfalls. In *TESOL symposium on dual language education: Teaching and learning two languages in the EFL setting.* Alexandria, VA: TESOL. Retrieved from https://www.tesol.org/docs/default-source/new-resource-library/symposium-on-dual-language-education-3.pdf?sfvrsn=0&sfvrsn=0

Daniel, A. M., Jiménez, R. T., Pray, L., & Pacheco, M. B. (2017). Scaffolding to make translanguaging a classroom norm. *TESOL Journal, 10*(1), e00361.

Davison, C., & Williams, A. (2013). Integrating language and content: Unresolved issues. In B. Mohan, C. Leung, & C. Davison (Eds.), *English as a second language in the mainstream: Teaching, learning and identity* (pp. 51–69). London, UK: Routledge.

de Jong, E. (2019, April). *Taking a multilingual stance.* Paper presented at the American Education Research Association meeting, Toronto, Canada.

de Mejía, A.-M. (2002). *Power, prestige, and bilingualism: International perspectives on elite bilingual education.* Clevedon, UK: Multilingual Matters.

Dewey, J. (1933). *How we think. A restatement of the relation of reflective thinking to the educative process* (Rev. ed.), Boston, MA: D. C. Heath.

Doran, G. T. (1981). There's a S.M.A.R.T. way to write management's goals and objectives. *Management Review, 70*(11), 35–36.

Douglas Fir Group. (2016). A transdisciplinary framework for SLA within a multilingual world. *Modern Language Journal, 100*(51), 19–47.

Dueck, M. (2020). Fishing for the right assessment language. *Educational Leadership, 77*(6), 20–26.

Escamilla, K. (2006). Semilingualism applied to the literacy behaviors of Spanish-speaking emerging bilinguals: Bi-illiteracy or emerging biliteracy? *Teacher College Record, 108*(11), 2329–2353.

Escamilla, K. (2016). Empirical applications of Ruiz's language orientations: From theory to practice. *The Bilingual Review, La Revista Bilingüe, 33*(3), 140–153.

Esteban-Guitart, M., & Moll, L. C. (2014). Funds of identity: A new concept based on the funds of knowledge approach. *Culture & Psychology, 20*(1), pp. 31–48.

Every Student Succeeds Act of 2015, Pub. L. No. 114-95, §114 Stat. 1177 (2015–2016).

Feldman, J. (2019). *Grading for equity: What it is, why it matters, and how it can transform schools and classrooms.* Thousand Oaks, CA: Corwin.

Fulcher, G. (2012). Assessment literacy for the language classroom. *Language Assessment Quarterly, 9*(2), 113–132.

Gándara, P. (2015). The implications of deeper learning for adolescent immigrants and English language learners. *Students at the Center.* Online publication. Retrieved from https://www.jff.org/resources/implications-deeper-learning-adolescent-immigrants-and-english-language-learners

García, O. (2009a). Education, multilingualism, and translanguaging in the 21st century. In A. Mohanty, M. Panda, R. Phillipson, & T. Skutnabb-Kangas (Eds.), *Multilingual education for social justice: Globalising the local* (pp. 128–145). New Delhi, India: Orient Blackswan.

García, O. (2009b). Emergent bilinguals and TESOL: What's in a name? *TESOL Quarterly, 43*(2), 322–326.

García, O., Ibarra Johnson, S., & Seltzer, K. (2017). *The translanguaging classroom: Leveraging student bilingualism for learning.* Philadelphia, PA: Caslon.

García, O., Kleifgen, J. A., & Fachi, L. (2008). From English language learners to emergent bilinguals. *Equity Matters: Research Review 1.* New York, NY: Teachers College, Columbia University.

García, O., & Wei, L. (2018). Translanguaging. In *The encyclopedia of applied linguistics.* Retrieved from https://onlinelibrary.wiley.com/doi/full/10.1002/9781405198431.wbeal1488

Genesee, F. (2006). What do we know about bilingual education for majority language students? In T. K. Bhatia & W. C. Ritchie (Eds.), *The handbook of bilingualism* (pp. 547–576). Hoboken, NJ: Blackwell.

Gibbons, P. (2015). *Scaffolding language, scaffolding learning: Teaching English language learners in the mainstream classroom* (2nd ed.). Portsmouth, NH: Heinemann.

González, N., Moll, L. C., & Amanti, C. (Eds.). (2005). *Funds of knowledge: Theorizing practices in households, communities, and classrooms.* Mahwah, NJ: Erlbaum.

Gottlieb, M. (2009). Standards: A metric for language teaching and learning. In *A TESOL symposium on English language teaching standards, Panama City, Panama* (pp. 15–23). Alexandria, VA: Teachers of English to Speakers of Other Languages.

Gottlieb, M. (2013). *Essential actions: A handbook for implementing WIDA's framework for English Language Development Standards.* Madison, WI: Board of Regents of the University of Wisconsin System on behalf of the WIDA Consortium.

Gottlieb, M. (2016). *Assessing English language learners: Bridges to equity: Connecting academic language proficiency to student achievement* (2nd ed.). Thousand Oaks, CA: Corwin.

Gottlieb, M. (2017). *Assessing multilingual learners: A month-by-month guide.* Alexandria, VA: ASCD.

Gottlieb, M., & Castro, M. (2017). *Language power: Key uses for accessing content.* Thousand Oaks, CA: Corwin.

Gottlieb, M., & Ernst-Slavit, G. (2014). *Academic language in diverse classrooms: Promoting content and language learning, Definitions and contexts.* Thousand Oaks, CA: Corwin.

Gottlieb, M., & Hilliard, J. (2019). A presentation at *La CLAVE: An Integration of Language, Culture, and the Arts.* Oaxaca, Mexico.

Gottlieb, M., & Honigsfeld, A. (2020). From assessment *of* learning to assessment *as* and *for* learning. In M. Calderón, M. Dove, M. Gottlieb, A. Honigsfeld, T. Singer, I. Soto, . . . D. Zacarian (Eds.), *Breaking down the wall: Essential shifts for English learner success* (pp. 135–160). Thousand Oaks, CA: Corwin.

Gottlieb, M., & Katz, A. (2020). Assessment in the classroom. In C. Chappelle (Ed.), *The concise encyclopedia of applied linguistics*. Hoboken, NJ: John Wiley & Sons.

Gottlieb, M., Katz, A., & Ernst-Slavit, G. (2009). *Paper to practice: Using the English language proficiency standards in preK–12 classrooms*. Alexandria, VA: Teachers of English to Speakers of Other Languages.

Gottlieb, M., & Noel, B. (2019). Character development in a multilingual international school and its use of self-assessment tools. *Sino-US English Teaching, 16*(9), 369–375.

Graves, K. (2008). The language curriculum: A social contextual perspective. *Language Teach, 41*(2), 147–181.

Graves, K. (2016). Language curriculum design: Possibilities and realities. In G. Hall (Ed.), *The Routledge handbook of English language teaching*. New York, NY: Routledge.

Grosjean, F. (1989). Neurolinguists, beware! The bilingual is not two monolinguals in one person. *Brain and Language, 36*(1), 3–15.

Gubbins, E. J., Siegle, D., Hamilton, R., Peters, P., Carpenter, A. Y., O'Rourke, P., . . . Estepar-Garcia, W. (2018, June). *Exploratory study on the identification of English learners for gifted and talented programs*. Storrs, CT: University of Connecticut, National Center for Research on Gifted Education.

Hammond, J., & Gibbons, P. (2005). Putting scaffolding to work: The contribution of scaffolding in articulating ESL education. *Prospect, 20*(1), 6–30.

Hattie, J. (2012). *Visible learning for teachers: Maximizing impact on learning*. London, UK: Routledge.

Hattie, J., & Temperley, H. (2007). The power of feedback. *Review of Educational Research, 77*, 81–112.

Hawkins, M. R. (2019). Plurilingual learners and schooling: A sociocultural perspective. In L. C. de Oliveira (Ed.), *The handbook of TESOL in K-12* (pp. 11–24). Hoboken, NJ: John Wiley & Sons.

Heritage, M. (2010). *Formative assessment: Making it happen in the classroom*. Thousand Oaks, CA: Corwin.

Heritage, M., Walqui, A., & Linquanti, R. (2013). *Formative assessment as contingent teaching and learning: Perspectives on assessment as and for learning*. Paper presented at the AERA meeting, San Francisco, CA.

Heritage, M., Walqui, A., & Linquanti, R. (2015). *English language learners and the new standards: Developing language, content knowledge, analytical practices in the classroom*. Cambridge, MA: Harvard University Press.

Hornberger, N. H. (Ed.). (2003). *Continua of biliteracy: An ecological framework for educational policy, research, and practice in multilingual settings.* Clevedon, UK: Multilingual Matters.

Hornberger, N. H. (2004). The continua of biliteracy and the bilingual educator: Educational linguistics in practice. *International Journal of Bilingual Education, 7*(2/3), 155–171.

International Literacy Association. (2017). Literacy assessment: What everyone needs to know. *Literacy Leadership Brief.* Retrieved from https://www.literacy worldwide.org/docs/default-source/where-we-stand/literacy-assessment-brief .pdf? sfvrsn=efd4a68e_4

Kalantzis, M., Cope, B., & Harvey, A. (2003). Assessing multiliteracies and the new basics. *Assessment in Education, 16*(1), 15–26.

Kaul, M. (2019, June). *Keeping students at the center with culturally relevant performance assessments.* Retrieved from https://www.nextgenlearning.org/ articles/keeping-students-at-the-center-with-culturally-relevant-performance-assessments

Kelleher, A. (2010). *Who is a heritage language learner?* Washington, DC: Center for Applied Linguistics. Retrieved from http://www.cal.org/heritage/ pdfs/briefs/Who-is-a-Heritage-Language-Learner.pdf

Kibler, A., K., & Valdés, G. (2016). Conceptualizing language learners: Socioinstitutional mechanisms and their consequences. *Modern Language Journal, 100*(S1), 96–116.

Ladson-Billings, G. (1994). *The dreamkeepers.* San Francisco, CA: Jossey-Bass.

Lambert, W. E., & Tucker, G. R. (1972). *Bilingual education of children: The St. Lambert experiment.* Rowley, MA: Newbury House. Retrieved from https://eric.ed.gov/?id=ED082573

Leung, C., & Valdés, G. (2019). Translanguaging and the transdisciplinary framework for language teaching and learning in a multilingual world. *Modern Language Journal, 103*(2), 348–370.

Lindholm-Leary, K. (2012). Successes and challenges in dual language education. *Theory Into Practice, 51*(4), 256–262.

López, A. A., Turkan, S., & Guzman-Orth, D. (2017). Assessing multilingual competence. In E. Shohamy, I. Or, & S. May (Eds.), *Language testing and assessment. Encyclopedia of language and education* (3rd ed., pp. 91–102). New York, NY: Springer.

MAEC. (2019). *Creating new futures for newcomers: Lessons from five schools that serve K-12 immigrants, refugees, and asylees.* Bethesda, MD: Author.

Mahboob, A. (2019). Beyond the native speaker in TESOL. *International Journal of Applied Linguistics, 12*(1), 74–109. Retrieved from http://citeseerx.ist.psu .edu/viewdoc/download?doi=10.1.1.510.2158&rep=rep1&type=pdf

Mann, S., & Walsh, S. (2017). *Reflective practice in English language teaching: Research-based principles and practices*. New York, NY: Routledge.

Marzano, R. J. (2010). *Formative assessment & standards-based grading: Classroom strategies that work*. Bloomington, IN: Marzano Research Laboratory.

Matlick, E. (2020). My greatest teaching problem was giving feedback. Here's how research helped me solve it. *EdSurge*. Retrieved from https://www.edsurge.com/news/2020-02-18-my-greatest-teaching-problem-was-feedback-here-s-how-research-helped-me-solve-it

McTighe, J., & Brookhart, S. (2019). *What we know about grading: What works, what doesn't, and what we can do about it*. Alexandria, VA: ASCD.

McTighe, J., & Wiggins, G. (2013). *Essential questions: Opening doors to student understanding*. Alexandria, VA: ASCD.

Menken, K., & Kleyn, T. (2009). The difficult road for long-term English learners. *Educational Leadership, 66*(7). Retrieved from http://www.ascd.org/publications/educational_leadership/apr09/vol66/num07/The_DifficultRoad_for_Long-Term_English_Learners.aspx

Menken, K., & Solorza, C. (2014). No child left bilingual: Accountability and the elimination of bilingual education programs in New York City Schools. *Educational Policy, 8*(1), 96–125.

Michigan Assessment Consortium. (2020). *Assessment literacy standards: A national imperative*. Mason, MI: Author.

Minaya-Rowe, L. (2014). A gothic story: "The Cask of Amontillado." In M. Gottlieb & G. Ernst Slavit (Eds.), *Academic language in diverse classrooms: English language arts, grades 6–8* (pp. 137–182). Thousand Oaks, CA: Corwin.

Mohan, B. (1986). *Language and content*. Reading, MA: Addison-Wesley.

Moll, L. C., Amanti, C., Neff, D., & Gonzalez, N. (1992). Funds of knowledge for teaching: Using a qualitative approach to connect homes and classrooms. *Theory Into Practice, 31*(2), 132–141.

Moss, C. M., & Brookhart, S. M. (2009). *Advancing formative assessment in every classroom: A guide for instructional leaders*. Alexandria, VA: ASCD.

Moss, P. (2008). Sociocultural implications for assessment: Classroom assessment. In P. Moss, D. C. Pullin, J. P. Gee, E. H. Haertel, & L. J. Young (Eds.), *Assessment, equity, and opportunity to learn* (pp. 222–258). Cambridge, UK: Cambridge University Press.

Mun, R. U., Dulong Langley, S., Ware, S., Gubbins, E. J., Siegle, D., Callahan, C. M., . . . Hamilton, R. (2016). *Effective practices for identifying and serving English learners in gifted education: A systematic review of the literature*. Storrs, CT: National Center for Research on Gifted Education.

Murphy, K. L. (2011). Student reflective practice: Building deeper connections to concepts. *ASCD Express, 6*(25). Retrieved from http://www.ascd.org/ascd-express/vol6/625-murphy.aspx

National Academies of Sciences and Engineering Medicine. (2017). Dual language learners and English learners with disabilities. In *Promoting the educational success of children and youth learning English* (pp. 351–408). Washington, DC: Author.

National Center for Education Statistics (NCES). (2013). *Participation in education. Elementary/secondary enrollment*. Retrieved from https://nces.ed.gov/programs/coe/pdf/Indicator_CGF/coe_cgf_2013_05.pdf

New London Group. (1996). A pedagogy of multiliteracies: Designing social futures. *Harvard Educational Review*, 66(1), 60–92.

Nieto, S. (2018). *Language, culture, and teaching: Critical perspectives* (3rd ed.). New York, NY: Routledge.

Otheguy, R., García, O., & Reid, W. (2015). Clarifying translanguaging and deconstructing languages: A perspective from linguistics. *Applied Linguistics Review, 6*(3), 8–19.

Palmer, D. K., Cervantes-Soon, C., Dorner, L., & Heiman, D. (2019). Bilingualism, biliteracy, biculturalism ... and critical consciousness for all: Proposing a fourth fundamental principle for two-way dual language education. *Theory Into Practice, 58*(2), 121–133.

Paris, D. (2012). Culturally sustaining pedagogy: A needed change in stance, terminology, and practice. *Educational Research, 41*(3), 93–97.

Percell, J. C. (2019). Strategies for diving into successful grading reform. *ASCD Express, 14*(31).

Phillipson, R. (1994). *Linguistic imperialism*. Oxford, UK: Oxford University Press.

Pimentel, S. (2018). *Policy brief: English learners and content-rich curricula*. Baltimore, MD: Johns Hopkins Institute for Education Policy.

Popham, W. J. (2009). All about assessment/A process—Not a test. *Educational Leadership, 66*(7), 85–86.

Popham, W. J. (2018). *Assessment literacy for educators in a hurry*. Alexandria, VA: ASCD.

Relyea, J. E., & Amendum, S. J. (2019). English reading growth in Spanish-speaking bilingual students: Moderating effect of English proficiency on cross-linguistic influence. *Child Development*. Retrieved from https://srcd.onlinelibrary.wiley.com/doi/epdf/10.1111/cdev.13288

Rewold, M. (2019, Summer). The question formulation technique: Validating students' voices. *Soleado*, pp. 2–3.

Reynolds, D. (2019). *Language policy in globalized contexts*. World Innovation Summit for Education (WISE) Carnegie Mellon University Qatar: WISE.

Robertson, K. (2014). *Essential actions: 15 research-based practices to increase ELL student achievement*. Retrieved from the Colorín Colorado! website:

https://www.colorincolorado.org/article/essential-actions-15-research-based-practices-increase-ell-student-achievement

Rogoff, B. (1994). Developing understanding of the idea of communities of learners. *Mind, Culture, and Activity, 1*(4), 209–229.

Ruíz, R. (1988). Orientations in language planning. *NABE Journal, 8*(2), 15–34.

Sahakyan, N., & Ryan, S. (2018, October). *Exploring the long-term English learner population across 15 WIDA states.* Madison: Wisconsin Center for Education Research, University of Wisconsin.

Sánchez, M. T., García, O., & Solorza, C. (2017). Reframing language allocation policy in dual language bilingual education. *Bilingual Research Journal, 41*(1), 1–15.

Schissel, J. L., De Korne, H., & López-Gopar, M. (2018). Grappling with trans-languaging for teaching and assessment in culturally and linguistically diverse contexts: Teacher perspectives from Oaxaca, Mexico. *International Journal of Bilingual Education and Bilingualism*, 1–17.

Shepard, L. A., Penuel, W. R., & Davidson, K. L. (2017). Design principles for new systems of assessment. *Phi Delta Kappan*, 98(6), 47–52.

Shohamy, E. (2011). Assessing multilingual competencies: Adopting construct valid assessment policies. *Modern Language Journal, 95*(3), 418–429.

Short, D. J., & Fitzsimmons, S. (2007). *Double the work: Challenges and solutions to acquiring language and academic literacy for adolescent English language learners.* New York, NY: Carnegie Corporation.

Sleeter, C. E., & Carmona, J. F. (2017). *Un-standardizing curriculum: Multicultural teaching in the standards-based classroom* (2nd ed.). New York, NY: Teachers College Press.

Smith, M. E., Teemant, A., & Pinnegar, S. (2004). Principles and practices of sociocultural assessment: Foundations for effective strategies for linguistically diverse classrooms. *Multicultural Perspectives, 6*(2), 38–46.

Snow, M. A., Met, M., & Genesee, F. (1989). A conceptual framework for the integration of language and content in second/ foreign language instruction. *TESOL Quarterly, 23*(2), 201–217.

Solano-Flores, G., & Nelson-Barber, S. (2001). On the cultural validity of science assessments. *Journal of Research in Science Teaching, 38*, 553–573.

Soto, I., & Gottlieb, M. (2020). *From monolingualism to multilingualism.* In M. Calderón, M. Dove, M. Gottlieb, A. Honigsfeld, T. Singer, I. Soto, . . . D. Zacarian, *Breaking down the wall: Essential shifts for English learner success* (pp. 161–182). Thousand Oaks, CA: Corwin.

Staehr Fenner, D. (2014). *Advocating for English learners: A guide for educators.* Thousand Oaks, CA: Corwin.

Stiggins, R. (2006, Nov/Dec). Assessment for learning: A key to motivation and achievement. *Phi Delta Kappa International, 2*(2), 1–19.

Stiggins, R. (2007). Assessment through the student's eyes. *Educational Leadership, 64*(8), 22–26.

Suskie, L. (2018). *Assessing student learning: A common sense guide* (3rd ed.). San Francisco, CA: Jossey-Bass.

Swain, M., Kinnear, P., & Steinman, L. (2011). *Sociocultural theory in second language education: An introduction through narratives*. Bristol, UK: Multilingual Matters.

Umansky, I., & Dumont, H. (2019). *English learner labeling: How English learner status shapes teacher perceptions of student skills and the moderating influence of bilingual instructional settings* (Ed Working Paper No. 19-94). Providence, RI: Annenberg Institute at Brown University.

Valdés, G. (2005). Bilingualism, heritage language learners, and SLA research: Opportunities lost or seized? *Modern Language Journal, 89*(3), 410–426.

Vygotsky, L. (1978). *Mind in society: The development of higher psychological processes*. Cambridge, MA: Harvard University Press.

Wajda, E. (2011). New perspectives in language assessment: The interpretivist revolution. In M. Pawlak (Ed.), *Extending the boundaries of research on second language learning and teaching* (pp. 275–285). Berlin, Germany: Springer.

Walqui, A., & van Lier, L. (2010). *Scaffolding the academic success of adolescent English language learners: A pedagogy of promise*. Oakland, CA: WestEd.

Walsh, S. (2011). *Exploring classroom discourse: Language in action*. New York, NY: Routledge.

Wiggins, G. (2012, September). Seven keys to effective feedback. *Educational Leadership, 70*(1), 10–16.

Wiggins, G., & McTighe, J. (2005). *Understanding by design*. Alexandria, VA: Association for Supervision and Curriculum Development.

Wiliam, D. (2017). *Embedded formative assessment* (2nd ed.). Bloomington, IN: Solution Tree.

Wiliam, D., & Leahy, S. (2015). *Embedding formative assessment: Practical techniques for K–12 classrooms*. West Palm Beach, FL: Learning Sciences International.

Wilson, D. M. (2011). Dual language programs on the rise. *Harvard Education Letter, 27*(2). Retrieved from https://www.hepg.org/hel-home/issues/27_2/helarticle/dual-language-programs-on-the-rise#home

Withycombe, A. (2019). Why we should test English language learners in their home language [Blog post]. *Getting Smart*. Retrieved from https://www.gettingsmart.com/2019/06/why-we-should-test-english-language-learners-in-their-home-language/

Wong, S. (2016). *Multilingualism as a tool for closing achievement gaps*. Retrieved from American Councils for International Education website: https://www.americancouncils.org/news/language-news/multilingualism-tool-closing-achievement-gaps

Zipke, M. (2007). The role of metalinguistic awareness in the reading comprehension of sixth and seventh graders. *Reading Psychology, 28*(4), 375–396.

Index

Note: The letter '*f*' following locators refers to figures respectively.

Student-led conferences, 139, 163
Student milestones, 143
Student samples in multiple
    languages, 97–104
  data collection during distance
      learning, 101–102
  data organizing in multiple
      languages, 102–104
  productive language data, 99–101
  receptive language data, 98–99
Student self-assessment of character
    traits, 133
Student self-reflection, 73, 152–157
  metacognitive awareness, 153–154
  metacultural awareness, 155
  metalinguistic awareness, 154
Student–student conversation, 73
Student with interrupted formal
    education (SIFE), 6
Success criteria, 70
Summative assessment, 37
Suskie, L., 64
Swain, M., 37

Teacher collaboration, 165–166
Teachers and other instructional
    leaders
  ask questions and listen to
      students, 76–77
  assets-driven philosophy, 20
  communities' connect, 105
  educators' connect, 105
  equitable assessment for
      multilingual learners, 188
  evaluating multilingual learners,
      167–168
  international network of
      educators, 140
  multilingual families' connect, 105
  multilingual learners with
      disabilities in the context,
      167–168
  multilingual resource bank, 43
Technologization, 4
Teemant, A., 11
Tests, 10
Theories of language learning, 8–10
Think-alouds, 72
  questions for building metacognitive
      awareness, 171
Thomas, W. P., 122
Timperley, H., 73

Translanguaging, 10–11, 21
  assessment *as*, *for*, and *of* learning,
      95–96
  curriculum, instruction, and
      assessment, 41–42
  data collection phase, 93–95
  generating and interpreting
      data, 128
  planning assessment, 75–76
Trumbull, E., 123
Tucker, G. R., 7
Turkan, S., 123

Umansky, I., 5
Understanding by design, 183
Undirected think-pair-share, 72
Unit-level reports, assessment *of*
    learning, 158–159
Universal Design for
    Learning (UDL), 89
Urow, C., 75
U.S. Constitution test, 27

Valdés, G., 5, 9, 123
Validity, 189
van Lier, L., 92
Vygotsky, L., 93, 130

Wajda, E., 10, 38
Walqui, A., 92, 134, 190
Walsh, S., 90, 184
Wei, L., 11
When I Listen, Read, and
    View, 113–114
When I Speak, Write, and Illustrate,
    117–118
Wiggins, G., 137, 182–183
Wiliam, D., 61, 73, 135
Williams, A., 64
Wilson, Daya. M., 32
Withycombe, A., 13
Wolstencroft, H., 96
Wong, S., 3
Woodfin, L., 14, 74
Written language feedback, 138
Wylie, C., 36

Younger multilingual learners
  ask questions and listen to
      students, 76
  assets-driven philosophy, 19
  communities' connect, 104–105

A SAGE Publishing Company

Helping educators make the greatest impact

CORWIN HAS ONE MISSION: to enhance education through intentional professional learning.

We build long-term relationships with our authors, educators, clients, and associations who partner with us to develop and continuously improve the best evidence-based practices that establish and support lifelong learning.

Solutions YOU WANT | Experts YOU TRUST | Results YOU NEED

EVENTS

>>> **INSTITUTES**

Corwin Institutes provide large regional events where educators collaborate with peers and learn from industry experts. Prepare to be recharged and motivated!

corwin.com/institutes

ON-SITE PD

>>> **ON-SITE PROFESSIONAL LEARNING**

Corwin on-site PD is delivered through high-energy keynotes, practical workshops, and custom coaching services designed to support knowledge development and implementation.

corwin.com/pd

>>> **PROFESSIONAL DEVELOPMENT RESOURCE CENTER**

The PD Resource Center provides school and district PD facilitators with the tools and resources needed to deliver effective PD.

corwin.com/pdrc

ONLINE

>>> **ADVANCE**

Designed for K–12 teachers, Advance offers a range of online learning options that can qualify for graduate-level credit and apply toward license renewal.

corwin.com/advance

Contact a PD Advisor at (800) 831-6640 or visit www.corwin.com for more information